LIGHTNING
THE OPERATIONAL HISTORY

KEV DARLING

Airlife
England

First published in the UK in 1995
by Airlife Publishing Ltd

British Library Cataloguing in Publication data
A catalogue record for this book
is available from the British Library

ISBN 1 85310 521 X

Typeset by Servis Filmsetting Ltd, Manchester

Printed by Butler & Tanner Ltd, Frome and London

Airlife Publishing Ltd

101 Longden Road, Shrewsbury SY3 9EB

Contents

Acknowledgements

No book of this nature can be compiled without the assistance of other interested parties. I would therefore like to use this space to thank all those that assisted me in this mammoth, but enjoyable task. Without them these stories would be less than complete.

Al Churchyard for all the Kuwait information, some brought out of that country at great risk. Graham Day of the AHB(RAF) for his assistance in filling the gaps of the early Lightning years. Wally Rouse of the BAe Warton for his help, encouragement, diagrams and photographs. Chris Chippington of the IWM at Duxford for help with their example. Flt Lt Dave Mason of XI Sqdn Leeming for the photograph. My old friend Peter Russell-Smith for letting me rampage through his photograph collection again! M.J. Smith of the Newark Air Museum for the information on their aircraft. Steve Buttriss for filling in those important gaps. Richard Simpson of the RAFM at Hendon who let me correct the history of their Lightning. Sqdn Ldr R.J. Major Retd. of the Museum of Flight at East Fortune for the photographs. Owen Morris for his help on the Saudi front. Jim Sheehan of FS (Stats) for his assistance once again and for putting up with my badgering. Tony Nuttall of the Solway Aviation Society for his help and photographs plus a prompt reply. Graham Jackson of the Lightning Preservation Group for answering a myriad of questions and for his help in general. Graham Morris of the East Midlands Aeropark for his help with the history of their aircraft.

Ian Bowers of NEAM, Sunderland for answering my letters. And last but not least to George Beck of Tanks and Vessels Industries Ltd for letting me know of their plans concerning the Rossington Lightning store. After all this more than generous help, any omissions or errors are therefore mine.

Finally my thanks are extended to all those that gave help in any way that they could, especially my wife Gina for tolerating my absences whilst writing this book.

Kev Darling
South Wales

Foreword

In the short history of aviation, there have been several evocative aircraft types which enthusiasts have raptured over, either in the spoken or written word, on cinema screen or television film. To include the Lightning amongst types such as the Avro 504K, Sopwith Camel, Gloster Gladiator, Supermarine Spitfire and Concorde is because it must surely merit the same special recognition within such a line-up.

It is forty years since the P.1 first flew and even though none of the noble breed have flown for five or six years, there remains plenty of anecdotal material from which to write another aviation book. Kev Darling has done much research and analysis in general, but in particular has examined in depth many facets of the Lightnings' operations, throughout its history and this book focuses on several incidents and periods of its folklore.

Even though I may not be a 'qualified' Lightning pilot to earn the honour of writing the foreword to this book, I commend it to all devotees that wish to keep the English Electric Lightning fresh in their minds.

M.V. Holden

FLASH OF FIRE, THE LIGHTNING PASSES
MIGHTY BEAST POWERED BY GASSES
INTO THE SKY TORN ASUNDER
IS THERE LIGHTNING AFTER THE THUNDER?

ANON

Introduction

THE LIGHTNING, a great success, a great fighter and now a great survivor. Designed and built by English Electric of Preston, the Lightning was destined to be the Royal Air Force's only Mach 2+ single-seat Interceptor and, although never having fired its guns in anger, it now joins such famous predecessors in the annals of RAF history as the Sopwith Camel, Gloster Gladiator, Supermarine Spitfire, Hawker Hurricane and the Hunter.

The story of such a famous and respected aircraft starts in the immediate post-war period when the results of German swept-wing research was beginning to be understood. Although Britain was close to bankruptcy, the government of the day conceded that the aviation industry should at least look at the practical applications of such research. The issuance of Experimental Requirement ER 103 brought forth submissions from many interested companies. Those of Fairey and English Electric were finally chosen as those most likely to succeed, although designs from AVRO, Hawkers and SARO were to at least reach the drawing-board stage and in some cases the flight test stage. Those from Fairey and English Electric finally emerged in hardware form as the FD.2 and the P.1A respectively. One was to set a world speed record and help in the Concorde programme whilst the other was to be the starting point for one of the most fiddled-with fighter programmes ever conceived. Mention should also be made at this point of the Short SB 5 which had been built to test a number of wing and tailplane layouts for the P.1A. This aircraft still survives in the Cosford Aerospace Museum collection.

Many will ask 'how did the Lightning survive the 1957 Defence White Paper?' The answer lies in the first flight of P.1B XA847 which flew just prior to the White Paper and successfully proved the concept of the supersonic manned interceptor. With so much money tied up in the project the government saw no other option than to proceed with a development batch of aircraft that were soon to be named Lightning. Contracts for in-service production versions were released in dribs and drabs, although English Electric were to seize the bull by the horns by offering slightly upgraded versions to fulfil each order. Once the foolishness of an all-missile defence had worn off, the company was able to offer better, and so they thought, more advanced versions of the Lightning. The first of these was the F.3 variant which unfortunately dispensed with cannons altogether, as air combat was thought to be the province of long-range missile engagements.

This theory was to collapse over Vietnam where much of the air-to-air combat was close-in dog-fighting or the missiles were launched at close range. The only Lightning version in service with the RAF at the time was the four cannon toting F.2 which, after conversion to approximately F.6 standard, became possibly the best of the breed and ideal for its role, that of patrolling the German Border. Hasty conversions of the definitive F.6 resulted in a cannon gunpack being installed in the forward section of the under-fuselage fuel tank. Carried out during the 1970s, the resultant loss in fuel capacity was more than compensated for by the increased ability of the Lightning to fight close-in. Other options offered by BAC were a missile pack that could carry four AIM-9 Sidewinders or one that could carry a pair of AIM-7 Sparrows.

The overwing mounts also came in for some scrutiny, missile fits also being offered for those positions. Although conversion costs to expand the Lightning's offensive capability would have been minimal, at every turn the company was turned down. Only the overseas versions delivered to Saudi Arabia and Kuwait were to be weapons-capable on the overwing mounts and represented the final and logical conclusion to the type.

Commonsense failure not withstanding, the Lightning remained a stalwart in RAF front-line service until it was finally replaced by the two-seat Panavia Tornado F.3. Upgrades throughout its working life kept the aircraft's detection and ranging systems as up-to-date as possible, although as a single-seater the cockpit work load was invariably high. As the airframes aged, plans were put in place to conserve the Lightnings' fatigue life. Rotation between storage and a Binbrook operator was a frequent event, this being backed-up by the strengthening of the wingroot areas that were becoming prone to cracking due to the types propensity to land in a form of controlled crash. Another option exercised on the Lightning fleet was the fitment of the overwing ferry tanks that had rarely seen usage since the overseas transit days of the 1960s/70s. With the tanks in place the Lightning could remain airborne longer, thus reducing the fatigue consumption experienced in the heavier air at lower altitudes and, more importantly, training and interception sortie times were extended, thus increasing the Lightning's effectiveness. Even so, ask any ex-Lightning pilot if he would fly anything else and the answer would be an emphatic 'NO!'

The future for the Lightning, at least in flying form, lies with the Lightning Flying Club currently based at Plymouth and Exeter, whose ambitious plans for flying either a single-seater or their T.5 appear to be coming to fruition. On the grounded front, those aircraft that are in the care of various museums appear to have secure, if not rosy, futures, although the cache of Lightnings at Cranfield appears to have been left to rot. Even so, the preserved Lightning front in this country appears to be in safe hands. As one early Lightning pilot said 'I was with it all the way to brakes off!'

This book is therefore dedicated to those that built, flew and maintained the aircraft in RAF service. It is especially for the latter, as the Lightning was reckoned by many to be one of the hardest aircraft to maintain to flying standard. This book is also dedicated to those brave souls who see nothing wrong in trying to put a Lightning back in the air again – who knows, we may yet again see the 'Frightning' tail skidding at high speed at air displays. To them a special word of thanks must go.

Part 1

Chapter 1
The Thunder Begins

Germany 1945, and the Allies in victory poke through the shattered remains of Hitler's Third Reich. From the British, and more importantly the Air Ministry point of view, the main areas of interest centred upon jet engine technology and developments in the aerodynamic field. Whilst the RAF had operated early examples of the Gloster Meteor F.Mk.1, the opposing Luftwaffe had been graced with Messerschmitt's Me 262 and Me 163 plus contributions from the Heinkel He 162 and the Arado Ar 234. Even as Germany teetered on the brink of collapse further designs, some utterly fantastic, were under construction or development. From the power-plant point of view centrifugal engine technology was fully understood in the UK. The trials and tribulations of Sir Frank Whittle in producing his examples are well documented. A field less appreciated was German advances in axial flow engine technology. Even with their propensity for failure after a short period in use, coupled to difficulties in starting, the axial engine had the potential to produce more thrust and had, in service, proved to be the faster of the two.

Aerodynamic advances covering the development of wing profiles and the streamlining of fuselages had begun to evolve into the shapes so familiar in the sky today. In the area of wing design, the German scientists had discovered the requirements for supersonic flight, that swept wings allied to the location of the centre of pressure as far aft as physically possible, reduced drag, increased lift and delayed the onset of the supersonic boundary wave layer breakaway. Early British designs, such as the Meteor, had concentrated the centre of pressure close to the leading edge, thus limiting the wing's ability to fly faster.

Taking their prizes home with them, the various Allies began to explore the potential of the information they had gained. In Britain various firms began construction of aircraft to investigate the realms opened up by the newly acquired data. As most of these were experimental, the Royal Air Force was initially gainsaid any direct benefits from the various research programmes, although at all times interested parties within the military were kept informed of progress. Earliest results saw various marques of Meteor flown, each slightly more refined than the last, to which should be added the de Havilland contribution of the Vampire and its more advanced successor the Venom which would be the first RAF fighter to exhibit any form of obvious sweepback in the wing planform. Further experiments in high-speed flight were to result in the aborted Supermarine Swift, dangerous in its earlier guises, and the far more successful Hawker Hunter – none of which were capable of level supersonic flight. This path of progression had encompassed such unfortunates as the Miles M.52 supersonic fighter, cancelled by a government and its advisors as too dangerous to fly.

In Britain the aviation industry manufacturers were becoming dissatisfied were the government's lack of interest in high-speed flight design. This was later to prove ironic, as English Electric had begun the development work on Specification B3/45, later to emerge as the Canberra, which laid the criteria for bomber designs to follow – that of penetration at fairly high speeds at great altitude. After the Canberra's first flight it soon became obvious that the Royal Air Force was in trouble; on the one hand it had a fast high-altitude bomber, on the other it was saddled with a collection of fighters which, even in their wildest dreams, were proving incapable of reaching the Canberra.

Across the Atlantic the United States manufacturers, with their usual customary enthusiasm for new ideas, had forged ahead through the first generation of straight winged fighters and were contemplating the next, swept-wing generation, capable of Mach 1 in level flight, the North American F-86 Sabre and the contemporary Republic F-84 Thunderstreak. Even as these new types were being developed for service, the next generation, the famous century series, was on the drawing boards.

In contrast to their outstanding Canberra, English Electric were also engaged in building Vampire fighters for the RAF and export on behalf of de Havilland. With the two mismatched types running side by side in the Preston factory it comes as no surprise to find that the chief designer W.E.W. 'Teddy' Petter, had already begun to outline a Mach 2 fighter design to combat his own bomber. Preliminary design and investigation had begun in 1946 with many radical swept-wing layouts being examined. However unusual the exterior was to appear, the internal fixtures and fittings were to incorporate the latest advances in design, but to avoid the pitfalls being experienced by others the 'keep it simple, stupid' rule was exercised. The first visual evidence of such a philosophy had of course been the Canberra, which outlasted all of its contemporaries by many years and the Folland Gnat, which although small in size, was a fairly simple design. Government indifference was the first reaction to Petter's proposals, English Electric continued to persevere with their high-speed flight trials using a Gloster Meteor F.Mk.4. Flown from the company's operating base at Warton, it did not take long to illustrate the 'modern' fighter's inability to reach an intruder flying at 50,000 ft and at M=0.85, both figures being the projected maximums for the forthcoming B3/45.

Although air resistance decreases as altitude increases the onset of compressibility at 40,000 ft and M=0.75, meant that such aircraft as the Meteor would be unable to carry out their primary task, that of defending British airspace. To answer these problems Petter and his Lancashire based design team settled on a swept-wing design that would delay the onset of compressibility. To breach the Mach 1 barrier it was proposed that two engines be installed – the theory being that the extra thrust would push the vehicle through the turbulent transonic range into the relative calm of the supersonic flight regime. It should also be borne in mind that during this period, axial flow engines were fairly crude in their capabilities and were still susceptible to in-flight failure. Location of the power-plants was also to play a crucial part in the design process, side by side as in the Javelin and wing mounted as in the Meteor, were quickly abandoned as inducing too much drag. Eventually a layout with the engines mounted one above the other and fed by a common ovoidal intake resulted. The latest craze of prone piloting was investigated and discarded as being both tiring and impractical in the face of the adopted engine positions. With many of the team's ideas coming together to form a cohesive whole, Petter felt confident enough to approach the Ministry of Supply in early 1947. As the government of the day was still exhibiting total indifference to air research and development he was most surprised to be given a study contract ER (Experimental Requirements) 103 to develop and produce a single trials aircraft. Operating parameters laid down in the contract included a maximum speed of Mach=1.5 at an altitude of 30,000 ft.

In May 1948 another link in the Lightning chain was forged when Wing Commander R.P. Beamont flew a North American XP-86 Sabre at Muroc (later Edwards AFB) Test Center in California. During this flight he successfully breached the mystical Mach 1 barrier, the first British pilot to do so. As the main test pilot involved in the ER103 project, his first action upon returning to the UK was to report his findings to the E.E. Co design team, thus paving the way for a new phenomenon in development work – that of a test pilot having an input into the design process right from the outset. This new policy, a British first, was to eliminate some design team quirks regarding systems and cockpit layout and resulted in a far better aircraft with less in-service refining required than had previously been the case. It is unfortunate that such a positive input was counterbalanced by the negativity generated by the politicians and their officials.

With the ER103 contract safely under their belts, the Petter-led design team began the enormous task of creating a Mach 2 test vehicle capable of front-line development. Working on the premise that the wing sweep-angle would be in the region of sixty degrees, Petter passed the intricacies of design to two aerodynamic specialists, Dai Ellis and Ray Creasey. With the wing progressing in safe hands the location of the tailpiece and its operating design was the next task to be overcome. Petter had, in common with others, favoured a 'T' tail configuration for the new aircraft. In order to prove that the theory was workable two paths of research were entered into. The first was to construct a wind tunnel at English Electric, using time-expired Rolls-Royce Nene engines as airflow generators. Into this would go scale models produced to give initial results of the various proposed layouts that would later be compared with flight-tested articles.

To complement the wind tunnel Short Bros. of Belfast were contracted to build an airborne test vehicle, the SB 5, an experimental aircraft that was unique in its ability to mount a varied selection of wing and tail layouts as required by the designers. The tailplane, in its various guises, was capable of installation on different parts of the fin and rear fuselage. Acting in parallel with the wind tunnel, the SB 5 either proved or disproved data coming from wind tunnel runs as experienced in the real world of flight. The aircraft had been built at the instigation of the RAE who had charged Shorts with providing a low-speed research aircraft.

The doyen of the Lightning, P.1A WG 760 poses for the English Electric photographer on an early test-flight. Of interest are the leading edge flaps that were soon to be deleted from the design as ineffective. (*BAe WARTON*)

The wing mountings were capable of adjustment over 50, 60 and 69 degrees depending on requirements.

On 2 December 1952 the SB 5, serialled WG768, made its maiden flight piloted by Tom Brooke-Smith, later to fly the unique VTOL SC 1 aircraft. Bearing a remarkable resemblance to the forthcoming E.E. Co P.1, the SB 5 first flew with its wings set at the 50 degrees position, the tailplane being set in the full 'T' position. Eventually the wing sweep-angle of 60 degrees was reached, this later being permanently coupled with a low set tailplane position. This final layout had been settled upon when it was realised that the sharply swept wings would blank out the effectiveness of a high mounted tailplane at high angles of attack. The idea of elevator control in pitch also disappeared at this time to be replaced with slab tailplanes. The whole ensemble, when tested, confounded the critics, not only by retaining control throughout the full range of flight manoeuvres, but eliminated any tendency to pitch up caused by trim changes. Deletion of the elevators simplified design by removing a separate tailplane trimming system from the design equation.

It is interesting to note that the company's nearest rivals in America, North American, had also opted for a low set slab tailplane for their F-100 fighter.

Aircraft designing up to the era of the Lightning had always placed the ailerons on the wing trailing edge. Such a feature on some earlier swept-wing designs had led to a loss of control during crosswind landings and pilot-induced high angles of attack, due to the wing itself blanking out the control surface. Determined that such a fate would not befall the P.1 the ailerons were placed on the wingtips, the trailing edges being used for the flaps alone.

Although frequently portrayed as a waste of money, the use of an actual flying test-bed did enable all interested parties to try out new ideas in the air and confirm the data gained from wind tunnel and water-tank testing. Once the aircraft's task on the P.1 programme had been completed WG768 was retained by the RAE for other low-speed trials work. Retirement came in 1968 and with the maintenance number 8005M it was deposited at Finningley for preservation before finally settling in the Aerospace Museum at Cosford in the hall dedicated to prototype and research aircraft.

Having ran the gamut of the various wing sweep ideas the design team finally settled upon a sweep of 60 degrees for the leading edge, with the trailing angle being fixed at 52 degrees. Wing thickness was set at five per cent with a taper ratio of 0.15. With the thickest part of the wing on the chord centreline coupled to the degree of sweepback, the aerodynamics team estimated that compressibility would be delayed beyond Mach 1. Petter was obviously happy enough with progress to approach the MOS in 1949. So impressed were they by the results that Specification F23/49 was issued. Although bringing great kudos to E.E. Co, it also presented another set of problems as they had to upgrade the airframe to withstand the rigours of fighter type manoeuvring.

These changes notwithstanding a contract was issued to the company on 1 April 1950 which called for two flying airframes and one static test specimen to be notated as the P.1, later P.1A. It is worth noting that the other protagonist in the ER103 programme, Fairey Aviation, had produced the record-breaking FD2 which achieved a world speed record on 10 March 1953 piloted by Peter Twiss. The Fairey aircraft had to await the arrival of the Anglo-French Concorde to fully justify its existence and bring its aerodynamic research results to full fruition.

Having decided where the wings, tailplane, engines and pilot would all be located, the designers turned to their next major problem – where to place the undercarriage. Early experiments for the Fleet Air Arm using a rubberised shock-absorbing runway were quickly discounted as impractical in everyday usage. Trials using a suitably modified Sea Vampire had shown the idea as feasible although excessive in cost, manpower and possible damage repair. Added to this of course was the increased weight and speed of the P.1, which would have made the whole concept very frightening indeed.

Awaiting pre-flight ground runs is the second P.1A WG763. The short fin is of note although the classic lines of the Lightning are already beginning to show through. (*BAe WARTON*)

The final solution was to feature a nose undercarriage with long, relatively spindly main legs at the extremities of which would be wheels large in diameter, but thin in cross-section.

Main leg mounting was along the centre of the chord line at the wing root, the whole ensemble retracting outwards to lie flat under the fairings and doors. The nose leg also received much attention. In the P.1 the distance between the outer skin and that of the intake tunnel was fairly marginal, therefore the leg was designed to retract forward with the wheel rotating 90 degrees to lie flat before the doors closed.

In 1950, much to everyone's surprise, Petter left English Electric to join Follands where he was to culminate his career with the Midge, later to evolve into the Gnat, the Royal Air Force's trainer stalwart for many years. Taking his place at the head of the design team was the Chief Stress Analyst, F.W. Page, who became project manager. Freddie, later Sir Fredrick, Chairman of the BAe group, soon added a new impetus to the design team's efforts. One of the first problems cured under his guidance was that of the complicated vortices and boundary layer breakaway generated by the severe sweepback of the wing. This had been discovered during trials flying with the SB 5, when a slight loss of lateral feel had been experienced during low-speed flight. Not wishing to mar the wing with ungainly fences the tried solution was to introduce notches, initially some six inches in depth, into the wing leading edge approximately two-thirds of the span from the wing root. The airflow thus generated presented the aileron with a steady air stream to act against and eliminated any tendency towards control loss. As development progressed these slots were slowly decreased in size, but were to remain, not only as a positive contribution to flight control, but also as an area where a fuel tank pressure vent could be located in a position free from excessive turbulence. The final wing and tailplane layout was test flown on the Shorts SB 5 during December 1953, all the way from full speed down to wing stalling conditions. Throughout the flight envelope the aircraft remained stable with pitch control readily available at all times.

It is of course all very well to design an aircraft complete with all necessary systems, but all are totally useless without a suitable power-plant.

Before his departure to Folland, Petter had settled on the Roll-Royce Avon as the P.1 powerplant. Unfortunately, delays in the development trials and already committed production capacity were to result in none being available for the proposed P.1 flight date. In order that flight testing could proceed on schedule, Armstrong Siddeley Sapphire S Assa.5 engines rated at 8,100 lb dry thrust were chosen as temporary replacements – the airframe and its mountings being altered accordingly. With its unique power-plant positioning, the growth of the intake for both engines had increased by only fifty per cent in contrast to that of a similar single engine equivalent. Although their rating was more than capable of pushing the P.1 beyond Mach=1 their slow acceleration coupled with the limited amount of fuel carried by the P.1 forestalled the airframe from reaching its limiting Mach number. This was later remedied when reheated versions were fitted to the second airframe. Fuel contents, not all useable, located in the wings, was calculated at 2,500 lb, and would in fact have been used before maximum speed was achieved.

The field of flight control was also a new area to be explored. Normal fighters during the Second World War had relied on fully manual systems for control in all

For a short period the first P.1A was housed at Binbrook before making its final move to Cosford. Of note are the trailing edge protectors for the safety of both the aircraft and personnel. (*STEVE BUTTRISS*)

three axes. As speeds increased it was discovered that complete lock out of the control surfaces could occur, this only being curable by slowing down or in many cases, until the phenomenon was further understood, by crashing. Assisted flight-control systems with hydraulic boosters had lately begun to appear on some aircraft, the boosted elevators of the Hawker Hunter being one such. As the P.1 was intended to fly faster than the speed of sound, irreversible hydraulic screw-jacks were proposed for all flight control surfaces. Unfortunately with such a system the pilot loses his sense of 'feel'.

To overcome this deficiency a collection of cogs, springs and cams – known as an artificial feel, or 'Q' feel unit – was installed in each control run. Not only did these units give the pilot control sense but it also stopped him from overstressing or destroying the airframe by placing a governor on the amount of control surface movement available as speed increased. This was achieved by including a pitot-static input into the unit which, coupled to an electronic sensor, told the unit how much control movement was available at any given airspeed. First tests of such a system had been carried out at Samlesbury in October 1948 using a Halifax equipped with a Fairey Hydraulics Servodyne fitted in the elevator control circuit. Trials were outstandingly successful, the crew including two stalwarts of the Lightning programme, J. Squier and R.P. Beamont. Parameters set for the 'Q' feel included an initial maximum speed of 650 kts IAS at a maximum altitude of 70,000 ft. Unfortunately the Halifax could not reach these extreme parts of the envelope, it did however prove the lower and slower sectors from which the rest were successfully projected. The units finally chosen for the P.1 were provided by Hobsons whose hydraulic controls also featured in the Folland Gnat system that was to prove such a trial to maintainance personnel in the years that followed.

With settlement of the locations for all the major components resolved, detail design work for installing hydraulic, pneumatic and electrical systems could begin. As any Lightning engineer will happily tell you, the whole lot is extremely compact and intertwined. Such is the close tolerance of many clearances that access to some valves and pipe-runs is only possible after the removal of one or both engines.

Landing and approach speeds were calculated at approximately 160 kts, an unheard of speed at the time. Allied to this was a heavy airframe with wings swept at 60 degrees and a loading of 70 lb/sq ft. With the possibility of some early landings being within the speed range of 180–200 kts its was felt that the 1,900 yard runway at Warton would be inadequate for the first flight of such an awesome beast. Although subsequent lengthening of the runway to 2,500 yards was carried out in time for the P.1B maiden flight, it was decided that the Boscombe Down runway would be ideal for the first flight and the initial series of twenty shake-down handling flights.

As with all prototypes the P.1 airframes were virtually hand-built at Samlesbury. Their assigned serials were WG760, WG763 and WG765, the last mentioned being the static-test airframe. WG763 was assigned, even before its maiden flight, to the general handling and performance role, whilst WG763 covered the tasks of structural stress-loading research and initial armament investigation. Throughout 1953 work progressed on the prototypes and their existence first rated a mention in the 1954 White Paper on Defence, although actual details and the manufacturer's name were deleted. By May 1954 WG760 was undergoing full ground-system testing at Warton prior to that all-important first flight. All possible ground testing completed, WG760 was then dismantled down to major assemblies. Complete with the requisite re-assembly jigs and jacks, the whole lot was loaded onto road trailers and moved to Boscombe Down in June.

Soon after arrival, re-assembly and functionals of the aircraft and systems began with a sense of vital urgency running through all operations as the race for the projected first flight in July loomed. Some minor hydraulic and engine problems delayed ground taxi trials until 24 July.

These first trials were required to prove the efficiency of the aircraft's braking system, especially as regards temperature control and heat dispersion. Testing of the tail brake-chute and the nose-wheel steering was also undertaken up to the threshold of the theoretical take-off speed. All the foregoing were completed satisfactorily between 24 July and 2 August. On at least one high-speed run during the early part of the taxi tests, with R.P. Beamont at the controls, WG760 achieved 125 kts and briefly flew. From that point onwards confidence in the aircraft grew and short down-the-runway hops were carried out that proved the design philosophy was correct and that the P.1 was stable about all axes at the low speeds to be encountered during approach and landing. Given the length of Boscombe Down's runway, all this could safely take place within the airfield's boundaries as – long as the brake-chute continued to function correctly. After each day's trials

Now resident in the Manchester Museum of Science and Technology, WG763 is pictured at Henlow in 1964. Displaced panels and ground equipment indicate that the aircraft is being used for engineering training purposes. Both P.1A prototypes spent some time at Henlow as parade ground backdrops before moving to their current homes. (*CP RUSSELL-SMITH*)

the whole team flew to Warton to analyse that day's results and lay out the programme for the morrow.

Mention should be made here of those personnel closely involved with the project at Boscombe Down. As noted R.P. Beamont was the Chief Test Pilot and overall controller of the trials and he was ably assisted by F. Bradford as Chief Engineer and D. Horsfield as Chief Flight Test Project Engineer. In charge of the all important ground crew, drawn from the works, was W. Evans.

As all the criterion for a test flight had by now been successfully met the decision was taken to fly WG760 on its maiden flight on 3 August. Unfortunately that great demon 'finger trouble' reared its ugly head. Checking over the cockpit and its controls for a final time 'Bee' Beamont inadvertantly fired-off the engine-bay fire extinguishers. Cleaning up the mess was to occupy the rest of the day, thus delaying the flight. The next day dawned with high cloud, although it was forecast to clear by mid-morning.

Priority cleared by Boscombe Down's Air Traffic Control, Beamont was strapped into the cockpit of WG760. Engines were started and the aircraft taxied to the runway threshold. Following closely behind WG760 was WD973 the company's Canberra chase-plane, At 0958 hrs on 4 August 1954 after a full power run-up against the brakes WG760, Britain's first true supersonic fighter roared down Boscombe Down's runway and lifted into the sky faultlessly. After years of trials and tribulations the thunder had truly begun.

Chapter 2
Cutting Metal

ALTHOUGH THE first flight of WG760 was to last no longer than thirty-three minutes, many of the aircraft's systems were given their first taste of operating in a flight regime. Overall the P.1 behaved much as expected, although 'Bee' Beamont did report that the prototype was very sensitive to aileron control and that with flaps and undercarriage retracted a tendency to pitch down was experienced. Deployment of the airbrakes also raised a few anomalies with heavy buffeting and erratic rolling in the yaw-sense noted as the main reactions. Maximum speed during this first flight was 450 kts at an altitude of 17,000 ft. Only one other technical difficulty arose from this momentous occasion – the radios all seemed to fail just after take-off.

The next day, after a night of engineering tweaking, WG760 was declared ready for more test flying. Investigations scheduled for August centred upon control operation and handling under a variety of G-force loads. It was whilst carrying out a 2G turn at 400 kts that the pilot, Beamont, experienced an aileron lock-up. Suspecting that bane of all aviators, FOD, he carefully flew the aircraft back to Boscombe Down. The in-depth investigations that followed revealed no foreign object lodged in an awkward place, but did point the engineering team towards the idea that careful balancing of the control circuits and their attendant hydraulic systems might in fact eliminate the problem before it grew worse. Further detailed examinations revealed that the aileron system had been set statistically using longitudinal accelerations as the guide-line, not as may be expected with those offsets required for high-speed banking.

Not wishing to ground the P.1 so early in its flight trials, the decision was taken to explore other flight parameters and return to manoeuvring under 'G' conditions once WG760 had undergone its first period of engineering modifications.

Accordingly on 11 August, WG760 climbed from Boscombe's runway, executing such a manner that was to become familiar to many Lightning pilots in later years, that of an express turbo lift! With all systems functioning as advertised, the throttles of the P.1 were advanced to maximum. On-board indicated airspeed finally settled at Mach=0.98 at 30,000 ft, WG760 seemingly reluctant to make that final leap from the realm of the transonic to that of the supersonic. With fuel getting low a return to base became a necessity, even so – a quick turn at full speed showed that this experimental test-bed had the making of a great fighter. Bee Beamont had to wait until the next day to find out that he had become the first British pilot to breach the supersonic barrier in level flight.

With this success under their belts the decision was made by the development team to delay flight No.4 so that many of the engineering glitches that had been building up could be rectified. On 13 August the P.1, now returned to tip-top condition, yet again took-off from the Boscombe Down runway like an express train. Levelling at 40,000 ft the throttles were yet again advanced and once more WG760 seemed to stall at the Mach=0.98 point. Continued thrust finally pushed the P.1 – with scarcely a tremor – through to Mach=1.01. Handling of the flight controls throughout all three axes was immediately carried out and revealed no adverse side-effects. Speed continued to climb finally passing Mach=1.08 by a small margin.

With its limited fuel load nearly expended the P.1 was pointed in the direction of Boscombe, a wise move as by now the fuel gauges were winding down faster than the speed was going up! Just to prove that it was all for real, Beamont overflew Boscombe at Mach=1.02 where all below were treated to a sonic boom – one of the less attractive benefits of high-speed flight. Continuing test flights, sometimes up to three a day, proved the soundness of the P.1 design. Unfortunately not enough flying hours were clocked-up to allow the aircraft to appear at the 1954 SBAC airshow at Farnborough.

A new idea always results in VIP visits and the advent of the latest English Electric product was to prove no different. Scheduled for 15 September, the first visit and flying display was for Prince Bernhardt of the Netherlands. Apparently on this occasion the government host failed to make an appearance, ironically it was Mr Duncan Sandys, later to be the presenter of the infamous 1957 Defence White Paper! A dynamic flying display by Beamont reportedly impressed the Prince, unfortunately no orders were forthcoming as the Royal Netherlands AF eventually selected the Lockheed F-104 Starfighter as its prime fighter-bomber. This decision was to prove very embarrassing when the Lockheed bribes scandal exploded across the front pages of the world's newspapers. Another upshot of the display was a letter of rebuke to the pilot for apparently endangering the visitors by low flying. Those familiar with Boscombe Down will be well aware that the runway is set 50 ft below the level of the operating apron.

It was soon after this that the lengthening of Warton's runway was completed, WG760 was then flown north by Beamont on 23 September where, soon after arrival, he was asked to fly a display for some VIP guests. Happily quoting the 'official letter' he needless to say, declined.

The whole sorry saga was eventually buried under a mound of redundant paperwork, strangely enough just in time for the visit of some American Generals, and never referred to again. Obviously such visits, although welcome, were not allowed to interrupt the programme. During its 50th flight on 28 November 1954 WG760 repeated its maximum speed run of Mach=1.22 – a benchmark that had first been passed a few days earlier. Pleased as the design and development teams were with the progress of WG760, it will come as no surprise to find that the next stage in the P.1 genesis was already under intense discussion. Designated P.1B, these next aircraft were regarded as the interim stage between pure development and trials and the 'real thing'. These were initially being envisaged as P.1B-type airframes built more on jigs than by hand, as was the case in the P.1 series. In an effort to overcome the short range of WG760, the second P.1, WG763, was built from the outset with mountings for the installation of a belly-mounted ventral fuel tank which, although it looked an integral part of the airframes, was in reality, detachable.

As with all such projects, no one man could or should be the linchpin. In the flight test department this meant the arrival of Desmond de Villiers as number two test pilot, whilst Peter Hillwood initially filled the vacant third slot. Arriving in December 1954, both pilots spent the early part of the following year becoming thoroughly familiar with their new mount. During 1955, with the future development of the P.1 looking hopeful, further work on ironing-out the engineering bugs continued. One area concentrated upon was that of tail brake-chute operation, which although working perfectly well most of the time, did on occasion fail to operate, much to the consternation of the pilots who then had to find extra braking power in the wheel brakes. Slight redesign and strengthening of the lower fuselage cleared the problem, enabling the 'chute to pop successfully every time.

With rectification and pilot conversion completed a return to development-trials flying began. Investigation into yaw roll coupling, aerodynamic flutter and the effect on other aircraft of supersonic flypasts were to occupy English Electric for much of that year. During these flights a persistent 'buzz' in certain parts of the speed range became noticeable in the area of the fin and rudder. Without fitting some sort of damping device to a fluttering control surface, the resulting vibrations can increase to such an extent that major structural failures can occur. In the P.1's case the problem was approached in two ways. The first involved complete redesign of the offending items, a lengthy and expensive business, or by the famous British habit of the quick fix. This latter course was adopted and a small viscous-oil filled damper produced by the Houdaille Hershey Company of America was fitted to the rudder. So successful was this solution that the redesign option was dropped, all production aircraft being fitted with the damper as standard during building.

During some of the 1955 test flights, problems with the canopy locking system began to occur. During one such flight, whilst operating airborne test equipment, a series of small explosions, deliberately set-off on the fin, was to be followed by one big one – definitely not deliberate. Once the pilot, Beamont, had recovered control and vision, he discovered that the canopy had completely disappeared – closely followed by his bonedome and visor. In similar circumstances, service pilots would have quite rightly ejected, but test pilots are by way of their occupation made of sterner stuff.

As full control was still available a cautious return to Warton was made. Investigations into the canopy detachment suggested that suction loads generated by high-speed flight had pulled the canopy rails clear of the locks and literally sucked it clear of the aeroplane. Rectification took the form of adjustments to the mechanism and after another canopy fit, WG760 was declared operational again. Unfortunately a few weeks later the canopy was to depart the aircraft again, this time de Villiers was the pilot. Yet again another successful return to base was made. Further tinkering with the canopy and its locking mechanism apparently cured the problem as further test flights were undertaken without incident. Test pilot de Villiers must have felt sorely put upon when a few weeks later WG760 self-jettisoned its canopy once again. Having failed a third time to cure the problem English Electric re-engineered the whole locking mechanism for greater loads, thus eliminating the problem completely.

By the summer of 1955 WG760 had achieved Mach=1.4 in a dive, this being the maximum speed attainable with the original thrust Sapphires then installed. With the second P.1, WG763, due to come into the test programme, the decision was taken to re-engine the first aircraft with re-heated Sapphires. The second aircraft, WG763, made its maiden flight on 18 July 1955 piloted by R.P. Beamont, this time from the revamped Warton runway. Subsequent to this first flight WG760, was grounded for the installation of its new power-plants and engineering modifications.

The second P.1 WG763, differed from the first aircraft in three main areas. The most obvious change was of course in the fitment of a ventral tank containing 2,000 lbs of fuel. Two 30mm Aden cannon adorned the upper nose area, one per side, whilst the flaps had reverted to the more common single piece hinged type, these were later to find usage as fuel tanks in the production aircraft. Unlike its predecessor WG763 was to be powered by unreheated Sapphires throughout its whole working life. Even so, these thirsty brutes managed to consume the wing fuel tank's usable contents in 55 minutes, hence the need for the ventral tank. One other, less obvious change, was the introduction of rudder-pedal-mounted toe brakes, common at the time in American aircraft, in place of the usually preferred control-column mounted handbrake lever. Evaluation at Boscombe Down concluded that the new installation operated well and without any problems, but was not so popular with pilots as was the earlier hand system.

WG760 resumed test flying on 31 January 1956, only this time a pair of reheated Sapphires replaced the 8,000 lbs dry thrust engines of earlier days. True, the replacements had a lower dry thrust rating of 5,500 lbs st, but with reheat engaged a respectable total of more than 18,000 lbs st was produced albeit via very crude fixed nozzles. Understandably the coarseness of the reheat system drained the usable fuel system quickly, but the advantages of the extra thrust, even for short periods, far outweighed any disadvantages. The lowered dry power thrust also reduced the single engine safety margin to zero, the possibility of a safe return on one engine was now regarded as a thing of the past. During its first flight in its new form WG760 gained an altitude of 40,000 ft in 3½ minutes, reaching Mach=1.4 with ease in the process. Further flight testing brought this up to a maximum of M=1.45, although at this speed longitudinal control had begun to decay. Further flights followed – finally producing a maximum speed of M=1.5.

At this point a definite intake buzz was discernable, indicating that perhaps the P.1 had reached its limit. In order to ascertain this, a further series of flights was undertaken during February 1956. It was during one of these high-speed runs that M=1.56 was reached.

The result of all this influx of data from the P.1A and the Shorts SB 5 was the determination of the specifications of the forthcoming P.1B. Before leaving the P.1A however, one other area of redesign deserves chronicling. During the latter part of 1956 WG760 was grounded for the fitment of a new pair of wings. In plan view the new wing set was cambered with a forward sweep of 55 degrees being incorporated outboard of the leading edge notch. Not only did this new shape promise greater stability, it also increased flying time, one benefit being the increased volume available for fuel carriage. The change in the wing's leading edge also led to the wingtip becoming squarer in profile. To accommodate this change the ailerons lost their prominent horns, presenting a straight leading edge to the airflow. Wind-tunnel testing on aerodynamic models had predicted an increase in stability in the transonic speed region, although on the negative side a slight decrease in top speed resulted. However, control surface handling became crisper, a bonus that was fully explored during the landing phase. Also deleted during this series of modifications were the leading edge flap sections which had proved to be of no benefit during the landing and take-off phases. Flight testing also revealed that at high speeds the onset of sonic shock waves and boundary layer buffet was delayed considerably.

Although the P.1A was flown to its maximum limiting speed with the new wing design, team leader F.W. Page delayed pushing its advantages until the Mach 2 barrier had been breached. This latter task was to be the major milestone set for the P.1B.

Ironically it took the governments that followed, of all political hues, many years to fund production Lightnings with cambered wings, even though the F.3 had been mooted with them as standard in 1958. It took the appearance of the F.6 and its derivatives – plus the rebuilt F.2s to repay the money expended during the research from the taxpayer.

On 4 April 1957 'Bee' Beamont lifted the latest stage in the Lightning's development from the Warton runway. Closely resembling the first production aircraft, this intermediate step in the programme was designated the P.1B. Design work for an advanced version of the P.1A incorporating those features deemed necessary in a fighter had begun in 1954. As data and flight test results were received in the drawing office, so refinements were incorporated in the new machines' specifications. Under the guidance of F.W. Page, the E.E. Co design team had advanced enough for the MoS to issue a contract in August 1955 for three hand-built specimens of the new design. Serialled XA847, 853 and 856 these three were followed by five more built in production-style jigging. A further fifteen were added to the contract in the following year.

Externally the main visual difference between the new P.1B and its predecessor was the replacement of the originals ovoidal intake by one of a circular section. Located in the centre of the pitot intake was the conical bullet designed to house the business end of the AI 23 AIRPASS radar system – a monopulse unit designed by Ferranti. As well as a redesigned canopy giving much greater all round vision, the pilot was provided with an early Head-Up-Display, HUD, data for which was partly fed from the on-board air data computer. All this electronic wizardry was incorporated to guide the aiming of the pair of 30mm Aden cannon installed in the upper nose section. On the lower forward fuselage, pylon mountings were built in as standard; these were later used to carry the DH Props Blue Jay, later Firestreak, infra-red homing air-to-air missile. Other weaponary designated suitable for mounting in the space occupied by the missile pack included drop-down packs containing FFARs or a further pair of cannon.

The greatest innovation in the P.1B was the fitment from the start of the designated power-plants, the Rolls-Royce Avon. Later designated the Model RA.24 Mk.210, these engines were the most powerful available for their size, being dry rated at 11,250 lbs st. In total contrast to the earlier fixed nozzle Sapphires, the new Avons featured a four-stage nozzle that improved engine performance at all settings. Engine starting was achieved through the usage of Plessey AVPIN (Isopropyl Nitrate) gas starters that were to prove occasionally troublesome in service use. As they were slightly larger than the earlier Sapphires, a complete redesign of the fuselage was required. This resulted in the characteristic deep slab-sided item that was to remain virtually unchanged throughout the production run. The pilots 'office' was also changed quite considerably, not only was it raised slightly higher in the fuselage, the canopy was also bulged to increase the vision area.

The appearance of the P.1B carried the Lightning's evolution one stage further. Here XA847 rolls along the Warton taxiway with brake-chute still attached. (*BAe WARTON*)

During wind-tunnel testing comparative trials between flush and bulged canopies had been carried out. Very little difference in their aerodynamic behaviour and efficiency had occurred, thus the bulged version appeared on the P.1B, faired into a dorsal fairing that stretched aft to the fin base. To assist the pilot in retaining his outside vision throughout all altitudes, an air bleed system for rain removal externally and a hot air demister internally were installed.

Electrical power supplies were provided using a hot air bleed turbine located in the rear fuselage, a change from the more normal practice of direct engine-driven shafts. To remove the buffeting caused by the airbrakes in the earlier P.1A the whole system was redesigned, the new installation being more efficient and more importantly reducing pitch changes to a minimum.

One feature carried over to the P.1B was the short fin which was later to prove troublesome due to the effect of the increased side area of the fuselage reducing the effect of the rudder. Changes to the undercarriage were also effected; the nose unit now retracted forwards without having to twist and lay flat, this simplified and lightened the whole assembly. Also omitted from the new design was the nose wheel steering system. Ground guidance was now controlled by differential braking, the nose wheel acting in a purely castoring manner.

The first flight of XA847 contrasted sharply with the Defence White Paper for 1957 delivered on that day by the Minister for Defence, Mr Duncan Sandys. As 'Bee' Beamont was exceeding Mach=1 on 1 March, the House of Commons was listening with incredulity to a speech that removed the manned fighter from Britain's air defence armoury. Many advanced and worthwhile programmes were axed, including the AVRO supersonic bomber, the Saunders Roe SR 53 and the thin-wing Javelin. To cap the Minister's naivety, those assembled heard him place his faith in a missile-based defensive and offensive system that was barely off the drawing-board, let alone ready to take over the role of defending the United Kingdom. Fortunately the Gods smiled upon English Electric and left their Lightning project alone, the reasons given including the costs already incurred during development and the need to produce a fighter capable of intercepting high-altitude attackers that were beyond the reach of the current crop of fighters – the Meteor F.Mk.8 and the Hunter.

A later product from the company was to

prove less fortunate, the TSR.2 being axed even though similar funds had been spent on its development and there was a proven need for such an aircraft.

Although the Lightning programme was allowed to continue, defence advisors initially ruled out developing it beyond the first generation. Fortunately wiser councils later prevailed and the missile defence system was junked. Further on the debit side, the Napier Double Scorpion rocket motor intended to boost the Lightning to great heights much faster than its Avons could was also axed. The irony of the situation was that the installation had virtually completed its test flying programme in one of the company's Canberras.

With the appearance of the P.1B on the test scene the share of work allocated to the earlier aircraft began to shrink. For WG760 this meant continuing as a general handling and conversion aircraft until 1962 when it was grounded. At Warton it was dismantled and transported to No.4 S of TT at RAF St Athan for use as a ground instructional airframe. By 1967 it had moved on to Henlow where it acted as a parade ground exhibit before moving to its present home in the Aerospace Museum at Cosford. The second P.1A, WG763, had achieved its first air-to-air cannon firing in 1956, which was followed by supersonic gun firing in 1957. Low-speed handling followed at the RAE where it remained until it was withdrawn from use, later joining WG760 at Henlow. When this station finally closed its gates for good, the airframe was moved to the Manchester Museum where it currently resides.

After this most successful of test flights in XA847 the test pilot team went onto complete a further thirty-seven sorties in the following two months. Comments from all sides were more than favourable concerning the P.1B's handling and performance which was similar to the earlier model, but with twice the engine power. The 100th test-flight was carried out in November 1957 during which speeds of M=1.7, 650 kts IAS at a turn rate of 6G were achieved.

These parameters were those that were initially laid down for the airframe, although the maximum speed soon rose to M=1.75 (1,161 mph). According to comments passed at the time, 'it was like riding a race-horse with the brakes on'. In order that the performance of the P.1B could be gauged correctly, flight trials were conducted with and without the ventral tank fitted and with aerodynamic dummy Blue Jay rounds on the fuselage pylons. In full war rig, with ventral tank and missiles, a slight loss of longitudinal control positiveness became apparent. This resulted in a small amount of weather cocking around the yaw axis. The E.E. Co, design team had already theorised that this problem would arise, therefore design work was well underway to produce a larger fin. First flight with the ventral tank fitted had taken place on 27 August 1957, the missile-fit following a few weeks later.

The first P.1B, shown as the third prototype in company records, was joined in September 1957 by the second example, XA853. The pilot on this occasion was Desmond de Villiers. Both P.1Bs then entered the pre-programmed phased flight-test programme that was intended to clear any airframe anomalies prior to the pre-production aircraft flying. Whilst both P.1B prototypes were busy clearing the airframe and system aspects of the new fighter, the third aircraft, XA856, was close to completion. The build process finally ended on 3 January 1958 when Beamont piloted the fifth P.1 from Warton's runway. After the usual series of shake-down flights XA856 was transferred to the Rolls-Royce test facility at Hucknall where it was flown at the end of its thirty-fifth flight. Having previously used Hunters and Canberras in the Avon development programme Rolls-Royce, not surprisingly, were eager to lay their hands on a supersonic test vehicle to extend the capabilities of the powerplant even further.

Throughout its period at Hucknall the fifth P.1 prototypes was in the care of Rolls-Royce test pilot J. Heyworth. On 23 October 1958 Chief of the Air Staff, Sir Dermot Boyle, broke a bottle of Champagne over the nose of prototype P.1B, XA847 at Farnborough – bestowing the name Lightning upon the whole of the breed.

The flight that was to justify the whole programme's existence took place on 25 November 1958 when 'Bee' Beamont flew XA847 through the Mach 2 barrier. To commemorate this outstanding achievement a plate was riveted to the port side of the nose. Although this was indeed a newsworthy item routine test flying to clear and expand the flight envelope for the forthcoming pre-production machines continued. Having passed Mach 2 in a clean condition, attention now turned to eliminating the weather cocking experienced with ventral tank and missiles fitted. On XA847 this was controlled by installing a dorsal extension to complement the aircraft's original short fin. For the pre-production series and later the first service aircraft, a taller fin was provided. From the start of the development programme it had always been recognised that the Lightning was going to suffer a range problem. To partially resolve this English Electric in co-operation with Flight Refuelling Ltd began developing a system for use in flight. Proving trials were carried out in 1959 using XA847 complete with pole probe under the port wing. The tanker aircraft was a converted Canberra B.2 WH734. For the period of the trials XA847 was painted with white fuel-sensitive paint on the port side of the fuselage. Intended to show the flow of waste fuel on connection and disconnection, it was somewhat overloaded when Beamont broke the tip off the probe during an early test flight. Fortunately damage was minimal and the trials resumed almost immediately, continuing on to a successful conclusion.

XA847 was also used for the development of a far more important system, the centralised warning panel. On an aircraft as complex as the Lightning, where systems and components are closely packed together, the possibility of fire was regarded as a real hazard. Unfortunately the early system was subject to malfunctions. So numerous were they that pilots and support crews alike developed a blasé attitude to this behaviour. This attitude changed radically on 8 May 1958 when XA853 returned to Warton with a fire warning caption lit on the panel. On touch-down the elevator control system seized and on stopping smoke was seen to be billowing from the rear of the aircraft. Inspection of the damage after the fire had been quenched revealed that a whole new rear fuselage would be required. The cause was later traced to a hot air leak from adjacent ducting that had ignited pockets of fuel and oil trapped in the various recesses in the structure. Much effort and energy was expended over the following fifteen months by English Electric and Rolls-Royce to solve the problem. Redesigning of the detection system and its feeds to the central panel was part of the solution, whilst the engine manufacturers placed a relight limitation of 20,000 ft for reheat restarts. All these delays, although not totally unexpected, did serve to slow the programme down, although it did pick up speed again once all the re-design work had been completed at the end of October 1959.

These set-backs however did not delay the deliveries of the pre-production P.1B/F.1 aircraft. The first of the twenty Lightnings ordered under this contract made its maiden flight on 3 April 1958, with the last appearing in September 1959.

It is interesting to note that as this batch progressed through Samlesbury more and more production-standard jigs were brought into use. When the last airframe was rolled out the door it had been built entirely to F.1 production standards.

The appearance of the pre-production Lightnings did not, however, mean the end of the P.1B's contributions. For XA853, complete with a four-cannon fit, this meant airborne firing in July 1959 – a task it was to remain associated with at A&AEE, Boscombe Down, until it was grounded on 3 May 1963 having flown 153 hours 25 minutes in a total of 296 flights. After dismantling, the airframe remained in use; the wings were returned to Warton for testing to destruction, whilst the remainder was given to the Boscombe Fire Service for them to practice their nefarious arts.

Meanwhile at Hucknall Rolls-Royce operated the fifth P.1, XA856, until 1 June 1967 exclusively on RA.24 Avon development flights, which finally reached a total of 296 before grounding. For the pioneer of the P.1Bs, flying continued until 1972 when, after 468 flights, it was finally withdrawn from use and placed on display in the RAFM at Hendon. One of its last trials was to air qualify the enlarged ventral tank that was to feature prominently in the F.2A and F.6 fighters. The appearance of the twin ventral fins at the rear of this tank owe much to the development work carried out on XA847. In-flight trials had revealed that a much greater fin area would be required to offset the aerodynamic influence of the tank. Two solutions were offered, the first entailed a complete re-design of the fin and its mountings, the second was for the neater and smaller ventral fins.

In the later variants of Lightning a larger squarer fin was to appear, but this still retained the original fixtures and provided enough longitudinal stability for the F.2A and F.6 to operate quite comfortably with missiles and tank fitted. A less glamorous task followed, that of trialing a method of stopping high-speed aircraft at the end of a runway after brake failure. Based on an original railway practice the trials were conducted at RAE Bedford during 1966 and entailed the aircraft taxying at high speeds into gravel-beds – the intention being that the resultant drag caused by the gravel would slow the aircraft down. Although a good idea, it was not adjudged a success as insufficient area was available on the aircraft's wheels to act as a brake.

Meanwhile the twenty development aircraft were being allocated and configured to carry out specific areas of the test programme. For the first two aircraft, XG307 and XG308, this involved flight handling trials which were to include stalling and spinning, although by 1960 XG307 was carrying out engine compartment gas leak investigations before its conversion to F.Mk.3 standard. Following conversion it was allocated to the Auto Attack trials of the F.3's weapons guidance system during the period 1963–65.

Weapons carriage and operation appeared very early on in the test programme with XA847 and XA853 already allocated. In addition, pre-production aircraft XG308, 309, 311 and 327 were soon involved. To the first three fell the tasks of carriage and release checks whilst the others were concentrated on establishing the operating parameters of the AI.23 radar system. Of all the allocated aircraft only XG309 remained totally dedicated to weapons development throughout its career. Of the others XG311 moved onto starter, cabin conditioning, engineering and tropical operations trials.

This was followed during 1962–63, by its usage as a high-speed target for the AI.23 carrier aircraft. This came to an abrupt halt on 31 July 1963 when it crashed after the starboard undercarriage had failed to lower, leaving the pilot, Don Knight, no other option than to eject. The abandoned Lightning finally crashed into the Ribble Estuary. XG327, the last of the weapons aircraft, was to continue in use as a systems' trials aircraft until 1967. On the way it had, during 1959–62, been employed in crash-barrier trials and was to suffer extensive damage during a landing in February 1960 that was serious enough to warrant attention by the manufacturers. By 1971 the aircraft was in store at Bedford having finished its last tests in the field of supersonic noise analysis. From the RAE XG327 was moved to 4 Sof TT at St Athan for use as a training aid with the maintainance number 8188M applied. Its final fate was a fiery one as it was moved to the Fire Training School at Manston in 1981 where it was used for brake fire training. After one brake fire too many it finally disappeared in 1992.

Trials flying of the Firestreak, as the Blue Jay had now become, was based at Warton with live firings being carried out at the ranges of Aberporth or Boulmer depending on the weather – diversion facilities were available at RNAS Brawdy for those aircraft involved if required. Of the six aircraft involved most of the work was the province of two, XA847 and XG308. To them fell the evaluation flights in the areas of flame-out after launch, vibration analysis, jettison characteristics, engineering support requirements and operational sortie profiles. Much was already known about the Firestreak's behaviour as early trials work had been carried out using Canberra test-beds.

An irony that arose from these trials was the revelation many years later, that English Electric were asked to pay the costs involved for services provided, even though the system was being developed specifically for the Royal Air Force, and later for export.

Another Lightning that spent some time engaged in the Firestreak programme was XG325 that had first flown with J. Squier at the controls on 26 February 1959. General handling and TACAN trials occupied the aircraft initially, before it moved onto IPN starter, radio bay cooling and auto-pilot evaluations. By 1962 XG325 was at Hatfield allocated to DH Props for Firestreak development. This was to be its dedicated task for the next four years until it was returned to Warton, being struck off charge in March 1966. After a career spanning 221 hours and 282 flights XG325 then suffered the indignity of being dismantled by a team from 60 MU, Leconfield, who removed the airframe to AWRE Shoeburyness. Placed in store, the Lightning escaped use as a target, being put up for disposal in October 1968. Most of the airframe went to the local scrapman although the nose escaped, being allocated to 1476 Sqdn ATC who later passed it onto 1312 Sqdn ATC at Southend. The appearance of XG310, the fourth aircraft in the batch, heralded the arrival of the tall pointed fin as standard. After its maiden flight on 17 July 1958 the F.1 was allocated to avionics development, mainly in the field of auto-pilot and ILS assessment and integration. This continued at various establishments until 1961 when it was returned to Warton for conversion to F.3 standard. Remodelled, XG310 resumed flying again in 1962, first with the manufacturers and later with the A&AEE at Boscombe Down. Once the flight parameters of the new fin had been established, flight trials with Red Top development rounds continued throughout 1963–64.

On 13 July 1964 XG310 ceased its flying career although it did continue in use at Warton for taxi tests. This was followed by a period in storage which lasted until 1968 when the aircraft was handed over to 60 MU at Leconfield for spares recovery. Now a hulk, the remains of XG310 were dispatched to the PEE Shoeburyness ranges (part of the AWRE) where it suffered the indignity of having cannon-shells fired at it, many of which came from weapons destined for the Lightning fleet. After three years use as a target XG310 was placed on the scrap list. The nose eventually came to rest in a scrapyard in Basildon, Essex, in December 1972. This most useful of development tools had flown 192 hours over 374 flights during the active part of its career.

The heart of the Lightning's attack system was the AI.23 AIRPASS radar system, aircraft assigned to this task included XG312, 326 and 331. In parallel with the fighters, development sets were also flown in Meteors, Dakotas and a much modified Canberra B.2. This particular airframe, WJ643, differed from the norm in sporting a B(I)8 nose which supposedly gave more room to the Ferranti radar observers. Unfortunately the remaining space available after installation of the AI.23 was so cramped that the possibility of abandonment in the event of an emergency was virtually impossible.

The first of the AIRPASS Lightnings, XG312 first flew on 29 December 1958. It began its radar assignment in the New Year, continuing in service with the various trials organisations until conversion to F.3 standard by Boulton Paul at Seighford during 1961. Upon completion XG312 returned to the radar trials programme, although it was now the test-bed for the more advanced AI.23B, a role it was to maintain until 1964. Still fitted with the upgraded radar XG312 then went on to provide target facilities for the Ferranti-crewed Canberra.

It was during one of these sorties that the windscreen shattered at 37,000 ft, Flying at Mach=0.9 the pilot, J. Cockburn, was obviously shocked, however professionalism took over and a successful recovery was made to base. This was to be the last flight of XG312 as it was withdrawn from flying on 12 October 1966 having achieved a total of 429 flights spread over 303 flying hours. After a further six years of ground testing followed by spares recovery, XG312 was finally scrapped in April 1972.

Also allocated to this programme was the ninth pre-production aircraft, XG326, which made its maiden flight on 14 March 1959. Throughout its flying career this Lightning was engaged in the more practical aspects of radar development which included weapons systems aiming trials at Boscombe Down and Firestreak carriage and guidance-head trials. Its role as a test vehicle ended at Warton on 6 October 1967. It was later dismantled by a team from 60 MU who then transported it to PEE Shoeburyness during June 1968 for possible use as a target. Before such a fate befell the aircraft however, XG326 appeared at Horse Guards Parade as part of a static display celebrating fifty years of the RAF in conjunction with that year's Battle of Britain display. By 1971 the remains were sold for scrap, the aircraft having flown some 416 hours in 551 flights.

The third AI.23 dedicated F.1 was XG331 which had first flown on 14 May 1959. Initial tasking for this, the 14th aircraft, over the twelve months that followed was engineering and operational reliability and assessment trials. Having practised everything in Britain, XG331 was flown to Aden in 1960 where it was all done again under tropical conditions. It was during this series of flights that the No.1 engine starter exploded, causing extensive damage to the rear fuselage. Rebuilt, XG331 rejoined the programme, this time testing the upgraded 'B' version of the Ferranti AI.23.

From basic radar trials XG331 progressed onto joint weapons systems trials which occupied the Lightning throughout 1964–65. Finally grounded in 1967 after 290 flights and 196 flying hours the aircraft's remains were shipped to the Shoeburyness ranges in 1968, finally being sold for scrap to a Basildon scrapyard in December 1972. The nose however went to the now defunct aviation museum at Long Marston.

One of the few pre-production Lightnings not to end its days as either a target or a crash rescue trainer was XG313 which was to finish its career far from these shores. First flown by R.P. Beamont on 2 February 1959 this, the 7th aircraft, spent its early days in the general handling role. This was mainly concerned with establishing the aft C of G safety margin. Following on from the various attempts to sit on its tail during flight, came the joys and delights of canopy jettison trials. Conducted mainly on the ground, this entailed firing the canopy clear of the aircraft so that an accurate path of trajectory could be established. Damage to both the canopy and aircraft was prevented by stringing nets over the area to catch the canopy when it landed. During this period XG313 was dispatched to the Paris Air Show to display English Electric's latest product alongside those of other nations. From 1960 the manufacturers used the aircraft in trials to prove the two inch rocket projectile packs that could be installed in lieu of the normal missile fit. Most firings were conducted, as before, at the Aberporth range. Once the company was satisfied as to the rocket performance the aircraft was handed over to the A&AEE where the installation underwent pre-service clearance trials in which it was successful.

The last flight of XG313 took place on 25 April 1968 when it left Boscombe Down for the Sydenham premises of Airworks Services for use as an instructional airframe, the Lightning having completed 361 hours of flying over 560 flights. Later allocated 'B' class marks as G-27-115 the Lightning was shipped to Dharan AB in Saudi Arabia for further usage as an instructional aid. Reports from the region indicate that XG313 was finally scrapped in the 1970s when more up-to-date training equipment was delivered.

In their earlier guises the P.1 series aircraft and those in the pre-production batch had all sported fairly basic flight control panels and navigation systems. To overcome the potential problem of becoming lost whilst on an interception the Air Staff issued Operational Requirement(OR)946. This called for an upgraded navigation suite that had update and guidance feeds to the main fire control system. Based largely on TACAN, OR946 also included an integrated flight instrument display, an air data system, master reference gyro and instrument landing system. The F.1 chosen to trial this equipment was the 11th example, XG328, which made its maiden flight on 18 June 1959 piloted by R.P. Beamont. Once company test flying had finished, assessment of the first OR946 package began. This continued throughout 1960–61 with the auto attack system phase being integrated at RAE Bedford during 1964, XG328 continued its avionics work until 20 January 1966 when it was grounded having flown 127 hours in 220 flights. Placed into store for possible future use it

Another stage in the Lightning's development was the appearance of the square topped fin. XG329, amongst others, was modified to this state for aerodynamic purposes to prove its viability for the forthcoming F.3. The F.1 is pictured at Swinderby in 1986 minus its ventral fuel tank which had been removed for its last flight – under a Chinook. (*CP RUSSELL-SMITH*)

remained at Bedford until August 1968 when it was acquired by the AWRE for target practice. By May 1972 the remains of XG328 were in the scrap compound at Farnborough where they remained until disposed of to a West Bromwich scrapyard twelve months later.

Joining XG328 on the OR946 trials was the 13th aircraft, XG330, which had first flown on 30 June 1959. For the next five years XG330 was engaged in proving the system before passing onto a task that was of equal importance. The shape of the fuselage and the diameter of the engines had resulted in some very close fitting of fuel, hot air and hydraulic pipework throughout the engine bays – obviously any fire in this region would be catastrophic and attempts were made continuously during the Lightning's career to control this problem. Improvements to the detection of fire and hot air leaks, allied to the upgrading of the fire suppression system, soon made the Lightning a far safer aircraft to fly. Also investigated at this time were servicing methods aimed at eliminating the human error factor from the equation. Once these investigations had been completed XG330, having flown 170 hours, was withdrawn from use eventually ending up on the Warton fire dump. By 1970 the remains had been disposed of to a Chorley scrap dealer.

Gun firing and harmonisation became the province of XG329 which first flew in April 1959. Joint development teams comprising personnel from the manufacturers, the RAE and the A&AEE carried out initial firing trials both in the air and on the ground, personnel from de Havilland were later to join the programme using XG329 exclusively during the last eight months of 1966. Data link trials on behalf of GEC also occupied the aircraft intermittently during 1963–66. Retired by 1969 XG329 became 8050M at the RAFC Cranwell Engineering School. Placed perpetually on jacks the aircraft was used to train young engineering officers in the principles of raising and lowering

Prior to its airlift to Swinderby XG329 had spent much of its grounded life on jacks being used in the training of Junior Engineering officers at Cranwell. The aircraft is now safely ensconsed at the Norfolk and Suffolk Museum at Flixton. (*CP RUSSELL-SMITH*)

aircraft, hydraulic system functionals including undercarriage operation plus the execution of all the relevant safety precautions.

XG329 was to undertake its last flight on 23 September 1986 as an underslung load for a 7 Sqdn Chinook to RAF Swinderby where the Lightning was placed alongside the resident Canberra PR 7, WT520. With Swinderby's closure as the recruit training school the Lightning was advertised for disposal. It finally came to rest at the Norfolk and Suffolk Museum at Flixton.

Subject of the most famous aircraft crashing picture to appear in the daily press XG332, the 15th pre-production airframe had first flown on 29 May 1959, the pilot being J.W.C. Squier. After initial flying as part of the Firestreak programme the Lightning had by 1960 moved onto Red Top development, still being operated jointly by E.E. Co. and D.H. Props. It was whilst flying on a post engine change test-flight that the pilot, George Aird of de Havilland, experienced a most unusual occurrence, that of a double engine reheat warning. As there appeared to be no other instruments indicating failure and handling seemed to be as advertised, he elected to return the Lightning to its base at Hatfield. Ten seconds from landing and 150 ft above ground XG332 responded to a sudden severe and undemanded pitch up. Wisely the pilot ejected, his egress being captured on film. Also in this photograph is a very startled tractor driver watching events unfold before him. The Martin Baker product worked perfectly, Mr Aird suffering injuries due to his using a green house to stop his descent. Crash investigations revealed that an intense flash fire in the lower engine bay had weakened a tailplane-operating tail jack to such an extent that it failed. Even though XG332 had only remained in existence for three years it did manage 214 flights in 138 hours.

To XG333, the 16th aircraft, fell the honour of being used by the Venezuelan Air Force for assessment flying, complete with the dubious support of British government officials. With such outstanding back-up it is not surprising that the sales drive pitched at this South American Air Force failed so dismally. Prior to this XG332 had made its maiden flight on 26 September 1959, the pilot being

T.M.S. Ferguson. Development flights to assess the UHF radio and LOX system followed, all previous aircraft having been dependent upon gaseous breathing equipment with its attendant weight penalty. Tropical trials of both systems took place in Aden during the period July-October 1961. Upon completion the Lightning was shipped home to the UK where it joined the test fleet at Boscombe Down for gun firing and radar assessment. These trials began in 1962 and continued until the Lightning's task was switched to that of operating with the Boeing rain repellent system in 1965. During this period the Venezuelans test-flew the aircraft and it continued in service at the A&AEE until being grounded and scrapped in the mid-1960s.

The first of the pre-production Lightnings for RAF use was XG334 which achieved a total of 23 hrs covering a total of 34 flights before being struck off charge. The Lightning had made its maiden flight from Samlesbury on 14 July 1959 piloted by J. Squier. Five months later it had been allocated to the AFDS (part of the CFE) at Coltishall where it received the code 'A'.

On 5 March 1960 whilst being piloted by Sqdn Ldr Harding of the AFDS the undercarriage of XG334 failed to lower properly on approach. Faced with the choice of a dangerous belly landing or ejection the pilot chose the latter course. After a successful egress the unmanned Lightning crashed near Wells-Near-The-Sea.

The next Lightning in the series, XG335, also proved unlucky, crashing on 11 January 1965 in the Larkhill ranges. Prior to that T.M.S. Ferguson had carried out a successful maiden flight on 7 August 1959. Early in 1960 XG335 joined the AFDS at Coltishall as 'B' remaining with them until transferring to the A&AEE in November 1962. At Boscombe Down the Lightning was engaged in weapons systems and Red Top missile trials. It was on one of these test flights that the aircraft suffered an undercarriage malfunction that left the pilot, Sqdn Ldr Whittaker with no option but to eject. During its flying career the Lightning had clocked up a total of 204 hours flying time that spanned 286 flights.

The third Lightning to join the AFDS was, not surprisingly, XG336 which became 'C' at Coltishall in December 1959 having first flown in August. A transfer to the A&AEE took place in November 1967, XG336 operating from Boscombe Down on weapons systems trials until grounding. Given the maintenance number 8091M the Lightning was transferred to Cosford for instructional use in 1970. A further move to 1 S of TT at Halton took place during November 1972, although the Lightning succumbed to the ministrations of the scrapman not long afterwards.

The last of the twenty pre-production aircraft, XG337, first flew on 5 September 1959 from Samlesbury piloted by J.K. Isherwood. A short period engaged in AVTAG fuel trials followed before a more permanent allocation to the Auto ILS evaluation trials which took place during 1960–61. This was followed by Red Top missile trials flights at Boscombe Down from 1963 until 1966. After 698 flights the Lightning was grounded and given the maintenance number 8056M for use by both Cosford and Halton as an instructional aid. Escaping the normal fate of scrapping, XG337 currently resides at Cosford as part of the Museum collection.

Chapter 3
Inside the Lightning

SITTING AWAITING its pilot or flashing through the air, the English Electric Lightning in all its guises presented a radical form to any onlooker. The slab-sided fuselage and dramatically swept wings notwithstanding, the Lightning followed many conventions in its construction and equipment fits. Even the new advanced systems such as cabin pressurisation, LOX and radar can trace their origins back to trials carried out in the Second World War. The placing of such a chapter at this particular point is to enable the reader to review the technical progress that has gone before and to understand the changes that were wrought later on in the development of, arguably, Britain's greatest fighter.

FUSELAGE

On all variants of the Lightning, including the two-seaters, the fuselage length was to remain constant at 55 feet three inches. Construction was based on ovoid frames, modified as required, which continued to just aft of the mainplane. From this point rearward they were basically double circular, or dogbone, in shape until the jet pipe end-cap mounting was reached. Longitudinal structure and shape was achieved by using mid-point longerons which were carried from the front pressure bulkhead aft to the forward fin mounting. Further shaping and strengthening was the responsibility of heavy and light gauge stringers applied where necessary.

Aluminium skin panels produced mainly by chemical etching were riveted to the basic structure thus creating even greater strength. The only major break point in the fuselage was at the aft cabin pressure bulkhead as the nose section was built in two halves. This was necessary due to the amount of wiring looms and hydraulic and pneumatic plumbing gathered in that area and the limited amount of access that was available when the whole assembly was complete. Major internal skinning was limited to the nose undercarriage bay, airbrake bays and the intake tunnels which were sheeted in aluminium, whilst the area surrounding the jet pipes was clad in heat resistant titanium. Further usage of titanium was around the engines themselves where the material was used as an explosion/debris suppression blanket. Lighter aluminium panelling appeared in the cockpit where it was mainly used to cover delicate items and protect them from damage. The fore and aft cabin pressure bulkheads were a different story altogether, as they were thick etched and machined plates punctuated by the minimum of holes.

The whole of the cabin was subject, after final assembly, to a pressure test that was at least two and a half times greater than any expected to be experienced in service. As part of the pressure cabin, the fixed windscreen and canopy were also of heavy duty construction, the frames of both items were manufactured from forgings whilst the vision areas were built up from stretched acrylic Perspex sandwich mouldings. The only exception to this standard of finish was the centre

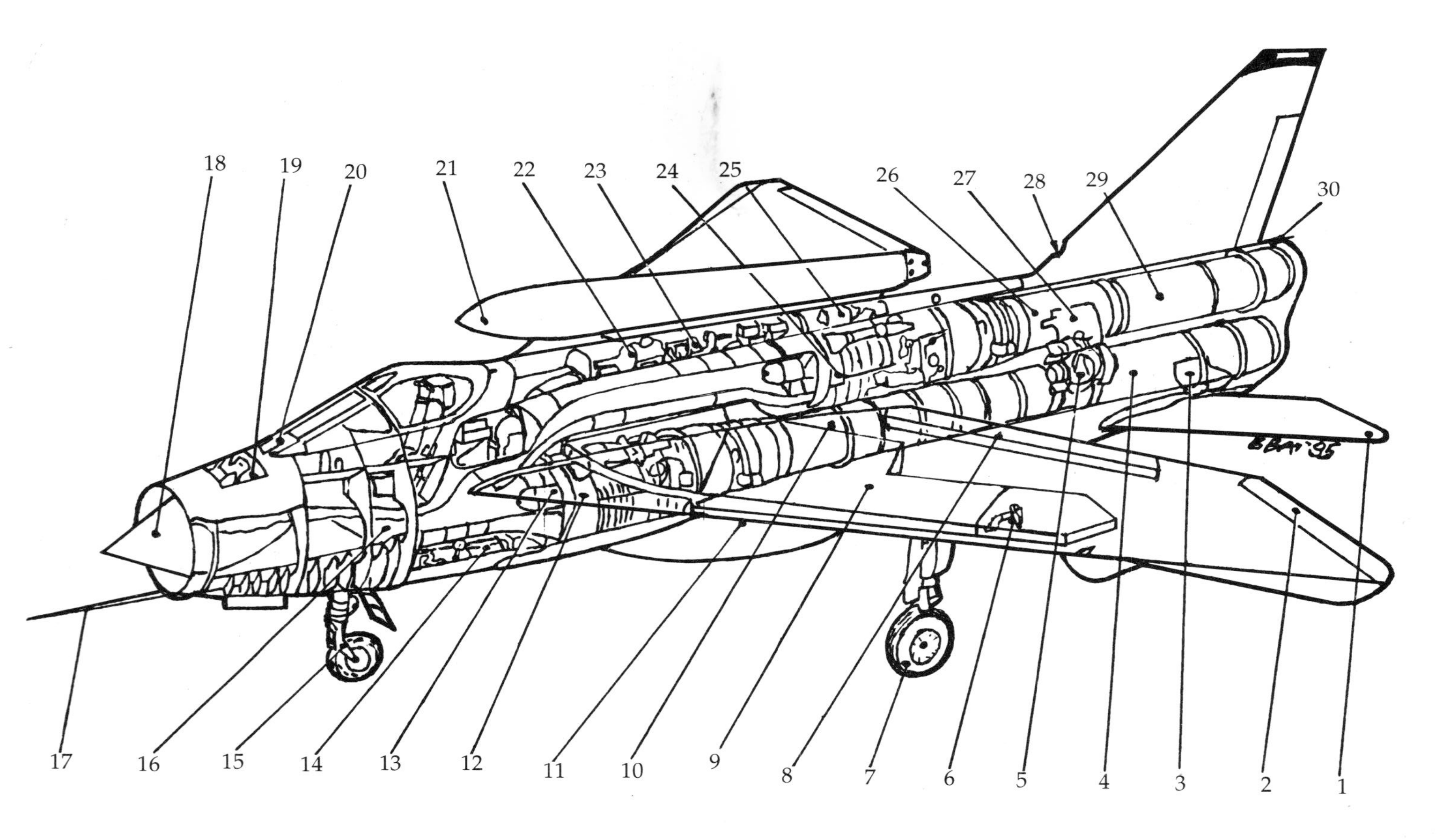

LIGHTNING MAIN COMPONENT LOCATIONS
1] All moving tailplane. 2] Aileron. 3] Brake parachute compartment. 4] No. 1 reheat jetpipe. 5] Alternator and generator air turbine unit. 6] Fueldraulic booster pump. 7] Main undercarriage. 8] Flap fuel tank. 9] Main fuel tank. 10] No. 1 intermediate jet pipe. 11] Ventral Fuel pack. 12] Leading edge fuel tank. 13] No. 1 engine. 14] Armament pack. 15] Nose wheel. 16] Air intake duct. 17] Pressure head. 18] Radar bullet. 19] LOX converter. 20] Rain dispersal nozzle. 21] Overwing fuel tank (other side similar). 22] AVPIN fuel tank 23] Engine starting system 24] No. 2 engine. 25] Standby DC generator. 26] No. 2 intermediate jetpipe. 27] Airbrakes. 28] Ram air cooling intake. 29] No. 2 reheat jet pipe. 30] Brake chute jettison release. *(information courtesy of BAe)*

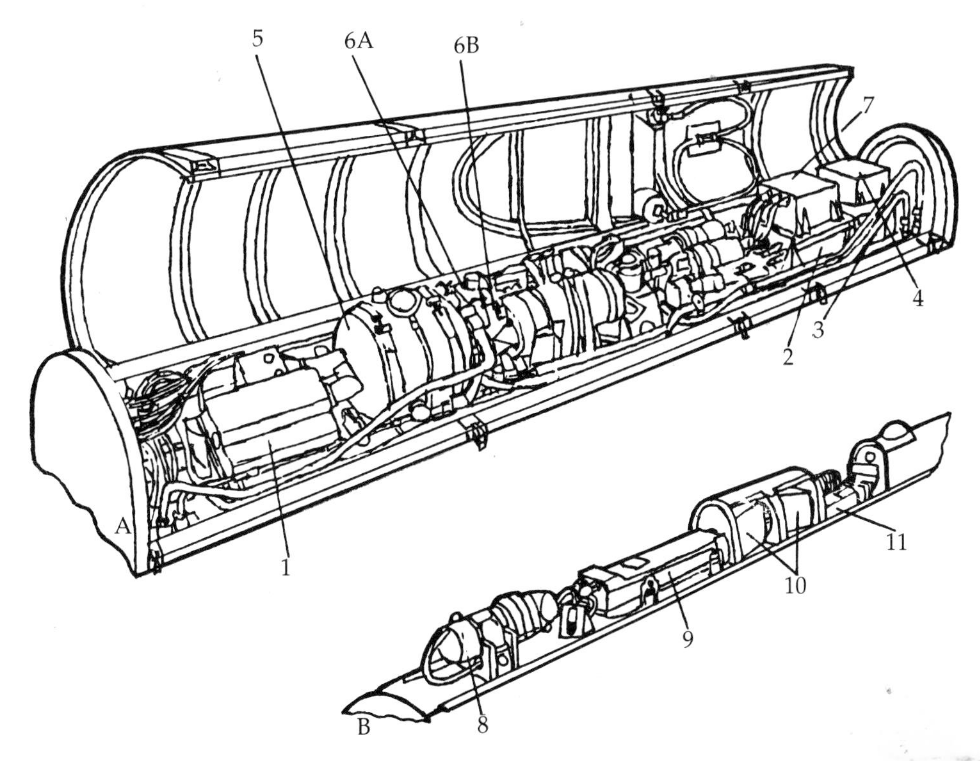

LIGHTNING UPPER SPINE DETAILS. Item 1 is the control panel for engine starting, whilst no's 2, 3, 4, & 7, are the H.F. ignition units and their control panels. No. 5 is the IPN starter fuel tank whilst 6A and 6B are the pumps for no.s 1 & 2 engines respectively. The smaller view reveals at 8, the standby generator, 9 the AIRPASS data recorder whilst no. 10 is the H.E. energy ignition units with their voltage regulator at no. 11. *(information courtesy of BAe)*

windscreen which was faced with optically aligned armoured glass, not only for strength but for clarity of the pilot's vision.

In the intake the radar pod with its fibreglass cone was mounted on a small vertically mounted wing on the centreline. Avionics and electrical compartments were lightly skinned and reinforced, mainly for protection against wandering fluids and less for strength. Access panels in the fuselage were normally produced by chemical etching/milling with stiffeners on the inside for rigidity. Their reception landings were also of a heavier gauge material, thus maintaining the integrity of the monocoque structure.

Wing, fin and tailplane mounting points were reinforced with machined castings lined with steel bushes. Using this method the possibility of fretting and wear damage was considerably reduced although reinforcing work to the wing root area was required on the surviving Lightnings during the late 1970s and early 1980s. Wing mounting was achieved by the usage of interference fit mounting pins which were finished with either a locknut or collar, both of which were split-pinned for added security. Fin mounting was similar although the pins were understandably smaller. The tailplanes on the other hand were mounted to the fuselage through bearings, their shafts being attached to the drive unit by bolts which were also securely locked. Steel was not used as extensively as aluminium in the Lightning although its denser and heavier attributes were employed to great usage in areas of high stress and heat. The nose undercarriage bay, wing and engine mounts, nose ring on frame 1 plus the jet pipe pen-nib fairing mounted on frame 62, an area of excessive heat, all featured steel in their construction. As with all such sharply angled structures, cracking was a persistent problem throughout the years and was subject to much attention by the gentlemen with their welding torches.

WING, FIN AND TAILPLANES

Mounted midway up the airframe the Lightning's wings feature a sixty degree sweepback which is modified on later models by a camber to the outer wing section introduced under Modification 2432. Construction of such a sharply swept structure called for a careful blending of wing flexibility coupled with enough rigidity, maintained by torsional stiffeners, to allow fighter-type manoeuvres to be carried out safely without nullifying the ailerons influence by flexing or cracking the wing during high 'G' operations.

The whole assemblage is based upon two primary spars to which are affixed a series of closely spaced ribs to which, in turn, stringers were riveted. In the areas outside those set aside for fuel containment the skeleton formed a series of box sections that gave great strength and allowed the designers to later fit pylons to the wings with few qualms. Wing fuel tankage was of the integral type and, although giving greater volume for fuel, caused in some aircraft great problems due to leakage through the sealant. The main undercarriage units were mounted in bays let into the lower surface of the wing, the legs themselves being mounted on to heavy-duty machined forgings mounted between the two spars. On all variants the leading edges were built as detachable items, a practice followed on the wingtips. For the F.6 and rebuilt F.2As the shape changed to compensate for the newly introduced cambered section. This resulted in the ailerons of the later aircraft having inset leading edges as against the earlier plain hinged items fitted to previous marques. In all cases the hinging line was at ninety degrees to the fuselage longitudinal axis. Structural strengthening was fairly localised being applied initially to the upper wing pylon mountings and under the port wing for the refuelling probe. In addition, overseas export aircraft featured further beefing up in the area of the underwing pylon mounts. Skinning of the wings was aluminium overall with a nominal thickness, after machining, of 0.2 inches.

The Lightning's flaps were of a similar construction to the parent body utilising a spar and ribs for strength and shaping. In the quest to improve and extend the Lightning's range these structures later found use as fuel tanks. Unfortunately leakage problems at the hinge point of flap and wing have, on some occasions, led to their being blanked off. The ailerons, whether of the inset or hinged type, were of mainly honeycomb construction with a leading edge spar and ribs interspersed.

The low-set tailplanes were fairly lightweight items being of similar construction to the wings. As in the latter's case the leading edges were made detachable for easy replacement purposes. Mounting on to the aircraft was achieved by the use of a steel shaft permanently affixed at the tailplane root, but detachable at the PFCU. Honeycomb structure featured heavily on the trailing edges. The fin was also of conventional construction although certain areas, such as the tip, were of fibreglass for the mounting of antennas. In keeping with the rest of the flight-control surfaces the rudder was of mainly honeycomb construction with the usual spar and ribs for strength and shape.

Unlike many other military aircraft, however, the Lightning's wings once assembled to the airframe were virtually a permanent fixture, designed to stay in place for the life of the aircraft. Such a method of construction resulted in many of those in preservation having the offending items amputated outboard of the undercarriage bays for ease of road transport.

UNDERCARRIAGE AND BRAKING

Given that the fuselage of the Lightning was exceptionally deep and that the wings were mounted at the mid point position, it is not surprising to find that the main legs were understandably tall. They, and the shorter nose unit, were products of the Gloucester based Dowty Rotol company. Damping of the main legs for landing and ground movement purposes was achieved hydraulically. Warning notices were placed prominently in various places to remind engineering staff not to overfill them as oscillation could be induced.

The nose leg shock-absorber was a separate item housed within the leg casting. It was mounted between the retraction mechanism and the nose wheel forks. To ensure that the nose wheel was aligned longitudinally for retraction, a straightening mechanism was installed inside the upper part of the leg, thus ensuring that fouling of the undercarriage doors was eliminated. It is interesting to note that a similar, although understandably smaller, nose leg was later fitted to the Samlesbury-built Jet Provost. Aluminium forgings were used wherever possible in the undercarriages although some steel was used in areas likely to suffer great pressure and stress. One such was the nose wheel fork mounting where the attachment pins and bushes were of this material. Clean and smooth operation is a prime factor in undercarriage operation. To ensure that this remains so, all jacks are fitted with a wiper ring at the ram entry point whilst the rams themselves are chrome-plated, or to use a more technical term fescalised. This ensures smooth operation and also helps to reduce the chances of corrosion. Upon retraction the nose leg moves forward and upwards into the undercarriage bay straightening the wheel as it does so. The rear door is hinged and connected to the leg by adjustable turnbarrels. The left and right forward doors move through their retraction sequence drawn by series of rods and cranks connected to the leg, the whole assemblage is operated by one jack.

Both main legs retract outwards, the inner section being covered by a fixed fairing and a sliding sprung cover that lies flush once the leg is fully retracted. The large 'D' shaped outer doors, dished on the inside face to clear the wheel/brake assembly, operate in a similar manner to those of the nose undercarriage.

As the retraction sequence is selector and sequence valve controlled the nose leg disappears first to be closely followed by the main legs in turn. This system in the early days of the Lightning was to cause a certain amount of trouble which was to result in the loss of at least two aircraft. Emergency lowering and retraction are also available by cockpit selection up to a limiting speed of 150 kts.

Braking is provided by hydraulically actuated Dunlop plate brakes that in the anti-skid mode are controlled by maxeret units. Nose wheel braking to stop the rotation of the wheel in the undercarriage bay was achieved by using a sprung steel plate that lightly touched the tyre thus slowing the assembly to a stop.

Possibly the hardest hit component in any undercarriage system is the wheel. In

As the Lightning developed so did its undercarriage legs. The first view is that fitted to the P.1A whilst the latter illustrates that fitted to the F.2A/F.3 and F.6 fighters. (*STEVE BUTTRISS*)

the Lightning's case this was even more so due to the thin cross section of the tyre. Manufactured by Dunlop the tyres were normally rated as good for seven landings although those aircraft of the OCU and later the LTF quite frequently managed less. The wheel hubs, also by Dunlop, were of aluminium construction and were subject to Non-Destructive Testing (NDT) at each tyre change as a hub failure could prove catastrophic. Tyre pressures recommended for these assemblies are 350 psi for the main wheels whilst the nose is pressurised to 240 psi. Load classification of the aircraft, rated by its 'footprint', was set at No. 35 for rigid pavements and No. 45 for more flexible surfaces. To combat the heat generated by excessive braking the hubs were fitted with fusible plugs designed to melt and deflate the tyre if the temperature became too great.

On many aircraft the brake-chute is designed as an emergency back-up; not so on the Lightning where it was regarded as the prime retarder and was rated up to 200 kts for deployment. In the case of an airborne deployment by accident, an emergency release was incorporated.

Steering of the aircraft was achieved using differential braking for directional control, leaving the nose wheel as purely castoring with a thirty degree movement either side of the centreline, thus the need for a nose wheel aligner.

With the increase in aircraft weights a further method of aircraft retardation was found to be necessary, especially as the ubiquitous barrier could prove dangerous to such aircraft as the Lightning with its numerous forward protuberences. Borrowing an idea from the Fleet Air Arm, the dry land designers evolved the Rotary Hydraulic Arrestor Gear, more commonly known as RHAG. To enable the Lightning to take advantage of this system a ventral arrester hook was fitted, as a modification, at the rear of the ventral tank. Using a hook mounted on a flat, fairly springy shaft, the system was designed as 'one shot' being lowered as required by the pilot, but being reset on the ground. RHAG systems cleared for use by the Lightning included the American 44B-3A and the Bliss 500S.

SYSTEMS

Systems is that well known euphemism for all those complicated sets of gubbins that make a modern (*sic*) aircraft work. At the heart of the Lightning pulses its life blood, the hydraulic system. Although designers have experimented with electrically operated undercarriages and flaps etc., witness the Valiant bomber, they have always returned in the end to the use of hydraulics, thus eliminating the weight problem engendered by the use of electric motors and their generators.

Driving this precious fluid around the Lightning's nether extremities are two Type 180 Mk.50/65 pumps, one per engine, which drive the undercarriage, flaps and airbrakes whilst power for the flying controls comes from a pair of Type 200 Mk.37 pumps, yet again one per engine. As leakage can cause no end of difficulties the designers attempted to build in some emergency back-up by making the pumps switchable between service and flying control circuits, thus retaining flight control and brake system

LIGHTNING SYSTEMS DUPLICATION FOR SAFETY PURPOSES.

1] Fuel system– engine-driven pumps use onboard fuel as a hydraulic source to drive the booster pumps. In the event of a pump failure the control valve rejigs the system to continue supply to both engines. 2] Hydraulic system– after the failure of an engine or hydraulic pump full aircraft control is maintained by the remaining pump. In the event of engines windmilling the accumulators will remain sufficiently charged for gentle manoeuvres to be carried out and a landing made. 3] Electrical systems– failure of an engine does not reduce electrical output. The emergency turbine can be driven by either engine in the event of a failure. (*information courtesy of BAe*)

1

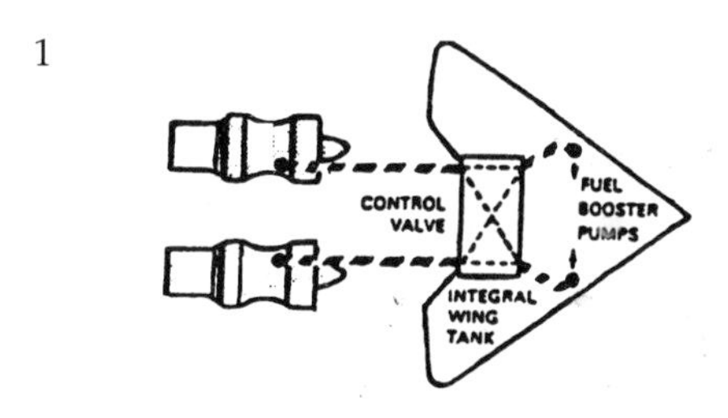

2

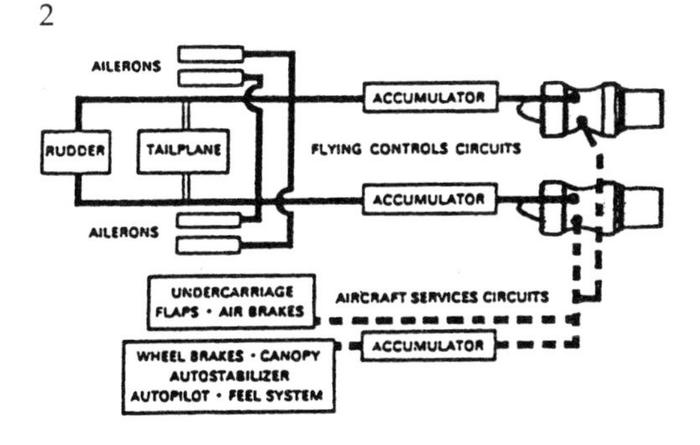

3

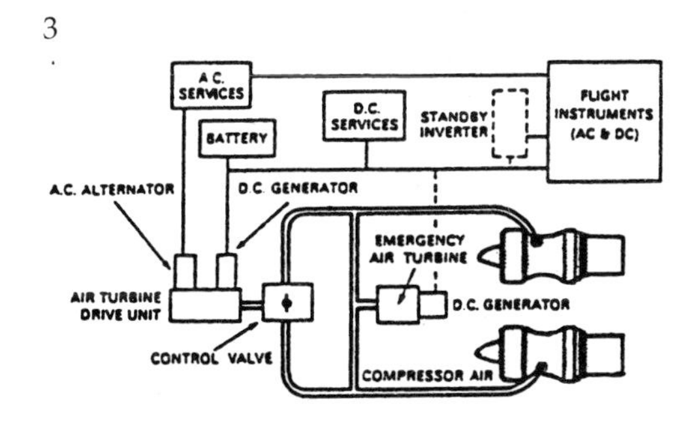

On the line and those stalwarts of any squadron engineering staff, the mechanics, prepare a T.5 for further flying. Below LOX is pumped into the airframe whilst above fluid for the AVPIN starter is poured into its tank. (*STEVE BUTTRISS*)

pressure as priorities. Operating pressure for the Lightning's hydraulics was a nominal 3,000 psi, with that for the brakes reducing to 1,500 psi accompanied by accumulator back-up. It was also possible to retain a goodly measure of control with both powerplants windmilling as the triple accumulators within the system supplied enough hydraulic pressure for some gentle manoeuvres and a landing. Fluid contained within the systems was Oil Hydraulic OM-15, a mineral-based product.

As the Lightning was intended as a Quick Reaction Alert aircraft the majority of replenishment points and contents gauges were located for easy ground access. This reduced the amount of ground-support equipment required, speeded up turn-round times and removed the hazard of stray steps etc from the flightline.

One fluid that has to be kept away from oil or grease is of course liquid oxygen, bringing both together can ruin anybody's day! The Lightning's breathing system was regulator controlled, the LOX container holding a maximum of 3.5 litres. LOX in its gaseous form is provided to the pilot's face-mask or partial pressure helmet, if worn, and to the pressure jerkin. Connection to the oxygen system is by a multi-connector at the ejection seat which is in turn connected to the aircraft in a similar manner.

Also integrated into the seat connector is an emergency supply gaseous oxygen bottle that is pressurised to a nominal 1,800 psi. This can provide either an emergency breathing capability should a fault occur in the main system or, as is more normally the case, will allow the pilot to breathe after ejection above 10,000 ft.

Although our intrepid pilot can now breathe, other physiological support services are required for comfortable flying. Cockpit pressurisation, air-conditioning plus canopy demisting are all gained from tappings taken from the engine compressor. Control is by electrically operated shut-off valves. If for any reason the cockpit becomes contaminated by either smoke or noxious fumes, a ram air valve mounted in the fuselage can in an emergency be opened to provide fresh air. Safety measures to safeguard the pressure cabin include an emergency pressure relief valve that supplements the normal inwards/outwards relief valve. Clear vision is obviously very important to our pilot, hence the electrical demisting facility

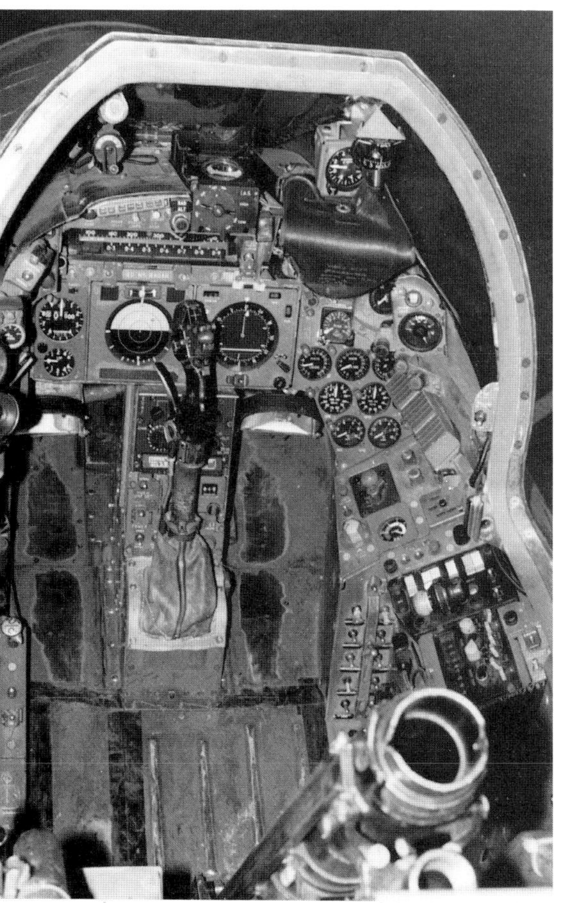

A contrast in cockpits between P.1A WG760 and Lightning F.6 XR728 both destined for preservation. (*STEVE BUTTRISS*)

built into the forward and port side windscreens.

Having provided our pilot with all the comforts of home to ease the execution of his air defence duties, it is imperative that he can see in all conditions, heavy rain even at high speeds is ever a problem. To counteract the rain, a unique dispersal system is employed which consists of a jet of compressed air blasted upwards from nozzles placed in front of the windscreens. Use of this method breaks up the droplets before they reach the screens.

If hydraulics are the lifeblood of any aircraft, then electrical power can be regarded as fulfiling the function of a nervous system. Power supplies in the Lightning are provided by an AC alternator and a DC generator, both driven by an air-turbine drive unit.

To enable supplies to be maintained in the event of an engine failure, air supplies routed from each engine are delivered to the drive unit via a control valve which rotates to which ever powerplant is still running. In the event of total engine-driven electrical failure an emergency ram air-turbine, complete with DC generator, is linked into the vital services busbar. Linkage to the system is via the stand-by inverter which, as its name suggests, provides direct DC power and the AC and DC electrical requirements for the cockpit instruments. Under normal circumstances the alternator and generator provide power to their respective services, the latter also maintaining the 28V DC charge in the aircraft battery. Lighting, both internal and external, consume a fair amount of the electrical energy produced by the generating system. In the Lightning internal lighting covers the instrument panels, general floodlighting, dimmer controlled high-intensity and emergency illumination. External lighting is restricted to the navigation lamps, anti-collision

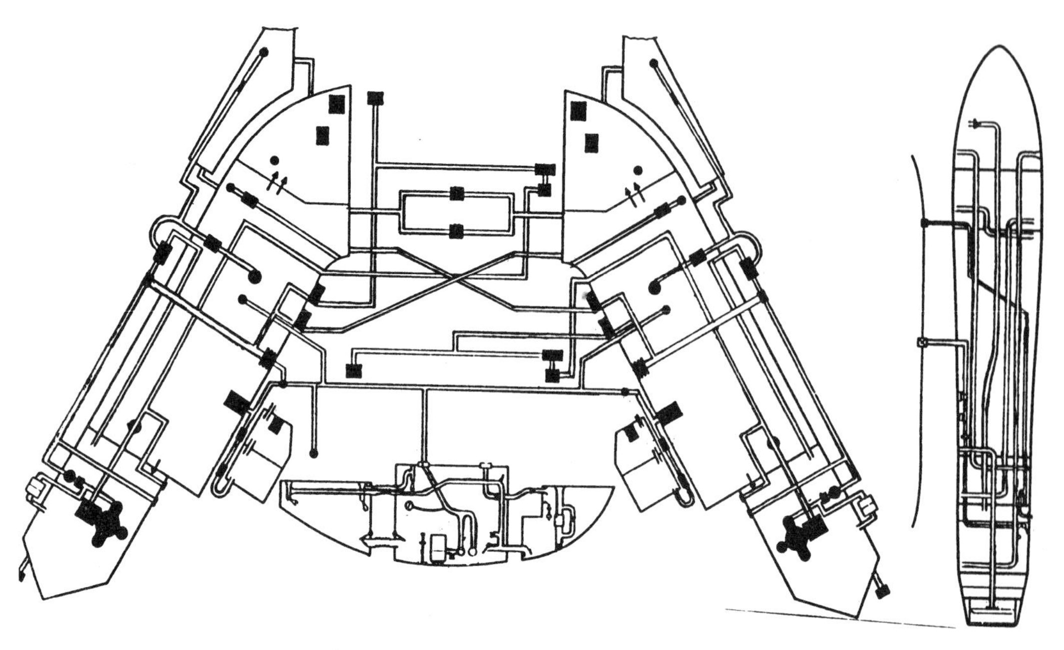

LIGHTNING WING FUEL SYSTEM
Although this diagram covers the F.6 variant with upper wing fuel tanks, much of the system shown was applicable to other marques. (*information courtesy of BAe*)

The heart of the Lightning's power was the Rolls-Royce Avon series of engines. This is an RA. 24 series 302 power-plant from an F.6 mounted on its special purpose transport trolley. (*STEVE BUTTRISS*)

Without the Avons installed the aircraft's fuselage appears cavernous. Of interest is the construction of the engine bays; similar methods were used throughout the whole fuselage. (*STEVE BUTTRISS*)

beacons, flight-refuelling probe plus taxi and spot-lights. Except for the 4V AC instrument lighting the remainder are all DC supplied. When main supplies fail, DC power can be supplied by the battery which supplies a selection of amber instrument floodlights and the integral light in the E2B stand-by compass and stand-by direction finder.

POWER-PLANT AND FUEL SYSTEMS

The increase in thrust of the engines that have propelled the P.1/Lightning series has been dramatic. Both P.1As were fitted with non-afterburning Sapphire 5 ECUs rated at 7,500 lbs st although, through development, this later grew to 9,200 lbs in the reheated version. The appearance of the P.1B saw the engine changing to that specified for the aircraft, the Rolls-Royce RA.24 Avon. Initially designated the series 24R the power-plants were dry rated, i.e., without reheat, at 11,250 lbs st. The subsequent installation of a four-stage afterburner resulted in an increase of available thrust to 13,300 lbs in the renamed Avon Mk.200R ECU. A further gain in available output power to 11,250 lbs, dry thrust, saw the appearance of the Mk.210 Avon that was to power the production F.1, F.1A and F.2. Fitted with a four-stage reheat, maximum output rose to 14,430 lbs st. The final Avon development was the series 301/302 engines that were capable of a maximum of 11,000 lbs dry thrust which rose to 16,300 lbs via the fully variable reheat. In the engine bays of the Lightning the temperatures generated quite often reached 600 degrees C, to protect the structure a special paint containing gold was applied to reflect the heat. Costing £75 per pound this made heat reflection a very expensive proposition.

Due to the unique shape of the Lightning the locations of the engines were staggered. The lower power-plant, No. 1, was mounted well forward of its companion, No.2. This resulted in the intermediate jet pipes between the rear of the engine and the reheat units being of different lengths. This discrepancy was to result in some spares problems in later years when usable quantities of either type fell to zero. According to E.E. Co., later BAC, an engine change could be accomplished in under four hours.

This was achieved in ideal conditions with all tools and equipment ready to hand. The upper engine lifted out through

Although not obvious in this view, this aircraft is only a couple of weeks away from flying again. The lower engine has been refitted and hydraulic test equipment is already plugged in for functional checks. (*STEVE BUTTRISS*)

the top of the fuselage after the roller equipped jet pipe had been rolled back and the four mounting points had been disconnected. For the lower engine, No.1, a similar practice was followed although in this case winches were used to lower the powerplant down into a special cradle.

After an engine component change on most aircraft, a full ground run of the engine and systems is normally standard practice. For the Lightning however, much of this requirement was eliminated by the use of ground test-rigs. Electrical and hydraulic test equipment was supplemented by rigs for ground operating the gas and air-turbine gearbox and ram air-turbine. Each item of test equipment was fitted with unique couplings so that the mistake of incorrect connections was avoided. Fuel boost pump checks could also be carried out without engine power. The connection points for these were located in each main undercarriage bay. Both high and low pressure ranges could be checked by the use of ground test equipment.

Engine starting on later marques was achieved by the use of AVPIN (Isopropyl Nitrate Mono Fuel). Each engine was fitted with an Impulse Turbine Starter and both were supplied by a common three-gallon tank that was located in the spine. A full tank was sufficient for six starts, although experience later in Saudi Arabia was to show that adjustments would be required for hot and high conditions. Each starter was fitted with an auto shut-off that came into use once the Avon had reached self-sustaining speed. Sometimes however the starter would fail to disengage, this normally resulted in shards of red-hot metal flying around the rear of the aeroplane and has been known to upset the ground crew.

One area of concern that had surfaced at the beginning of the P.1/Lightning programme was the lack of fuel that could be carried in such a tightly packed airframe. In the early stages of development the Lightning's fuel contents, about 5000 lbs, meant that as an interceptor it was going to have a very short range coupled to an equally short airborne loiter time. Thus the designers set about trying to squeeze as much fuel as they could into any available space. Redesign of the wings eventually placed fuel in the leading edges and the flaps; there was even talk at one time of turning the main undercarriage 'D' doors into small fuel tanks. Total wing fuel was finally raised to a grand total of 5,728 lbs (2,597 kg). To extend the range further a ventral fuel tank was developed and these appeared, not only on the prototypes and development aircraft, but on the F.1 through to the T.5. This, the smaller of the two types eventually fitted, was jettisonable in the air and held 2,000 lbs of much needed fuel. With the advent of the more advanced F.6 and its rebuilt counterpart in Germany, the F.2A, a larger tank containing 4,880 lbs was introduced by Modification 2433. Non-jettisonable, it was however removable on the ground for maintainance purposes. When the Aden cannon package was installed in the front portion of those carried by the F.6, usable fuel dropped to 4,280 lbs. As the F.6 was intended for the overseas rapid re-inforcement role, provision for the fitment of over-wing tanks and pylons was included in the main build run.

This extra fuel provision was also highlighted by those charged with selling the Lightning in the export markets of the world. With the over-wing tanks installed a further 2,160 lbs per side was available and they were made jettisonable in the event of combat.

The heart of the Lightning's fuel system is the wing collector box, one per side, that receives fuel delivered by gravity, air pressure or electric transfer pumps from the wing tanks. To move the fuel to the engines and their reheat pumps, inline booster pumps are fitted within the collector box. These are hydraulically driven using the fuel as a propulsive medium. Fuel flow rates are controlled by the engines themselves as they control the rates of delivery via a drive shaft to the pumps, thus an increase in throttle results in an increase in fuel flow, one always matching the other.

In the event of a pump failure, a cockpit controlled change-over valve can be opened; this allows both collector boxes to be operated by one pump. The types of pumps installed in the Lightning are: Booster(2)Lucas Type GBB 131 and (2) FBP 104/111 whilst the Transfer pumps are Type TPE 101. The boosters were set to operate at a maximum pressure of 1,600 psi and 60 psi respectively whilst the transfer pumps operated at a lowly maximum of 14 psi. Jet fuel for the Lightning was AVTUR 50 with FSII (fuel systems icing inhibitor) or its NATO equivalent AVTAG. Refuelling was by gravity through the over-wing points, or more commonly pressure refuelling was used via the couplings under the wings. In exceptional circumstances provision was made for using the refuelling probe.

In-flight refuelling has become an important part of fighter deployments overseas and in the Lightning's case it was an important part of day-to-day operations.

Although nominally detachable, the supersonically cleared probe, once fitted, tended to stay as part of the airframe, only being removed when required for maintainance. This most useful of range-extending items first appeared as standard on the F.1A and continued with only minor changes throughout the entire spectrum of variants. Matching up with the tanker aircraft was initially accomplished using the VHF homing facility, part of the onboard comprehensive navigation suite. Once plugged-in the fuel flow rate could be run at a maximum of 1,360 lbs/617 kgs per minute. Ferry ranges using the probe were calculated to give a point of no return of 1,830 nm on one airborne refuel. For those aircraft fitted with over-wing tanks this increased to 2,200 nm, both sets of figures including a 1,000 lbs diversion reserve and five per cent headwind allowance.

AVIONICS

Sitting at the metaphorical centre of the Lightning and its *raison d'etre* is the integrated weapons system. This draws together data from the AIRPASS radar, pitot statics and air data computer, TACAN,

LIGHTNING AVIONICS DIAGRAM.
The following items of equipment feature in the F.6 and overseas aircraft. MFD–Magnetic flux detector. TA–TACAN. MRG–Master reference gyro. CA–Compass amplifier. FCC/AP Flight control computer/Autopilot with outputs to AS–Autostabilizer, RG–3-axis rate gyros and A–ailerons, R–rudder, TA–tailplane and TH–throttle. ILS–instrument landing system. PDI–pilot data inputs. FDS–Flight director and MRG signals. In the cockpit are RD–Radar display, LFS–Light fighter sight, WS–weapons selector plus items 1–6 which are; altitude indicator and director, standby instruments, strip speed display, navigation display, height display and autopilot display respectively. PS–is the pilot and static inputs into the ADC–air data computer. Radar data comes from the STR–search track radar which is controlled by RSC–radar steering control. Allied to the radar is the IFF. The WLU–weapons launch unit is controlled by the WS in the cockpit. (*information courtesy of BAe*)

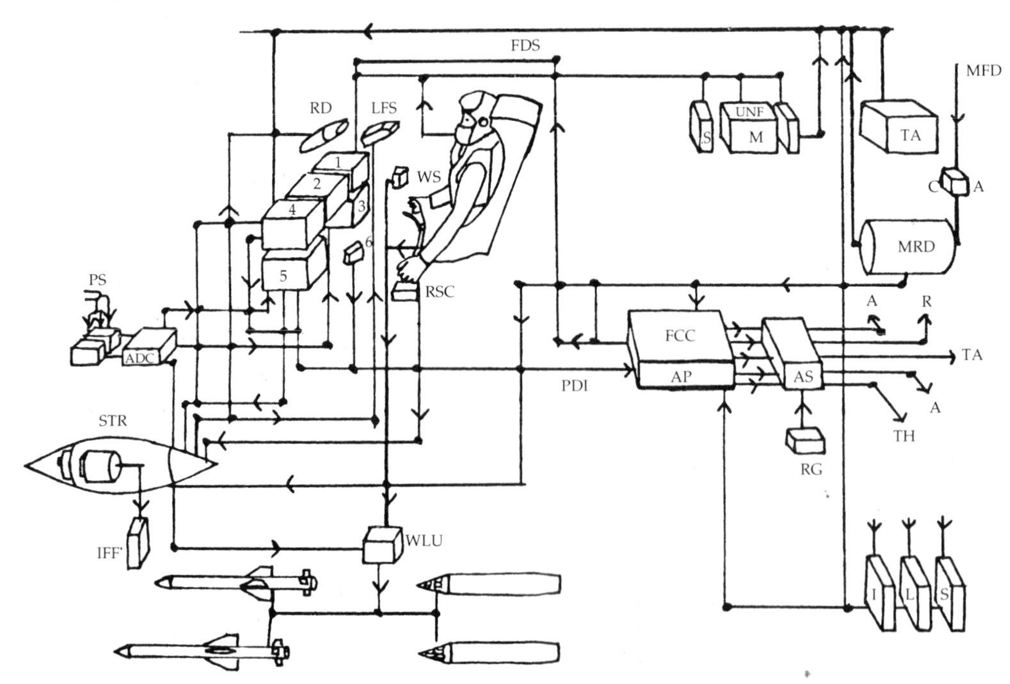

flight control computer plus a myriad of other devices to present to the pilot an overall picture on his CRT and flight instruments of the situation facing him. This information is also fed to the weapons launch unit and can be used to update any active weapons carried, i.e. missiles.

The primary source of navigation rests with the TACAN. Working in conjunction with an off-set computer which receives signals from a remote transmitter and allows for such natural deviations as wind-drift, the TACAN's range is effectively increased to 400 nm. An outstanding feature of this system is its ability to produce a reciprocal heading for a return to base. To supplement and sometimes replace the TACAN in the event of failure is the homing facility incorporated in the VHF radio installation. For guidance during landing an ILS unit is carried and this will respond to signals generated by ground control. Audio signals are transmitted for the outer and middle markers whilst visual displays indicate localiser, glide-path and beacon reception.

Communications are available through multi-channel VHF and UHF transmitter/receivers that have a nominal range of 200 nm plus along the line-of-sight transmission plane. Auto channel selection of up to nineteen separate inputs will result in the appearance of communications on a pre-set frequency. Manual dialling for other locations is available on 1,750 channels that cover the range 225–299.9 mHz. In the case of a total or partial failure a pre-tuned standby VHF receiver comes into use and provides two emergency frequencies. One is normally set to the base frequency whilst the other is locked onto 243 mHz which is the international distress frequency.

Early-on in the Lightning programme the chosen radar system was introduced for evaluation. Designed by Ferranti the AIRPASS AI.23 reached its final variant in the 'B' series with the introduction of the Lightning F.6/F.53. The scanner, complete with its wave guide generator, is housed in a demountable bullet fairing in the nose intake, whilst the CRT indicator is placed directly in front of the pilot. Used in both the search and guidance role the system has proved eminently reliable, although the lack of an auto-search facility does increase the pilots workload. Control of the scanner's direction is by a single lever in the cockpit located next to the pilot's left hand. Moving the lever fore and aft puts the system into search mode, whilst movement from side-to-side engages target acquisition mode. Linked into the radar and its electronics is the Mk.10 IFF which, upon interrogation, will identify the Lightning as a friendly through activation of the secondary radar responder.

As the flight control surfaces of the Lightning are controlled by PFCUs an electronics-based flight control system is required to provide position and pilot data. At the heart of this system is a collection of four instruments. The first is the strip speed indicator, below which is mounted a rate of climb indicator and a digital altimeter. To the right of this is the combined altitude and TACAN indicator. Introduced by OR946 the strip speed indicator gives it readings in both knots and Mach numbers, whilst the altitude indicator displays pitch, bank and sideslip. The navigation display gives compass, ILS, TACAN offset and TACAN upon selection. Much of the data for the flight information suite comes from the air data computer. Inputs include the air data system which provides computer-corrected measurement of barometric height, Mach number and rate of descent and climb.

Pitch and roll acceleration is provided by the master reference gyro which has a fast erection button in the cockpit to reset it should toppling occur, whilst azimuth heading comes from continuous magnetic updating of the main reference gyro by a fluxgate sensor. Any transient inputs of roll and yaw are sensed by the rate gyros, their inputs into the air computer enable it to damp out their effects using optional auto stabilisation, or during weapon firing their inputs will help maintain the aircraft in a stable position. Much of this equipment would of course be useless without externally transmitted radio signals. These external additions are available to the TACAN, localizer, glide-path beacon and ILS.

Having achieved flight in our Lightning it is time to explore its fire control system. The avionic developments during the aircraft's lifespan has resulted in a proven, reliable and efficient method of weapons control. The prime source of data for the fire control system is the radar which, with its computer-generated aids enables the pilot to search, lock-on and with steering guidance attack his target with missiles, cannon and rockets. The last is of course an operational option on overseas-sales aircraft only, its general use not having been adopted by the RAF.

All the data coming from all the previously described systems is calculated by the onboard computers. These in turn generate the necessary displays for the optimum steering course which appears on the CRT. Once acquisition has been achieved by the missiles this is then signalled in the cockpit and this will remain the position until launch.

At that point the display cancels and a caption appears warning the pilot to change course to avoid flying debris. To aid the pilot and reduce some of the cockpit workload the autopilot includes selections for flight direction and auto flight. One can be used to change course manually or update the other whilst the auto flight, when selected, will follow a pre-programmed route. For visual engagements the aircraft is fitted with a light fighter sight which is a gyroscopically-stabilised reflecting optical display. Although intended primarily for cannon and rocket sighting, the system can be used for missile guidance in the event of a CRT failure. An optically generated ring graticule-sight comes complete with horizontal and vertical sighting bars that can be superimposed over the target. Range judgement gives a 60 ft target filling the ring at 1,000 ft whilst a 180 yd target would fill the full width of the display at the same distance. Using missile-firing mode event-markers, generated by the radar, will indicate target acquisition and ranging.

With all this clever electronic equipment within its skin it is obvious that some form of externally attached test system should be available. Unfortunately, development funding – or rather lack of it – delayed such a unit until fairly late in the aircraft's life. The test equipment that did appear rejoiced in the name of 'Transportable Automatic Self-Checking Unit.' This plugged into various test points dotted about the airframe. Upon activation the unit tested the different avionic sub-systems before running the suite as a whole. At any point when an incorrect value is detected the auto check will run through the individual components one by one until the item at fault is discovered.

Within the Ferranti AI.23B radar system itself there are numerous modes of operation. These cover approach and attack, search and attack, radar control and mode selection, visual display, cine recording and the light fighter sight. The flight control system consists of an Integrated Flight Instrument Display. Type OR946 phase 2, Air Data System Mk.2, Navigation Display Unit, Master Reference Gyro and ILS. Stand-by instrumentation covers the artificial horizon Type 'H', Directional Gyro Indicator Type B, Compass Type E2B, Altimeter Mk.26 and Air Speed Indicator Mk.18. Navigation aids comprise a compass with remote flux indicator, TACAN, UHF homing and IFF Mk.10. Radio communications are the province of a PTR 175 combined UHF/VHF transmitter/receiver with 1,750 channels. Stand-by radio cover has two emergency channels whilst for QRA duties a tele-briefing system, which will automatically disconnect on taxi, is fitted.

WEAPONS, RECONNAISSANCE AND EJECTION SEATS

For an aircraft that was designed for a defensive interception role, the variety of weapons available to the Lightning operator was very small. Those overseas buyers did slightly better than their RAF counterparts as a fairly extensive ground-attack capability was added to those machines. Much of this lack could originally be put down to the earlier aircraft having such a short range and endurance, thus increased stores would have increased the drag coefficient and increased fuel consumption. However, many of these deficiencies were overcome with the appearance of the better equipped F.6. It is still strange to note however that no attempt was made to integrate the AIM-9 Sidewinder into the armoury, although such a plan was mooted in the 1970s.

The projected loads for aircraft up to and including the F.3 was for four missiles on the fuselage pylons whilst the later F.6 was to have carried a further four, mounted on launch rails attached to the over-wing pylons. A similar installation finally made its RAF debut during the Gulf War when RAF Jaguars carried over-wing Sidewinders, albeit on single rail mounts only. As successive governments, throughout the 1970s, proclaimed that the Lightning would be leaving the service 'next year' a great opportunity was lost to sell the aircraft to the world's markets as an outstanding dog-fighter.

Aircraft-mounted cannon, as subsequent events in Vietnam were to prove, are a vital accessory for any aircraft that finds itself engaged in close air combat. Unfortunately for the Lightning and its designers the fitment of such useful weapons became very much a stop-go affair. From the start of the development programme, when the advice of pilots was listened to very closely, cannon were seen as a vital part of the Lightning's weaponry, unfortunately armchair tacticians began to interfere and the option was dropped leaving the aircraft armed with a missile that, in its early years was unreliable.

English Electric chose for their latest product the ubiquitous Aden 30 mm cannon which was normally belt fed with approximately 130 rounds of ammunition. As fitted to the early Lightnings the cannons were mounted in the upper nose decking, one per side. After successful air firing the installation appeared in the P.1 Bs, the twenty pre-production aircraft and the F.1/F.1A production Lightnings. For the F.2 variant a fit of four weapons was introduced, the second pair being located in a similar position to the first pair, only in the lower fuselage. Even after conversion to F.2A standard, the fighters retained their cannon armament, although most only had weapons in the lower positions.

With the cannon in the lower fuselage the hazard of muzzle flash that had so distracted, and sometimes disorientated pilots, was removed. When the F.3 appeared the provision for close-combat weapons had been deleted and, unlike the later F.6, was never re-instated. Very much on the horns of a dilemma were the two trainer versions, the T.4 and T.5. No

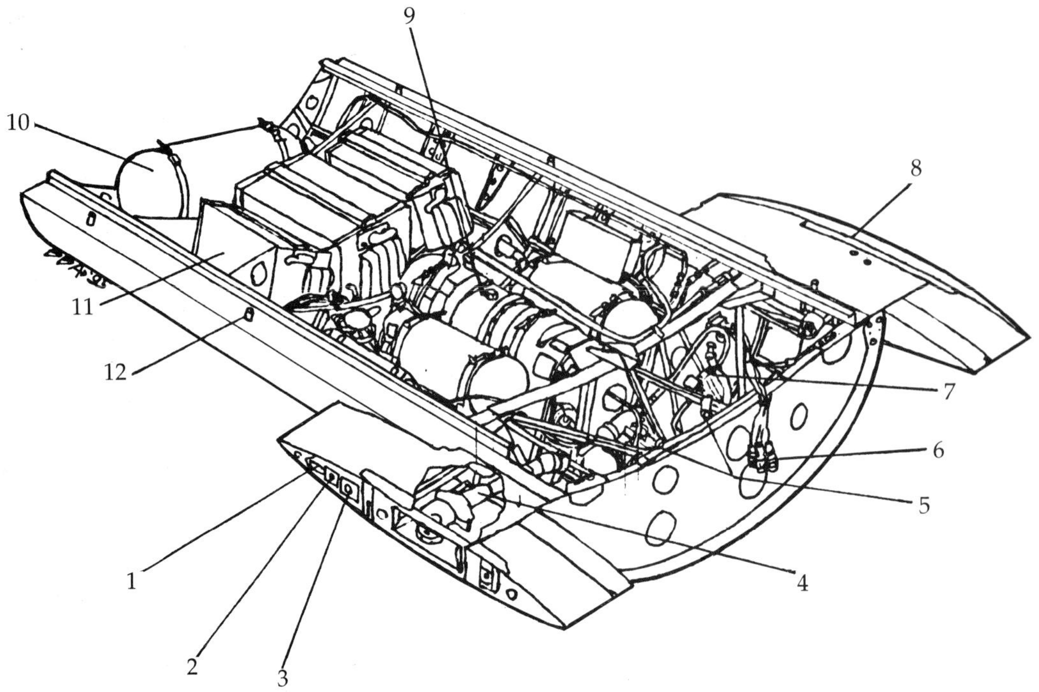

LIGHTNING MISSILE PACK DETAILS.
A similar mounting pack was available for both Firestreak and Red Top missiles. 1] Electrical interface. 2] Cold air connection 3] Hot air connection. 4] Missile ejector release unit. 5] Hydraulic connections to aircraft. 6] Electrical connections to aircraft. 7] Hot air connections to aircraft. 8] Pylon fairing, missiles not fitted. 9] Pack alternator. 10] Pack locating/mounting bolts. *(information courtesy of BAe)*

provision for cannon armament was made in either, which was a strange omission bearing in mind that both types not only had a basic training mission, but were also capable of reinforcement duties and airborne weapons training. However this was the age where the missile was king so their omission should come as no surprise.

On the final RAF version, the F.6, no provision for cannon was made initially, it took the lessons learned by the USAF in Vietnam to filter through for any change to occur. As no space was available in the fuselage for their fitment BAC, which had taken over E.E. Co, opted to install them in the forward section of the ventral fuel tank introduced by Modification 4243. Into this compartment was shoehorned a pair of 30 mm Aden cannon with a fire rate of 1,400 rounds per minute plus their associated ammunition feeds and gas expulsion vents. Extra reinforcement was required to maintain the integrity of the tank and eliminate, as far as possible, the fire risk. As with the F.2A, mounting the cannon underneath the airframe eliminated the hazard of flash blindness to the pilot. Those Lightnings sold overseas were also equipped to carry the ventral gun/fuel pack although this version of the installation had a dual air/ground-attack role.

Conceived as an interceptor, the Lightning with its limited range, had to extend its offensive reach by the use of missiles. Both types developed for the aircraft relied on infra-red homing – this reducing the dependence upon radar for both target-acquisition and guidance.

Air-to-Air missile development had begun in Britain during the 1950s. The first missile chosen to arm the early Lightnings was the de Havilland Propeller Company's Firestreak, which had originally rejoiced in the designation of Blue Jay. Developed almost in parallel with the English Electric programme, design and development had begun in 1951 with the assistance of the RAE, RRE and RARDE. Infra-red seeker head development was the responsibility of the Mullard Co. First firings of guided tests rounds were undertaken in 1954 at the RAE Aberporth range in Wales. This and subsequent firings were an outstanding success. Unfortunately later hiccups in guidance and propulsion were to catch the developers unawares. The seeker head developed a propensity to chase the sun, not the drone it was fired at. This led to the development of a lead sulphide seeker head that was virtually impervious to nature's biggest heat generator. Actual firings of the fully fettled missile took place in 1955 from a Venom carrier aircraft at Aberporth. This was completely successful, the Firefly V.9 drone being downed. Further test firings took place at Woomera in Australia using N.A. Sabres matched against Jindvik drones. Production versions of the Firestreak Mk.1 entered service with the Sea Venom squadrons of the Fleet Air Arm in 1958. The Lightning began to receive their allocation as the aircraft entered service in 1959. With a length of 10 ft 5.5 inches, a diameter of 8.75 inches and a wingspan of 2ft 5.5 inches the missile was carried in pairs by the Lightning.

For quick turn-round purposes the lower fuselage section, complete with pylons, was built as a pack. The option existed therefore of changing a complete package or of loading the missiles separately. The layout of the Firestreak has sometimes been described as backwards. Motive power is provided by a solid-propellant motor mounted amidships. Arranged around the motor and its jet pipe are the rear fin actuators which are driven by an air motor which also provides power to the turbo generator. Guidance was the responsibility of a cassegrain IR telescope with fifteen degree squint angle that was located behind an eight faceted nose-cone.

LIGHTNING RECONNAISSANCE PACK.
Low Level Sorties 1] Lower oblique 6"–f2.8 lens 2] Port oblique 3"–f2.0 lens 3] Stbd oblique 3"–f2.0 lens 4] Port split vertical 1.75"–f2.8 lens 5] Stbd split vertical 1.75"–f2.8 lens.
High Level Sorties 4A] Split vertical 12"–f2.0 lens 5A] Split vertical 12"–f2,0 lens
Other Items 6] Detachable fairing 7] Rotatable camera pack. (*information courtesy of BAe*)

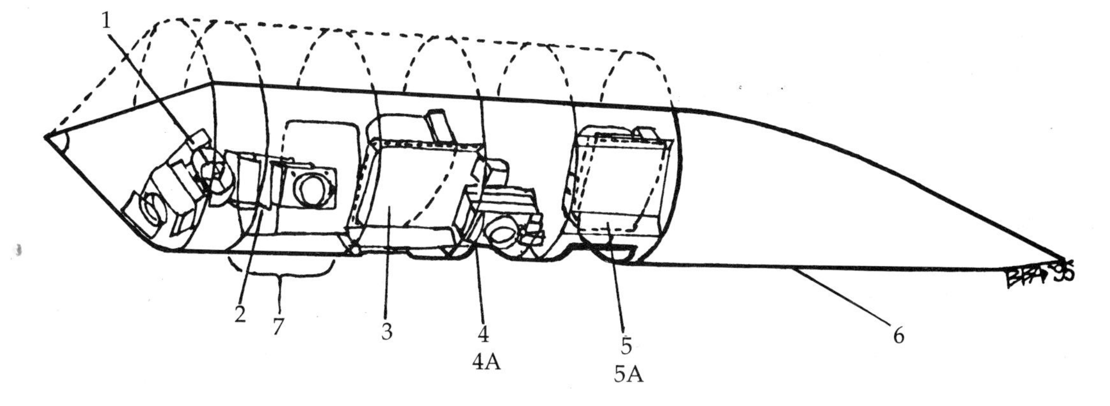

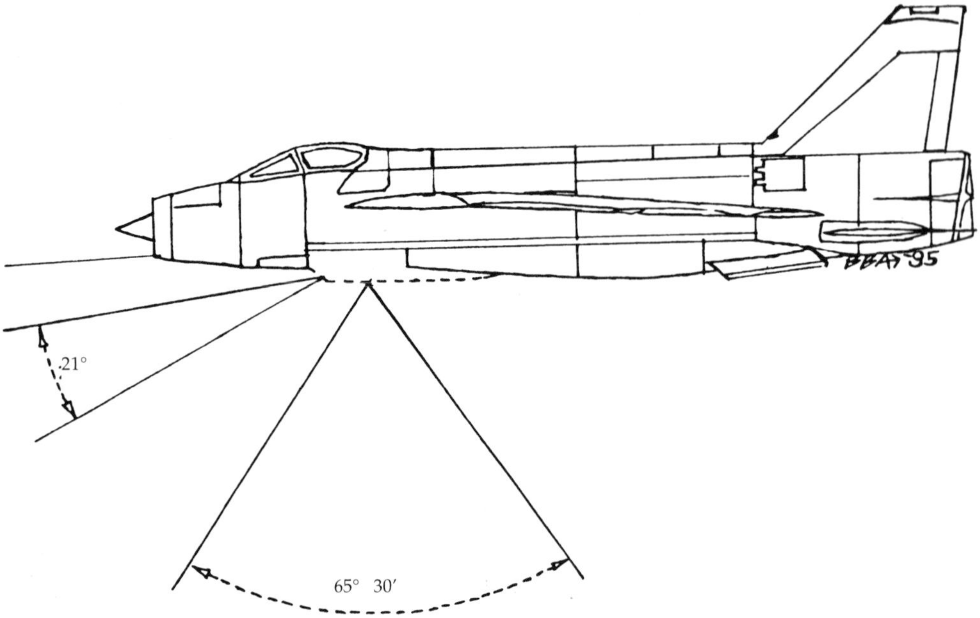

LIGHTNING RECONNAISSANCE PACK PERFORMANCE.
Inside the rotating capsule the forward oblique lens is 6″ in length whilst the lower lens can either be a 1.75″ item for low level work or a 12″ one for high level work.

Cooling of both the seeker head and onboard electronics was carried out using nitrogen stored onboard the carrier aircraft.

Target lock-on came not from the seeker head itself, but from two rings of sensors located behind the main seeker head. These latched onto a target and produced the necessary signals for the course corrections required to place the proximity fuse and warhead into the correct position for detonation. Weighing in at 50 lbs the warhead was wrapped around the motor tube just forward of the fins. Launch weight was 300 lbs, the motor being capable of boosting the weapon to Mach=3 over a range of 0.75 to 5 miles. Although the Firestreak finally achieved a kill probability of eighty-five per cent its main drawback always remained its limited seeker aspect – this being confined to rear only attacks.

As a first generation missile the Firestreak proved adequate to its task, although by 1956 advances in seeker technology were beginning to overshadow those in service. Originally designated the Firestreak Mk. IV, the Red Top, also a D.H. Prop product, was a successful exercise in rationalisation and logic. The major difference between the missiles was the new seeker head which because of its advanced all-aspect design was not only able to lock onto the heat generated by the target aircraft's engines, but to the friction hot spots created by its passage through the air. This eliminated the limiting rear only attack profile of the Firestreak, the new missile being capable of acquisition from any angle. Design studies began in 1957 with first details being released by an American magazine – much of which at the time was classified as secret.

Externally the Red Top lost the faceted head of the Firestreak, replacing it with one of a far more rounded appearance. An improved rocket motor increased the top speed past Mach=3, whilst in-control range was increased to seven miles.

Control surfaces were still small triangular fins at the rear of the body, although the forward wings had become cruciform in shape. Careful redesign of the body resulted in the warhead increasing to 68 lbs of high explosive. Dimensionally the Red Top was 10.57ft in length with a body diameter of 8.75 inches. Wingspan had increased to 2 ft 11.5 inches whilst the weight had grown to slightly over 330 lbs. The first Red Top entered RAF service with the Lightning F.6s of No. 74 Sqdn in 1964. Mode of carriage was similar to the earlier Firestreak, both missiles finding sales overseas with foreign Lightning operators.

Missile effectiveness in kill is rated as follows: at Mach=1.5 at an altitude of 45,000 ft over a distance of 300 nm a kill is possible with Firestreak whilst with rockets this is increased to 390 nm. At the slower speed of Mach=0.9 at an altitude of 36,000 ft this increases to 480 nm with either rockets or missiles. Firing at a hostile flying at 350 kts at a height of 20,000 ft the kill radius is 475 nm with both weapons. It is interesting to note that results of the lethality of the Red Top and its seeker are not available for publication. Both remain on the secret list.

Although never carried operationally by RAF Lightnings, the export F.53 was offered with a reconnaissance capability. This system replaced the missile package and extended aft to encompass the forward part of the ventral fuel tank. Contained within the rotatable section of the pod were five Type 360, 70 mm Vinten cameras which are directed left, right, fore, aft and centre-giving complete coverage. To eliminate humidity problems a self-contained de-mister was provided as was a range of lenses for use at different heights. Depending on lens-fit the system was designed for operation between altitudes of 200 and 30,000 ft. Film magazines held 500 ft of film each which enabled the Lightning to cover a strip of land 87 nm long with a camera angle of 186 degrees at a height of 200 ft . At 30,000 ft, strip width is increased to 1.74 nm with a length of 195 nm.

One other mode of operation that was exploited to the full in the export Lightnings was that of ground-attack using both rocket pods and bombs. First developments in this field were the Micro-Cell rocket pods fitted in the missile pack position. Although initially developed for mass airborne usage against large bomber formations, they were soon adapted to the ground-attack role, sighting being carried out using the Light Fighter Sight system. A total of forty-four 2-inch rockets were contained in the two drop-down packs. Wing pylons, stressed to a minimum of 1,000 lbs, were provided with strengthened pick-up points outboard of the main undercarriage doors. Equipped with standard NATO pick-up shackles these pylons could carry either a 1,000 lbs bomb or alternatively a SNEB MATRA Type 155 launch pod containing thirty-six rockets.

Other projected weapons fits included twin bombs or rocket mounts on the underwing pylons or fitment of MATRA L100 rocket pods, singly or in pairs containing eighteen projectiles and 500 gallons of fuel, to the over-wing pylon positions. Weapons aiming in ground-attack mode is by the depressed sight-line method where the pilot, using information projected by the radar onto the sight glass, descends in a gentle dive. Exposure to hostile fire is limited to a maximum of eight seconds as the lock-on mode of the attack system should have in fact acquired the target before this, leaving the pilot free to manoeuvre and to choose his weapons.

Combat air patrol, enhanced by flight refuelling, enabled the Lightning to loiter 100 nm from its base for sixty minutes before intercepting a target some 50 nm further away. Alternatively, on point defence it can intercept a target flying at Mach=1.3 at an altitude of 36,000 ft at a distance of 450 nm on internal fuel alone. Without external refuelling, ranges can be increased to a maximum of 524 nm at 36,000 ft with no loiter time in pursuit of a subsonic target. Overhead loiter time can however be as long as eighty-five minutes, but leaves the aircraft capable of only one interception up to 150 nm away.

On QRA using alternative weapons the following are theoretically possible: (a) An intruder travelling at Mach=1.5 at an altitude of 45,000 ft can be destroyed in six minutes using Micro Cell rockets or in eight minutes using Firestreaks. (b) For a hostile moving at Mach=0.9 at 36,000 ft this drops to three minutes using either weapon, whilst (c) supposes that a slower target moving at 360 kts at 20,000 ft can be destroyed in two minutes using either weapon.

Over the years the Lightning has been equipped with variations of the Martin-Baker Mk.4 ejection seat. Variants fitted include the Mks, 4BS, 4BSA, 4BSC and 4BST, all of which operate in a similar manner. Developed in its turn from the Mk.3 lightweight seat the later type was considerably modified. One major advance was the substitution of an 80 ft/sec ejection gun for the earlier slower version and the installation of a duplex parachute drogue extraction system in place of the earlier single unit. The original rail mounting was replaced in its turn by channel members mounted on the sides of the seat. These contained all the required switches to actuate various sequences as the seat left the aircraft.

Initially face-blind actuation was regarded as the main operating genre, the seat-pan handle being regarded as a back-up although its inclusion was regarded as a boon by any pilot unable to reach the face blind due to excess 'G' forces. Careful redesign of the seat packs resulted in a greater degree of comfort than ever before. This was achieved by completely relocating the survival equipment in the packs. Airborne use is available within the manufacturer's specified envelope; for ground operation a minimum speed of ninety knots is required to lift the seat clear of the aircraft.

When operated, the face-blind first initiated the cartridge ejection of the canopy which was followed by the release of the seat interlocks that stop it moving until the canopy has gone. For external rescue a handle located on the outside of the nose can initiate canopy ejection without firing the seat, a similar handle is located within the cockpit and has sometimes been used to assist pilots trapped in their aircraft due to a failure in the normal operating mechanism. Although the Martin-Baker seat is more than reliable, its use for escape by Lightning operators has been considerably less than those of its contemporaries. This must in turn say something for the reliability of the aircraft.

Air combat training is an important part of a fighter pilot's training, but shooting down his opposition, except in time of war, is officially frowned upon. Therefore many aircraft are fitted with a camera gun. That of the Lightning is the Type G90 which is located in a fairing below the pod for the AIRPASS radar and is operable in both auto and manual modes.

Chapter 4
From Hand to Jig: The Tall Tails

English Electric, and its supporters within government and military circles, were more than pleased to receive a contract for Lightning F.1 fighters in November 1956. The programme had been very much touch and go since the 1957 Defence Estimates White Paper had been presented to the House of Commons, only the development funds already invested coupled to excellent progress had diverted outright cancellation. Contract No. 6/acft/12715 called for twenty aircraft in this first batch. Basically production versions of the preceding P.1/F.1 development aircraft, first deliveries followed straight on from the earlier variant. The first production Lightning F.1 to fly was XM134 which made its maiden flight in the hands of R.P. Beamont, from Samlesbury to Warton on 3 October 1959. Shakedown flights, totalling fourteen in all, occupied the F.1 until it was declared ready for collection. During the company trials-flying the starboard undercarriage managed to shed part of its fairing whilst No.1 ECU starter had burnt-out after overspeeding during start-up. These minor problems notwithstanding, the Lightning was ready for other operators by 31 March 1960, being flown by 'Jimmy' Dell to A&AEE at Boscombe Down for pre-service evaluation. As most of the type's handling characteristics were already on record, much had been gleaned from the P.1Bs, the time spent by XM134 in Wiltshire was understandably short. Coltishall was the next stop for the aircraft where it arrived for use by the AFDS in July. Although the East Anglian flying period was short, a move to Warton in November curbing its time, much was learned and tactics developed for the new art of air combat up to Mach 2.

In June 1960 No. 74 'Tiger' Sqdn was declared ready for operations by Fighter Command, having given up its earlier Hunters with glee soon after arrival at Coltishall in mid-1959. No. 74 Sqdn was the only front-line unit to retain this first production variant in service, until they moved north to Leuchars in March 1964 for eventual re-equipment with the more advanced F.3. It is worth noting that of the twenty airframes built, the squadron successfully operated nineteen of them only missing out on XM168 which remained at Warton for use as a static fatigue test-bed. The first F.1, XM134, spent only a short time with the Tigers at Coltishall where it became 'A' after arrival on 2 September 1963. When 74 Sqdn left their East Anglian base for greater things their discarded mounts remained, being destined to form the core of the emergent 226 OCU. It was whilst on a training flight in XM134 that Flt Lt Bond became aware of control problems in pitch. Choosing wisely, he safely ejected leaving the abandoned Lightning to crash into the Wash. Obviously disturbed by this turn of events the RAF made every effort to recover the wreckage. Working in conjunction with the manufacturers and the AIB from Farnborough the cause was eventually postulated as a fire in the rear fuselage which had burned through the

Into service and F.1A XM135 looks resplendent in 74 Sqdn colour at Coltishall in September 1963. *(CP RUSSELL-SMITH)*

tailplane control runs. The remains were eventually divided between Warton and Farnborough in 1966 from whence they were eventually sold for scrap. During its short service life XM134 had achieved a total flight time of 229 hours.

With the first production F.1 safely in service, deliveries continued at a steady pace with Lightnings XM135 and 136 arriving at the CFE, Coltishall, as 'D' and 'E' respectively in May 1960. Both later appeared in 74 Sqdn colours as 'B' and 'C' before their ways parted. XM135 was to end its career on the strength of the Leuchars TFF before finally finding a permanent home as part of the IWM

With the signs of its previous ownership removed XM135 is seen on show as the 60 MU, Leconfield, 'hack'. *(CP RUSSELL-SMITH)*

The nose marking of 60 MU is well illustrated here in this view of the preserved aircraft. (*STEVE BUTTRISS*)

collection at Duxford. In contrast XM136 was to stay in the south joining the Wattisham TFF before coming to rest, in pieces, on 13 September 1967 having suffered a reheat fire that preceded a loss of control. To complete the story the pilot ejected safely, courtesy of Martin-Baker.

Further deliveries in June saw XM137 and 138 following the CFE route into Royal Air Force service. Coded 'F' and 'G' respectively, they later changed identities to 'D' (later 'T') and 'E' upon joining 74 Sqdn. As with others in this batch XM137 ended its RAF flying career in the service of the TFFs, this time at Binbrook in March 1966, before moving to join the 23 Sqdn parented TFF at Leuchars in 1971 as 'Y'. Finally withdrawn from use its last flight took it to Leconfield where storage awaited, although unlike others it was used as a guinea-pig for various novel forms of aircraft conservation by 60 MU before meeting its end at the hands of the scrapman. XM138 managed only a short period in 74 Sqdn service before succumbing to extensive fire damage discovered during a landing. Although the resultant inferno was successfully quenched, the extent of the aircraft's injuries was such that its only future use was in the instructional role. When the early Lightnings finally left RAF service XM138 found its nose going to Farnborough while the rest ended up on the Coltishall dump.

The next aircraft in line, XM139, took nearly eight months to deliver, having first flown in January 1960, as the number of flights to clear it for delivery finally totalled twenty. This Lightning is unique in that it was the first to be delivered by a service pilot, Sqdn Ldr Nicholls, direct to 74 Sqdn where it was first coded 'C', this later changing to 'F'.

In keeping with the other F.1s XM139 joined 226 OCU at Coltishall when 74 Sqdn decamped north. A year later the Lightning had followed northward, only its destination was the Leuchars TFF where it later acquired the nose marking 'Royal Scottish Air Force'. By 1969 a tour at Wattisham had been followed by a visit to Warton for a Cat 4 wing change. Being virtually a new aircraft it was a natural for the RAF fighter display slot. Piloted by Flt Lt R. Pengelly, XM139 put up spirited performances at the SBAC shows at Farnborough in 1970 and 1972. In the intervening year it had graced the Paris Air Show for the same purpose. After withdrawal the Lightning became 8411M at Wattisham where ground instruction became its forte, a duty it successfully carried out before scrapping.

In the first three months of 1960 the next seven Lightnings for the RAF had been test-flown and were soon ready for 74 Sqdn service. Arrivals at Coltishall followed some six months later with XM140, 141 and 142 arriving to take up the 'M', 'D' and 'B' slots respectively. In September XM143 and 144 joined the squadron as 'A' and 'J'. All were to move to 226 OCU before dispersing to other operators, XM140 joining 111 Sqdn as a high-speed target and general use trainer before withdrawal for scrapping. XM141 was damaged beyond economic repair in a landing accident, being reduced to spares at Lyneham before the remains were scrapped. XM142 crashed near Cromer in 1963 whilst XM144 was to do the rounds of the TFF units at Leconfield, Wattisham and Leuchars before returning south to 60 MU for use as a hack. Originally slated for gate guard purposes at Leuchars it has since moved onto a private owner cum scrapyard at Burntwood, Staffs.

From this point Lightning F.1 deliveries become somewhat erratic as the next in series, XM145, had to wait until May 1962 to reach Coltishall. The delay was the result of rear-end damage caused by a fire during ground reheat runs. A more normal service was resumed with XM146 which became 'L' of 74 Sqdn in September 1960. Before reaching the front-line at Coltishall the next aircraft, XM147, was employed by the AFDS for tactics development. In service this Lightning was unlucky, requiring extensive repairs by 33 MU, Lyneham, during 1969–70, the result of a heavy landing. After a period in store XM147 was allocated to the Binbrook TFF although much of its first eighteen months were spent under repair, the mainplanes being completely replaced whilst the fin and rudder assemblies underwent the same treatment having become detached in flight. What was left of the airframe finally became an instructional tool at Wattisham as 8412M.

Of the later serialled F.1s, XM163–XM168, the last, as already noted was retained as a structural test airframe at Warton. Of the others all eventually joined 74 Sqdn although XM165 has the honour of being the first Lightning delivered directly for squadron service. XM163 arrived via the AFDS while XM164 was routed via the A&AEE. Most were to pass to 226 OCU although XM164 did spend some time with the FCTU at Binbrook. After their flying service all were dispersed to the Maintenance Units at Lyneham and Leconfield where, after storage and eventual spares recovery they were scrapped.

In the Lightning's early months of service with the 'Tigers' the squadron's new mounts were to prove difficult to master. Ground crews were having to work exceptionally hard to maintain a flying programme as well as learning the intricacies of their latest challenge.

To achieve the things that they did does them great credit, bearing in mind that the simpler Hawker Hunter had served the squadron previously. Even so after six months of hard graft from both air and ground crew, 74 Sqdn finally achieved 100 hours of flying in a calendar month. This period of glee came to a shuddering halt at the end of February 1961 when a serious defect in the ventral fuel tank feed system was discovered. Caused by vibration and airflow disturbances, cracking pipework was allowing fuel to leak out under pressure in the vicinity of the engines. To overcome this set-back the temporary measure of flying the Lightnings without the tanks was adopted. This allowed the pilots to maintain type currency, but seriously curtailed their adventures beyond the airfield's boundaries. Fortunately the E.E. Co. came up with a modification (STI/120) that was to cure the problem. Quickly embodied, the squadron's aircraft were all available to take part in Exercise Matador that took place in April. Basically an air defence exercise, 74 Sqdn achieved ten simulated kills against intruding bombers operating at all altitudes and using every penetration tactic in the book.

Air displays at Farnborough for the

SBAC show were also a highlight of the squadron's year in 1961. During 1962 the first squadron commander, Sqdn Ldr Howe, was replaced by Sqdn Ldr Botterill. After the change-over the Lightnings of 74 Sqdn entered their most colourful phase. Black fins and spines predominated with the Tiger badge writ large upon the fin.

Contrary to all uninformed opinion the Lightning proved to be a dramatic success at formation aerobatics. No. 74 Sqdn began performing with a seven-strong team during 1962. From the outset the display was noisy, beginning with a mass reheat formation take-off. Having personally experienced the heat, noise and vibrations caused by a pairs take-off close at hand, seven must have been truly mind shattering. Flypasts low and slow with everything out and down were normally followed by slow wing-overs and rolls – the whole show finally ending with a bomb burst. Foreshadowing the Red Arrows by many years, 74 Sqdn took their circus overseas to tour Europe before culminating their season at the Royal Air Force's 50th Anniversary show at Upavon.

Farnborough and the 1962 SBAC show must surely be regarded as the greatest achievement of 74 Squadron's aerobatic prowess. With ten Lightnings in the air, the team was joined by the sixteen all-blue Hunters of 92 Sqdn. Unfortunately such manoeuvres generate high 'G' forces that can cause unforeseen airframe distortions. Such an occurrence overtook XM147 during a practice display. Pulling out of a sharp manoeuvre, the pilot encountered control column restrictions and wisely returned to base. Investigation found that the balance weights fitted at the column's base had fouled the distorted cabin floor structure at 2G plus. Modification work to strengthen the floor was carried out and the lessons learned applied to the aircraft that followed.

Having been thwarted in their plans to cancel the Lightning, the government of the day were to resort to indifference and obstruction to defeat sales of the aircraft. The first victims of this policy was the Indian Air Force which was shopping around for a new high-performance fighter. Queries from the sub-continent began in 1961, with a first batch of a dozen aircraft being mooted. Government support for this venture was not forthcoming and the deal fell through. India eventually bought the MiG-21, although they were later to return to Warton to buy the Jaguar.

During 1963 No. 74 Sqdn was looking forward to re-equipping with the more advanced Lightning F.3. Prior to that however the Fighter Command version of a no-notice TACEVAL had to be endured. Beginning in the afternoon of 23 March the squadron started off with only its pair of QRA aircraft fully serviceable. Over the next couple of hours hard graft by air and ground crews brought the total up to the eighty per cent required. The result although outstanding, was not unexpected from a unit that had operated the type for three years. Less than a year later 74 Sqdn left Coltishall and its faithful F.1s behind to join the Scottish Air Force at Leuchars with the F.3.

This did not mean that the career of these first Lightnings was ended. Far from it as a need for a dedicated type OCU had been identified early in the programme. The first appearance of a training unit, an OCU in embryo form, was the Lightning Conversion Unit that had appeared as part of the OCU at Middleton St. George in June 1962. As the fighter pilots moved north their tyro replacements began to flog their former mounts around the sky under the aegis of 226 OCU. Previously based at Middleton St. George as the Hunter OCU, with the shadow designation of 145 Sqdn,

After their front-line service the discarded F.1As found favour with 226 OCU at Coltishall. XM173 taxies past the photographer wearing the markings of 145 (Shadow) Sqdn in 1968. (*CP RUSSELL-SMITH*)

they had moved to Coltishall in April 1964. Their new charges were soon resplendent in the cross of St. George nose bars, these later being supplemented by red and white markings on the fin and spine. Until disbanding as 145 Sqdn in May 1971, the OCU spent all its time at Coltishall except for a short period at Leconfield, home of 60 MU the Lightning major unit, whilst the runway and infrastructure of its home base was refurbished.

High-speed fighters eventually need high-speed targets. The doctrine of mass or single bomber raids had faded with the appearance of reliable surface-to-air missiles. Their replacement was to be the medium to low level high-speed intruder. To simulate and develop tactics to counter these postulated forms of aerial attack, the RAF created the Target (Dual) Facilities Flights. More commonly known as TFFs their allotted task was to provide high-speed targets capable of cine-gun recorder dog-fights as well as providing aircraft, as required, for on-station convertion and continuation training. Target Facilities Flights appeared at Leuchars, Wattisham and Binbrook during 1966, that at Leuchars being parented for a short while by 23 Sqdn. Their sojourn with these flights lasted until 1972 – the eight aircraft involved, XM136, 137, 139, 144, 145, 147, 163 and 164 moving in the main to 60 MU for storage and eventual scrapping. Their places were later taken by the slightly more advanced F.1A. Other units that used the Lightning F.1 for varying periods of time included the AFDS/CFE which formed at Binbrook in August 1959 before moving to Coltishall in 1962. In February 1966 this unit became the FCTU, later to emerge as the far better known Lightning Training Flight.

Initially major servicing support had been the responsibility of 33 MU at Lyneham, however by 1965 the unit was in the process of winding down. Aircraft in store were either being scrapped or prepared for further service before Lyneham's duties were finally transferred to Leconfield.

Some of the stored Lightning F.1s were scrapped on-site although others such as XM135 were being prepared for aerial transit. It was during this period, on 29

Possibly the most colourful markings ever sported were those applied to the 56 Sqdn 'Firebirds' aerobatic aircraft illustrated here by XM172 at the 1963 Paris Air Show. (*CP RUSSELL-SMITH*)

June 1965, that Wing Commander 'Taffy' Holden (the writer of the foreword) undertook the only recorded unqualified Lightning flight. Whilst undertaking engine high-power ground runs in XM135 at the end of Lyneham's runway in an effort to trace an inverter problem that only appeared at high RPM, the Wing Cdr inadvertantly pushed the throttles through the reheat detent gate. As the aircraft was not tied down, due to the taxying requirements of the engine runs, the Lightning jumped the chocks and accelerated rapidly down the tarmac. Quickly realising that stopping distance was rapidly slipping away there was little alternative but to pull the control column back and take-off. Once airborne our intrepid pilot took stock of his situation. Due to the nature of the ground runs 'Taffy' Holden had not been wearing a headset, the ejection seat was fully pinned and therefore unusable and the Lightning had no canopy. All in all a perilous situation.

Fortunately some solo flying in a Harvard, some Javelin T.3 experience, plus the pilot's notes came in quite handy when controlling XM135. After three attempts at landing the impromptu pilot changed his approach pattern to match that of the alternate runway. Putting the Lightning through some strange gyrations to line it up, a further attempt was made. The fifth was successful although the Lightning did suffer some rear fuselage damage on touch down causing the brake-chute to fail. Heavy braking was applied, this finally bringing the Lightning to a shuddering halt complete with trailing plumes of smoke, fire-engines and ambulances. Thus ended for both parties twelve minutes of most unusual flying. Further inspection after the dust had settled revealed Cat 3 rear end damage that was subsequently repaired on site by a team from 60 MU. Successfully completed XM135 re-entered RAF service continuing to fly until gifted to the IWM at Duxford.

Although the Lightning F.1 was only ordered in small numbers and only lasted in service for twelve years, their contribution to the development of the supersonic air defence of Britain is inestimable.

Progression and development is an integral part of any aircraft's genesis, so it was with the Lightning. Major differences between the F.1 and the F.1A were minimal. Externally the main visible change introduced external cable ducting that ran, port and starboard, from the rear of the missile pylon to the rear fuselage. In-flight refuelling had become an intimate part of fighter operations and the Lightning F.1A was summarily equipped with a probe, complete with lights, mounted inboard under the port wing. Tanking facilities were provided care of 214 Sqdn from Marham equipped with Valiant B(K).1 tankers. Internally only the addition of a UHF radio system added to the clutter in the cockpit. Weaponry and fixed armament remained unchanged as did the power-plants, a pair of Avon 210s with four-stage reheat.

With No. 74 Sqdn successfully established as a fully functional fighter unit, it became the turn of an equally famous fighter squadron to relinquish its Hawker Hunters for the Lightning. A paltry total of twenty-eight aircraft, serialled XM169–XM192 and XM213–XM216, were ordered under contract 6/acft/12715 placed with E.E. Co. in 1956. Thirty aircraft were originally envisaged, but XM217 and XM218 were to remain unbuilt. First deliveries to the Royal Air Force began with XM172 to 56 Sqdn as 'B' on 14 December 1960. Prior to that the first three aircraft had flown, XM169 becoming airborne on 16 August. Delivery of this Lightning to the RAF did not take place until 1964 as it was first used by both A&AEE and the manufacturers to prove the in-flight refuelling system. Further trials concerning cabin pressurisation and improved windscreen rain dispersal followed.

The next aircraft, XM170, made its maiden flight on 12 September and managed to clock up a total of fourteen minutes flying time. And the reason for such a brief career? Mercury contamination which literally eats aluminium and similar alloys. Safety and the difficult and expensive task of removal successfully grounded XM170. Use as an instructional airframe and an appearance as a static display during the Lord Mayor's Show was followed by a return to instructional duties at RAF Newton. Complete with the maintenance number 7877M the Lightning eventually ended its days at Swinderby. Placed on the fire dump for eventual disposal, the defunct Lightning still had one vital task to perform. Contaminated parts of the airframe were removed and transported carefully to No.1 S. of TT, Halton, where they were used in the instruction of the Royal Air Force's future engineers. Its remains still lingered at Swinderby in 1973 when the author joined the RAF, although by this time much myth and legend had grown about its presence at this training base.

The third F.1A was also a late entrant into RAF service, XM171 had first flown in September 1960 being dispatched immediately to Boscombe Down where it was used as a cross-check aircraft in the trials concerning XM169. This part of its career was short however, as in February 1961 the Lightning had joined 56 Sqdn at Wattisham as 'R', later changed to 'A'.

No 56 Sqdn RAF had moved from Waterbeach on 10 July 1959 to Wattisham in anticipation of receiving its new equipment. With XM172, 174 'D' and 175 'E' safely on board before year's end in 1960, the next delivery occurred early in the New Year when XM173 'C' arrived on 2 January. Further deliveries occurred throughout the early part of 1961 with XM176, 177, 178, 179, 180, 182 and XM185 arriving in quick succession, the latter three appearing in March. The squadron's final Hunter F.6 departed in January 1961 leaving the unit fully supersonically equipped for the second time in its history.

F.6 XS928 completed its flying programme for the Tornado F.3 radar trials before becoming the Warton gate guard. Prior to appearing on the gate however much of the systems and equipment were removed for the LFC fleet. *(BAe Warton)*

On its way by heavy transport is F.53 ZF583 once 53-681 of the RSAF. Its current home is the Solway Aviation Society at Carlisle. *(Solway Aviation Society)*

Another ex-Saudi, ex-Warton escapee is F.53 ZF588, currently resident at the East Midlands Airport Aeropark – it was once 53-693. *(Via EMAP)*

Warton has an F.6 on its gate whilst Samlesbury uses ZF580, ex-Saudi 53-672, as its gate guardian. *(BAe Warton)*

Into the blue flies Kuwaiti AF T.55 No.410 wearing 'B' class markings as G-27-78 on a pre-delivery test-flight. *(BAe Warton)*

Lima and Juliet with everything out and down approach Dharan after an air defence training sortie. *(BAe Warton)*

Beautifully posed over the Saudi desert is T.55 No.711. This Lightning later returned to Warton before departing, allegedly, to the USA via the Haydn-Ballie collection. *(BAe Warton)*

A classic sight for any Lightning buff. An F.53 of the RSAF cleans up straight after take-off from Dharan. *(BAe Warton)*

Once destined for BDR duties, F.6 XR753 was rescued by 11 Sqdn at Leeming and now resides outside their HQ. *(11 Sqdn Leeming)*

Flying by the SNCO's mess at Boscombe Down is the second T.4 prototype XL629, the only complete example in preservation. *(Author's Collection)*

Bathed in the bright Cyprus sunshine, TV star F.6 XS929 (it had a cameo role in *Soldier Soldier!*) is resplendent in 56 Sqdn markings. *(Author's Collection)*

T.5 XV328 is currently awaiting sale from the Arnold Glass collection at Cranfield. In its RAF days the aircraft wears the markings of 11 Sqdn and is seen undergoing pre-flight servicing at Binbrook. *(Steve Buttriss)*

Heading the Cranfield line-up is redundant F.6 XS899 pictured in 1988.
(Author's Collection)

Prepared and awaiting its pilot is F.6 XS903 'BA' the 11 Sqdn Commander's machine. *(Steve Buttriss)*

Still wearing the earlier grey/green finish is F.6 XR769, being prepared for flight at Binbrook in March 1988. *(Steve Buttriss)*

F.6 XS904 is now owned by the Lightning Preservation Group at Bruntingthorpe. Although low on remaining fatigue-life and engine hours the aircraft is maintained in taxiable condition. It is pictured here at Warton awaiting engine ground runs. *(BAe Warton)*

The earlier occasion had involved the Supermarine Swift which had quickly, and thankfully, faded from the scene. In contrast, the Lightning proved a great and positive step forward. Achieving their full operational capability was made easier by the practice of using experienced personnel to form the basis of the squadron. For the pilots, including those transferred from 74 Sqdn, the first technique to be mastered was in-flight refuelling. The culmination of all this intensive training was a two-aircraft flight to Akrotiri, Cyprus, that took place on 23 July 1962. Lasting four hours 22 minutes the Lightnings were ably supported by Valiant tankers drawn from 90 and 214 Sqdns. The success of this mission prompted MoD to issue a statement that the squadron would repeat the performance again, this time with four aircraft, in October. This operation too was a success and helped formulate the basis for any future requirements that would be needed for the other Lightning deployments that were to follow.

Even in RAF circles glamour must be equalled by hard work. Exercise Matador in April 1961 alongside 74 Sqdn soon proved that the F.1A operator was as good as its rival. Like the Tigers, the aircraft of 56 Sqdn had been subject to the fuel system modification that had earlier restricted their operations.

Fortunately their aircraft were also modified in time for the exercise. Air displays also formed part of 56 Sqdn's early public appearances. The first such events graced were Bentwaters and Mildenhall in 1961 when XM182 and XM177 were displayed. This was followed by appearances at the many other shows throughout Britain. Possibly the ultimate accolade granted to any fighter squadron is to be nominated as the Fighter Command display team.

In acknowledgement of their previous outstanding performances No.56 Sqdn assumed this mantle in 1963, replacing the previous holders 92 Sqdn who were in the process of trading their all-blue Hunters for the Lightning F.2 (of which more later). Although the aircraft of the Firebird Squadron still retained their familiar red and white nose checks, the rest of the aircraft was to become brightly coloured. Bright red adorned the leading edges of wings and tailplanes, whilst the fin and spine were also similarly finished. With a large 'Firebirds' badge and swept back flash on the fin the Lightnings of this squadron were most striking. Fin codes were originally black outlined white on the fin, but later became red outlined white on the airbrakes. It was during this period that the aircraft were recoded thus XM172 changed from 'S' to 'B' in 1962.

One concession to the world of aerobatics was made, the removal of the in-flight refuelling probe was sanctioned for displays and their practices. Air displays and formation flying have their inherent risks, mainly that of collision. And so it was to prove on 6 June 1963 when two of the squadron's aircraft collided. During a bomb burst over Wattisham XM179 slammed into XM171. The latter aircraft made an eventual, and eventful, safe landing whilst the other, totally out of control left the pilot with no other option but to eject. This he did, unfortunately the ejection seat was operating outside of its design parameters and, although he survived he suffered serious injury.

With deliveries of the far more advanced Lightning F.3 commencing, the earlier variant was replaced in 56 Sqdn service in 1965. Of the aircraft on inventory, Lightnings XM172, 174, 177, 178, 180, 182 and XM183 were to transfer to 226 OCU at Coltishall. Life after the OCU continued for most of these aircraft when they followed the earlier F.1s into the service of the Target Facilities Flights at Binbrook, Wattisham and Leuchars. At the Scottish base XM174 was to end its career in an abrupt and fiery manner, crashing near its home base on 29 November 1968, the pilot ejecting safely. In contrast XM177 of the Wattisham TFF continued in use until withdrawn to 60 MU for storage and spares recovery in 1974. Other Lightnings of 56 Sqdn did not even advance that far, XM176 suffered such severe damage due to an intense ground fire that it was fit only for spares recovery and fire practice being deemed beyond economic repair.

A far more dramatic fate overtook XM185 on 28 June 1961 when Flying Officer Ginger discovered that his delightful mount was no longer behaving in the manner to which he had become accustomed. With hydraulic failure warning captions illuminating the cockpit he elected to eject, leaving the doomed Lightning to end its career after thirty-nine flying hours. In total contrast to the foregoing, the final fates of XM172 and XM173 are almost pastoral, both are gate guardians at Coltishall and Bentley Priory respectively.

There can be few squadrons in the Royal Air Force that can boast that their latest aeroplane is a model kit! The squadron was No.111 which re-equipped from the Hunter at Wattisham in April 1961 whilst the aircraft was F.1A XM192 , which, after a long and illustrious career graced Wattisham's gate.

The kit manufacturer was of course Airfix whose kit is unfortunately no longer available in F.1A form. From the total batch of twenty-eight aircraft produced 111 Sqdn was to operate fourteen at one time or another. Some were from early-on in the production run such as XM169 which arrived fairly late at Wattisham in October 1964. Four months later the F.1A had been supplanted by the more advanced F.3 in 111 Sqdn service. XM169 moved to Binbrook where it was on the strength of the TFF. After withdrawal the Lightning was renumbered 8422M for instructional use at Leuchars. Three other Lightnings joined 111 Sqdn at a later date than their maiden flights would suggest. XM188–190 had been retained at Warton by English Electric for evaluation flights by the SAAF, USAF and the Indian Air Force respectively. XM188 reached Wattisham in May, but was to end its career not long afterwards when it ploughed into the squadron buildings after brake failure.

The F.1A differed little from the preceding F.1, the most obvious difference being the external cable ducts, and when required a demountable in-flight refuelling probe. XM192 'K', the subject of the Airfix kit, undergoes pre-flight checks by its pilot at Middleton St. George in 1961. (*CP RUSSELL-SMITH*)

XM189 also joined 111 Sqdn that month and remained with them until relocating to 226 OCU in 1964. The last of this trio, XM190, also came to an inglorious end. Having served 111 Sqdn well, it too was transferred to the OCU, crashing in the sea near Cromer on 15 March 1966. The pilot, a USAF exchange officer, ejected safely.

The first Lightnings to appear on the 111 Sqdn inventory were XM184 and XM186. Both arrived on 13 April 1961 and were followed in rapid succession by XM178 (24 April), XM191 and XM192 (28 June), XM181 (29 June), XM213 (30 June), XM214 (1 August), XM215 (2 August) and XM216 (29 August).

Once the squadron's air and ground crews had mastered the technicalities of their new charges, helped no doubt by an influx of experienced personnel from other sources, their main task began. Not for them the joys and delights of thrilling massive crowds. To 111 Sqdn fell the lot of air-to-air and ground-attack tactics.

Prior to that however, flight refuelled trips to Germany, Cyprus and Malta were undertaken, as were dog-fight combat exercises with aircraft of other squadrons and other nations within NATO. All this intense hard work resulted in the squadron being declared fully operational on 29 September 1961. The next month however was very quiet for the Lightning fleet as all extant aircraft were grounded for emergency remedial work on the hydraulic system pipelines. Centred mainly in the engine bays this consisted of separating the pipes by mounting them in Paxolin clamps to eliminate the chafing problem that had come to light. Some rerouting and replacement of the pipe-runs also took place. Heat was another problem that faced the pipework in the engine bays. To counteract this the affected pipes were either lagged or had shielding fitted. Such was the urgency of the task, Britain being virtually undefended in the air, that an intensive programme of works was instigated. By mid-November all the affected Lightnings were declared ready for use, although some had been repaired within days to retain a QRA presence on each squadron.

During 1963 and 1964 detachments from the squadron found themselves at El Adem in Libya. Here, above the desert sands, they practiced air-to-air firing with cannon, rockets and Firestreak missiles. Ground-attack work included strafing passes using the permanently installed cannon to which was added an Aden package instead of the usual missiles. Even the two-inch Micro Cell rocket packs were used – a very rare occurrence. Much of the air-to-air gunnery was carried out at Mach=0.9 at an altitude of 36,000 ft although at least one aircraft managed one attack at a higher altitude at a speed in excess of Mach 1.

Airborne refuelling exercises to gauge the loiter verses pilot-endurance ratio were also undertaken – tanking facilities being courtesy of the Fleet Air Arm that supplied suitably equipped Sea Vixens for the purpose. The famous lightning flash on 111 Sqdn's aircraft continued to dart about the skies of the world until they too transferred their skills to the Lightning F.3.

From their lofty perch as Britain's front-line fighters the displaced F.1As were passed onto the OCU for the mundane task of pilot training. Some of course never survived that long, XM191 being seriously damaged by fire that virtually destroyed the rear fuselage by the time it landed again at Wattisham in June 1964. Although a write-off its nose still survives as an exhibit with the RAFEF which is currently resident at St. Athan. The last three aircraft in the contract, XM214–216, were to end their lives at the scrap merchants having passed through the hands of the OCU and the different TFFs along the way. XM214 has one minor claim to fame as this was the aircraft upon which the standard Lightning brake-parachute coupling was introduced. This design was perpetuated throughout the rest of the type's production and also retrospectively fitted to the earlier aircraft.

At various times throughout their existence the Lightning F.1As were operated in small numbers for short time periods by the Lightning Conversion Squadron and the AFDS, part of the CFE at Binbrook.

Looking at the Lightning F.2, when first rolled out, most observers would have been forgiven for writing it off as a slightly upgraded F.1A. Nothing could be further from the truth, in looks certainly the external visage was at least unaltered except for a small intake duct on the spine. Under the skin however, it was another story altogether, for the F.2 combined the basic elements of the earlier versions with the first inklings of the advanced radar and navigation equipment that was to feature in the later square-tailed Lightnings. Always a pilot's aeroplane in the truest sense of the word, the Lightning F.2 in both its original and rebuilt forms was regarded by many as the pinnacle development of both eras.

In comparison with the first Lightnings the F.2, although retaining the Rolls-Royce Avon series 210 engine, featured a fully variable reheat, a standard four-cannon armament that left the missile pack untouched, plus an upgraded AI.23 radar. Partial incorporation of OR946, minus the speed strip indicator improved the navigation potential of the type appreciably, it also benefited the pilot by reducing some of his in-house workload. To make way for all these extras the early Lightning gaseous oxygen system, heavy and cumbersome with lots of vulnerable pipework, was replaced by a more compact liquid oxygen (LOX) pack. Based upon a 3.5-litre container, whose contents expand by 800% upon becoming gaseous, only two short sets of pipework were required. One led to the combined fill and vent valve used for replenishment, whilst the other – via a series of coils – released oxygen in gaseous form to the pilot. For those imagining that neat LOX could be fed to the pilot a check valve was fitted to prevent that happening. As the pack was removable it became a common sight to see a Land Rover or tractor pulling a special trolley containing freshly charged, 'pots' up and down the flightline delivering them to the aircraft scheduled for that day's flying.

Ordered as part of contract KC/2D/03/CB7(b) dated for December 1959, the first F.2 made its maiden flight piloted by J. Dell. As with other firsts XN723 was, after company flying, delivered to A&AEE Boscombe Down for C(A) pre-service release testing in February 1962. Whilst at the Wiltshire test facility XN723 undertook cannon-firing trials and general handling evaluation. Over a year later this first F.2 moved on, this time to the Rolls-Royce flight test base at Hucknall. Arriving on 2 April 1963 XN723 was never destined to enter RAF service, managing less than twelve months with its new employers. A fire in No.2 engine bay rendered the Lightning uncontrollable leaving the pilot, D. Withnall, with no other option than to eject – this he did successfully.

Of the next forty-three aircraft (the last six originally provisioned were cancelled) a further five were to find themselves involved in trials work of one kind or another. The second F.2, XN724, having first flown in September 1961 was allocated to Boscombe Down for general handling and avionic assessment. Completed by September 1963 the Lightning was despatched to 33 MU for storage, a state it was to remain in until returned to Warton for F.2A conversion in October 1966.

Another F.2 that avoided service with the RAF was the third machine, XN725. After its first flight on 31 March 1962 trials work covering engine performance and possible intake buzz occupied it until 1963. With Samlesbury backed up with production aircraft, the decision was taken to transfer the aircraft to Filton for conversion to F.3 standard.

Complete with the obligatory square fin and Avon 301 series engines, the revamped F.2, now the F.3 development airframe, made its 'second' first flight in early 1964. General handling and brake assessment followed throughout 1964 before XN725 moved onto ventral arrester-hook development trials in 1965. A return to BAC (which had been formed from E.E. Co., Hunting and Vickers) saw XN725 fitted with a pair of cambered wings and for a short time, dummy overwing tank installations that were being aerodynamically proven. By 1967 the Lightning was at RAE Bedford where it was fitted with a variety of ventral tanks containing various recording devices. For the next few years it acted as a Concorde chaseplane recording both noise and air vibrations generated by this magnificent airliner. Modified beyond any common standard XN725 was deemed unfit for RAF service and eventually it was scrapped.

Another F.2 destined to avoid RAF usage was the 12th production example, XN734. After its first flight in July 1962 the Lighting was transferred to Rolls-Royce at Hucknall where it was to join the ill-fated XN723 in 1963. Engaged in reheat development trials, not only for the series 210 Avons, but for the forthcoming series 301 powerplants destined for the F.3, XN734 spent 1964 shuttling between Hucknall and the A&AEE for assessment and any required modifications to the fitted engines. A more permanent allocation, for consolidation work, occupied the Lightning during the next three years before it was returned to Warton on 18 September 1968. Fitted with a ventral hook it too went to RAE Bedford for trials and assessment. Later withdrawn in February 1970 XN734 was placed in storage at 60 MU Leconfield to await disposal. The Lightning's time in store was to be foreshortened by a requirement by BAC for a ground systems trainer for use in its Saudi Arabian training programme. Wearing the 'B' class registration G-27-239 the Lightning was used for many years at Warton as a ground training aid before being put up for disposal. After a short period in the ownership of Aces High, XN734 is currently in residence with the Vintage Aircraft Team at Cranfield.

The 20th production airframe, XN773, had to wait until 1967 before joining the Royal Air Force. First flown in June 1962 this Lightning too became part of the Rolls-Royce line-up at Hucknall where it was used for engine development. Prior to that transfer however, it has spent much of the previous year at Boscombe Down engaged in Auto ILS trials. Having undertaken its share of the development load XN773 was delivered to 60 MU in March 1965 for storage. Here it remained until moving to Warton for F.2A conversion in July 1967.

With more aircraft than squadron slots available it is hardly surprising to find many aircraft from the end of the F.2 production entering storage for some considerable period of time before entering full RAF service. Such a fate overtook the 42nd airframe, XN795. Having first flown on 30 May 1963, the pilot being J. Carrodus, its first port of call was 33 MU at Lyneham for storing. By July 1964, as no front-line slot was available, the decision was taken to transfer the Lightning to Warton where

Resplendent with blue fin and red/yellow arrow-head is F.2 XN785 'C' of 92 Sqdn captured returning to the flight-line at Leconfield in September 1963. (*CP RUSSELL-SMITH*)

it was to undergo partial F.2A conversion. This entailed changing the fin and ventral tank to the new format whilst the wing platform was to remain unchanged. Very much a hybrid of the F.2A/F3 XN795 undertook some flying trials work before entering storage again, this time at Warton. Here it remained until 1968 before BAC passed it to A&AEE for chase-plane work. This lasted until 1972 when XN795 returned to Warton for use in the MRCA development programme. Well underway by this date, various aircraft types were being allocated to develop aspects of this advanced programme.

To XN795 fell the task of trialing the intended cannon fit of the 27 mm Mauser cannon. This continued to be the Lightning's lot until 1980 when it was diverted to fulfil other MoD sponsored contracts. By late 1980 XN795 had been grounded and transported to the weapons range at PEE Foulness Island. After some years as a target, its remains were finally sold off as scrap.

It is fairly obvious that from the numbers ordered there had been at one time an intention to form a third F.2 squadron. Peacetime financial stringency made its mark upon the Royal Air Force, the third unit failing to materialise. Having disposed of five aircraft to various trials programmes it is not surprising that further aircraft surplus to requirements were being allocated to other spheres of operation. An unusual example of this was the decision to release five further aircraft from the RAF inventory for sale overseas. The purchaser was the Royal Saudi Arabian Air Force. On initial observation this would appear a strange sale given the government's lethargy towards aircraft sales in general and the Lightning in particular. Until of course the magic word 'oil' is mentioned!

Of the five, XN729 was the only Saudi F.2 to have seen some RAF service, firstly with the AFDS/CFE at Binbrook during 1963–67 and later at Wattisham for in-flight refuelling trials. Purchased from the MoD at the end of 1967 it joined the other four aircraft, XN767, XN770, XN796 and XN797 at Warton to await conversion to F.52 standard. Their further exploits are continued in a later chapter.

On 29 June 1959, No.19 Sqdn RAF moved from its old home at Church Fenton, where it had resided for the past ten years, to its new base at Leconfield. For the next three years the 'Dolphins' continued to fly their trusty Hawker Hunters before being stood down to re-equip with the Lightning F.2. Their first aircraft, XN775, arrived on 17 December 1962 although Christmas and New Year were to pass before squadron acceptance flights were made. The squadron's second F.2, XN778 struggled to reach Leconfield as it had diverted to Finningley on its 9 January delivery flight. Soon rectified, the Lightning finally made Leconfield where it and the earlier aircraft were soon joined by others. During February XN774 'C', XN779 'G', XN780, XN782 'K' arrived being followed in March by XN730 'B', XN776 'E', XN787 'M' and XN791 'N'. The final allocated Lightning XN785 reached Leconfield on 5 April 1963. It should be noted that deliveries to both 19 and 92 Sqdns were not in sequential order. This was possible because many of the early-build Lightning F.2s had been held in storage for up to two years. When the late-build aircraft were ready at Warton for despatch, all aircraft were released in one glorious flood to equip the Leconfield Wing.

Intensive flying became the order of the day for 19 Sqdn, thus they were able to achieve full operational status by March 1963. Fully equipped in April the squadron was allocated to the air defence role. Training accelerated over the year to reach a set target of 300 hrs/month spread over more than 350 sorties. In-flight refuelling in the F.2 played a prominent part in air defence operations, much as it had with the earlier F.1A. Practising this art began in January 1964, culminating in the usual celebratory trip to Cyprus in June. Support, as before, came courtesy of the Valiant tanker Wing, although in the following year 19 Sqdn was acting as the trials unit for the Victor K.1. Unfortunately even in-flight refuelling can generate risk, witness the loss of XN785 on 27 April 1964. After attempting a number of unsuccessful probes at the tanker, the Lightning pilot pulled clear due to decreasing available fuel. Unable to reach Leconfield he

Lightning F.2 XN790 'E' of 92 Sqdn lands at Farnborough during the 1964 SBAC show. By now the blue painted area had spread to encompass the whole spine. (*CP RUSSELL SMITH*)

attempted to make an emergency landing at the disused airfield at Hutton Cranswick. Although such a feat is possible in such a high-performance aircraft as the Lightning, in this case it was not to be and the aircraft crashed killing the pilot, Fg. Off. Davey.

When 19 Sqdn had arrived at Leconfield in June 1959 it had been followed in May 1961 by 92 Sqdn. Although two years late in arriving at its new base the squadron was to be no laggard in replacing its famous blue Hunters with the far more capable Lightning. Coded 'A', the first arrival was XN727 which was delivered from Warton by E.E. Co. pilot J.K. Isherwood on 23 January 1963. It was soon followed by XN728 'B', XN732 'H', XN786 'D', XN789 'G' and XN790 throughout April whilst in May XN735 'J', XN783 'A' (replacing XN727) and XN788 arrived. Three others followed in June these being XN733 'C', XN792 'N' and XN793 'K'. One final straggler, XN731, arrived during August having been in service with the Handling Squadron at Boscombe Down in the meantime.

Adorning their aircrafts' noses with their famous red and yellow checks, 92 Sqdn settled-down to follow a similar path to that taken by 19 Sqdn towards operational readiness. Conversion work was courtesy of the two-seaters of 226 OCU with which all pilots were conversant before they flew any of the fighters. By the start of 1964 the intensive work-up period was completed and 92 Sqdn was declared ready. Having supplied an official aerobatic team in the days of the Hunter it came as no surprise to find the squadron filling a similar slot with their newer and faster mounts. Resplendent in blue tails and spines, with a red and yellow arrowhead replacing the checks on the nose, these thunderous beasts thrilled and delighted the crowds wherever they performed. Possibly the highlight of 1964 was their performance at the 1964 SBAC show at Farnborough.

Although QRA interceptions and aerobatics were important facets of a Lightning fighter pilot's life, the extra cannon and a mooted move to Germany saw both squadrons active in training for the ground-attack role. Once completed 19 Sqdn packed its bags and began its move to Germany on 23 September 1965. Home was to be Gütersloh for the next twelve years as part of the NATO assigned 2TAF. No.92 Sqdn was also quick off the mark in joining 2TAF arriving at Geilenkirchen from 29 December onwards. Their stay at Geilenkirchen lasted until 24 January 1968, when they officially moved to Gutersloh thus consolidating the F.2 assets at one base. Both squadrons were to remain active with both the F.2 and F.2A training for a war that thankfully never came. This was not to say that life was ever boring – far from it – as the numerous incursions by various forms of MiG fighters were to prove. Scrambled to intercept these strong target blips they inevitably turned out to be young pilots that claimed they were lost, although some were definitely identified as probing flights to evaluate NATO reaction times.

During 1967/68 the F.2 aircraft of both squadrons were rotated through to Warton for conversion to F.2A standard. In the event only twenty-eight aircraft were converted out of a total of forty-four built. A few remained unconverted, these being XN768, XN769, XN779 and XN794. All remained at Gutersloh for use in the TFF and conversion/continuation training role. Three were eventually scrapped after the squadrons disbanded in 1977. One however escaped, this being XN769 which until 1993 was placed on display outside the air traffic control centre at West Drayton wearing both 19 and 92 Sqdn colours. Although no complete example of the F.2 now exists, preservationists were fortunately able to save the nose from the scrapman's axe.

Study of the Lightning F.2 records show that quite a few were in storage at 33MU Lyneham, before issue to either of the squadrons. To obviate waiting time in store and to reduce the possibility of leaks, mainly caused by the drying out of seals in the fuel and hydraulic systems, many were passed onto minor units for weapons and tactics development. One of these units was the Air Fighting Development Squadron, part of the Central Fighting Establishment at Binbrook. One of their first F.2s was XN726 which arrived in Lincolnshire on 14 February 1963 which, having first flown on 29 September 1961 had remained at Warton ever since. Having evaluated the full range of tactics possible with the F.2 it was returned to BAC for F.2A conversion in 1968. Operating alongside XN726 was XN729 which eventually left the service of the Royal Air Force to join the RSAF as an F.52. XN771 also remained clear of RAF usage until passed to BAC for F.2A conversion. Prior to that it was also in use at Binbrook where it was coded 'M'. During its time with the CFE, flying had been so intensive that 33 MU were obliged to carry out a major servicing on the aircraft. Boscombe Down also acquired an F.2 when XN772 joined the A&AEE on 7 November 1963. It continued to fly from Wiltshire until 1967 when the Lightning was returned to Warton for conversion. A similar fate befell XN773 which was operated on behalf of Rolls-Royce. Unfortunately engine development work does not always last a long time and as result XN773 was in storage at 60 MU by March 1965. By 1967 however the Lightning was at Warton awaiting upgrading to F.2A standard.

On 21 December 1962 XN777 finished its remarkably short career with the AFDS when it was rendered Cat 4 during landing when the nose leg sheared off. Obviously beyond Binbrook's capacity to repair, it was shipped to Lyneham where rectification was effected. As the Lightning F.2's days were drawing to a close XN777 was flown to Warton for conversion, having achieved only five months of flying to that date, October 1966. In both its guises the Lightning F.2 served the RAF well and we are indeed fortunate that a number survive in preservation for future generations. After their careers were over in 1977 many of the redundant Lightnings ended up at various RAFG airfields as decoys although some did appear in the UK for the same purpose.

Was the Lightning F.2 overordered? Were there plans to form a third squadron? Probably we shall never know. What is obvious however is that the F.2 variant was the pinnacle of the pointed tail Lightnings and that in its converted form would probably have been better suited as the basis for the multi-role version that was eventually sold overseas.

Chapter 5: The Thunderous T-Birds

SOMEWHERE ALONG the learning curve most air forces realise that they need a two-seat trainer version of their latest fighter. The first Lightning pilots were chosen from aircrew with a minimum of 1,000 hours fast jet flying. Obviously such a resource is finite, thus the E.E. Co. began developing a two-seat trainer designated P.11 – later to become the T.4 in RAF parlance. Initial design work at Preston looked at producing a tandem-seat aircraft. This, although the favoured solution, was abandoned when it was realised that the extended fuselage required would call for considerable redesign of the rear fuselage and engines that were far more powerful than those currently available. Eventually ingenuity came to the fore and evolved a solution that widened the forward fuselage by only 11.5 inches, but quite happily contained a crew of two mounted upon ejection seats. A widened and deepened fairing blended the new nose and canopy profile into the spine and remainder of the airframe. The remainder of the P.11 was to remain virtually unchanged from the production F.1A single-seater. Major changes only involved those frames numbered from No.1 at the extreme nose to No.25 at the rear cabin pressure bulkhead. To equalise the C of G trim changes engendered by the addition of a second ejection seat, widened fuselage and additional equipment, the cannon armament was completely deleted. One other bonus that stemmed from the final design chosen was the application of area rule to the fuselage which maintained supersonic performance and aerodynamic handling. Fitted with the then standard Avon 210 power-plants, the new P.11 also retained the single-seater's AI.23 radar and sighting systems, albeit that they were optimised for Firestreak use only. This gave the forthcoming trainer an air defence capability that would have been much appreciated in time of war.

The Air Ministry's Operational Requirements Branch finally took an interest in the project and issued Specification T178 D&D to cover development. Full-scale design work began in 1954 and progressed well until the full-scale mock-up was unveiled. As no input had been drawn from the flying test team, certain aspects drew criticism from the pilots. The major flaw was the canopy framing which would have had a tendency to blot out certain parts of the pilots field of vision. Fortunately these blind areas were quickly realised as a hazard by Freddie Page and the design team and the framing was altered accordingly.

Two aircraft, XL628 and XL629, were ordered under this specification, the first being completed in April 1959. Taxi tests and brake-parachute deployment trials followed over the next few weeks until all activity ceased on 1 May whilst the P.11 was prepared for its first flight. On 6 May 1959 XL628 in clean configuration, piloted by Roland Beamont, took to the air for the first time. Lift off (V2) was achieved at 145 kts IAS and the first thing that the pilot was to comment upon was the lightness of

With the demise of the first T.4 prototype XL628, its sister ship XL629 was left to shoulder the burden of the development programme. Replete with Firestreaks the Lightning is captured at Farnborough in September 1960. (*CP RUSSELL-SMITH*)

the controls in comparison with the single-seaters. A full range of manoeuvres at varying speeds was carried out on this maiden flight, all of which were later reported as satisfactory. Maximum speed attained was Mach=1.2.

Having achieved enough flying hours to prove the safety of the design, XL628 was diverted away from the evaluation programme to take part in the 1959 SBAC show at Farnborough. Resplendent in polished aluminium offset by the yellow trainer bands currently in vogue, the Lightning also toted a pair of Firestreaks and the legend 'Lightning T.4' below the cockpit.

The days of two-seat glory were nearly to end in tragedy however when on 1 October, disaster struck. Piloted by John Squier XL628 left Warton that morning to carry out engine handling and manoeuvring trials over the Irish Sea. Part of the specified test included an aileron controlled roll of 360 degrees at M=1.7 at an altitude of 40,000 ft. As this had already been carried out in the preceding single-seaters no problems were expected. Therefore feet were removed from the rudder pedals and the control column moved fully right. The T.4 entered a maximum rate roll, stopping it required the controls to be centralised. This the pilot duly did, his action being accompanied by a mighty bang followed by a total loss of control. With the Lightning tumbling about the sky and on the edge of consciousness he took the only possible option and pulled the face blind handle on the ejection seat. As advertised, the canopy and seat separated from the doomed aircraft and thus began the longest and hardest hours of John Squier's life. Unable to despatch a distress signal his only hope of rescue was to be the aids included in the seat's survival pack. Apparently as he was to find out later, the dinghy-mounted SARAH beacon was useless. Having deployed his chute and eventually landing in the water he rigged his useless SARAH and settled down in his dinghy to await rescue. After three attempts with rockets, two of which failed to attract the attention of searching aircraft, Squier was left with no option but to wait the night out upon the sea. In the morning's early light he spotted a coastline and with paddle power provided by a piece of driftwood he made his way towards it. After thirty-six hours at sea and much struggling, John Squier eventually reached dry land and civilisation at Wigtown Bay on the Solway Firth. Medical checks by various interested parties followed, including those of the Institute of Aviation Medicine. It was to be nearly a year before he flew again.

Investigation of the accident concluded that there had been a major structural failure of the fin at its base, brought on by unrecognised increased side loads generated by the new nose shape. A subsidiary investigation into the pilot's safety and survival equipment was to order changes in oxygen mask design, ejection seat sequencing and rigorous checks on time-servicing of the survival equipment. The Air Sea Rescue service was also to learn some valuable lessons from the episode, especially in the field of area-based searching. Although John Squier had spent a long time at sea his ejection and subsequent survival taught aircraft and equipment designers some valuable lessons that were readily absorbed by the industry.

With only ninety-four flights and forty hours flying time the loss of XL628 was to leave the second T.4 prototype to carry the brunt of two-seat development. The second T.4, XL629, had flown on 29 September 1959 and was thus able to shoulder the burden almost immediately. With the results of the accident that had overtaken XL628 safely incorporated in the airframe, handling and performance trials continued. Not all was plain sailing however as an accident that took place on 19 November illustrates. Rotating clear of Warton's runway the on-board crew, Beamont and de Villiers, became aware of a slight whistle coupled to a drop in cabin pressure. Seconds later the canopy had broken clear of the airframe and correctly the aircraft was returned to Warton for investigation. Their only comment afterwards being that in spite of the wind and its associated noise the T.4 handled well. With the trauma of the canopy corrected a tour at A&AEE followed in 1960 for stability and handling trials.

During 1961 evaluation of the AI.23 radar and the Auto ILS was added to the programme. The avionics trials continued until mid 1962 after which XL629 resumed its role in pure handling trials. These continued into early 1966 and involved at various times, stalling, spinning, rolling and the investigation of the interaction between all three flight axes.

After 187 hours of evaluation flying XL629 was transferred to the Empire Test Pilots School on a permanent loan basis. Arriving at Farnborough on 13 May 1966 the T.4 was allocated the fleet code '23'. In company with the rest of the ETPS fleet XL629 returned to Boscombe Down on 20 December 1967 to take up permanent residence. Training future test pilots continued until the Lightning was grounded on 3 November 1975. By this time a T.5, XS422, was carrying out similar duties and this left XL629 to see out its days as an instructional airframe for apprentices. These duties continued until February 1977 when the decision was made to externally refurbish the airframe and use it as a gate guard at Boscombe Down. As initially mounted the Lightning was unarmed, although this deficiency was soon rectified by the acquisition of a pair of Firestreak missiles that were awaiting disposal from the recently closed Missile Training School at Newton. Refurbished just prior to the school's move to Cosford, the weapons were fitted to the airframe in 1991.

Production Lightning T.4s were covered by contract No.6/acft/15445 issued in July 1958 and initially covered thirty aircraft although this was later reduced. A total of twenty were finally delivered in the serial range XM966 to XM974 and XM987 to XM997. The first two XM966 and 967 were in fact diverted from this contract to act as the prototypes in the T.5 programme. This left XM968 as the first pure T.4 to fly.

By this time in the company's history the E.E. Co. had become part of the British Aircraft Corporation in company with Vickers (40%) and the Bristol Aeroplane Company (20%). Later the Hunting Aircraft Company was to become part of this organisation, thus leading to the successful Jet Provost joining the BAC stable. First flight of XM968 took place on 9 November 1960. After shakedown flying it was used by both BAC and the various trials organisations for handling and pre-service release trials. During 1961–62 the Lightning was in the hands of the A&AEE for radio, avionics and handling trials, this being followed by the investigation of aquaplaning and its affects on Maxaret braking systems during 1963. With the commencement of TSR2 flight-trials in 1964, involving XR219 the first prototype, the T.4 was co-opted as a performance measuring chase plane. Entry into RAF service took place during 1965 initially with 226 OCU followed by a spell in 56 Sqdn's line-up. From Wattisham XM968 moved to 92 Sqdn in Germany where its tasks included conversion, continuation and target facilities training. It was on one of these flights on 24 February 1977, that this T.4 experienced serious hydraulic failure. With control becoming marginal and no hope of recovery to base possible the crew ejected safely, their abandoned aircraft crashing near their home base at Gütersloh.

Prior to joining the T.5 programme XM966 had been operated by BAC and the A&AEE for evaluating the type with the canopy removed deliberately, the accidental version had already been carried out on XL629! C(A) release flying occupied the Lightning throughout 1961 before departing to Filton for T.5 conversion.

The prime operator of the two-seat Lightnings was not surprisingly 226 OCU at Coltishall where it was considered the equal of F.1, F.1A, F.2 and F.2A single-seaters. Resplendent in their aluminium finish with yellow trainer bands, the T.4s began their RAF career with the LCS at Middleton St. George. Aircraft delivered to the LCS included XM969 which appeared after seventy shakedown flights and XM970 which had achieved twenty-six such flights and an appearance at the 1962 Paris Air Show. Further deliveries during 1962 saw XM971, XM972, XM987, XM988, XM990, XM991 and XM993 arriving between July and October. The squadron's final aircraft, XM996 and 997, appeared in January of the following year. Five months after the final pair had arrived the LCS became 226 OCU with the shadow identity of 145 Sqdn. Operating alongside displaced F.1 and F.1A fighters, the T.4s wore their last three as a fin identification code. This was also the most colourful period in the Royal Air Force's post-war history, the trainers especially

This is a very confused aircraft. Belonging to 92 Sqdn XM968 'Q' is still unpainted, but wears toned-down national insignia and spine panel. *(CP RUSSELL-SMITH)*

bright in their red and white painted fins and spines. A move en masse to Coltishall in April 1964 was to eventually result in the disappearance of these bright finishes although the 145 Sqdn bars either side of the roundel were to remain.

1972/73 saw the rundown of the T.4 fleet, some were dispatched to other units for fire practice whilst those in better condition joined the two RAFG squadrons, Nos. 19 and 92. Some of course failed to survive that long, examples of those lost in service include XM971 which crashed after ingesting parts of the radar bullet after a bird strike. Both pilots ejected safely. Soon after XM988 also crashed in the North Sea after entering a spin that followed a spiral dive. The lessons learned from the loss of XL628 had been fully assimilated, the pilot Wing Commander Bruce ejecting safely – being rescued quickly by the SAR services.

Two-seat trainers quite often have the reputation of being slow and steady, not so the T.4 which proved as quick, lethal and agile as any of the fighters. On 19 September 1970 XM990 was taking part in the Coltishall Battle of Britain display when it entered an uncontrollable roll overhead East Plumstead close to its home base. Having proved to both crew that the Lightning could bite, they were left with no other option than to abandon the trainer. Bearing in mind that OCU aircraft take such a hammering from tyro fighter pilots it is surprising that more were not lost in landing accidents. One that did expire was XM993 which lost a tyre on landing at Middleton St. George on 12 December 1962. Even though differential braking was applied XM993 continued its inexorable progress towards the runway edge. Coming to a grinding halt the crew quickly evacuated. Before fire and rescue

Inbound to the Gütersloh runway is 19 Sqdn T.4 XM973 'V' in the later toned-down camouflage scheme which appeared in the early 1970s. (*CP RUSSELL-SMITH*)

services could arrive the T.4 was well alight and burned out completely.

With deliveries to the OCU continuing steadily some aircraft were transferred to front-line squadrons. No.74 Sqdn with its F.1 fighters at Coltishall received XM973 on 3 August 1962 after twenty-seven shakedown flights. Also joining the Tigers on the same day was the next T.4 in sequence, XM974. Having appeared at the SBAC show in 1961 XM974 was to remain in 74 Sqdn service until they transferred to Leuchars to convert to the F.3. The move made by the aircraft itself was sideways to the OCU. It was on a training flight from Coltishall on 14 December 1972 that a serious fire developed in both engine reheat systems and No.2 engine itself. Obviously unrecoverable the crew wisely abandoned their doomed aircraft. After 1,753 flying hours the T.4 finally came to rest near Happisburgh, Norfolk.

The Firebirds, No.56 Sqdn at Wattisham, received XM989 on 5 September 1962. With the replacement of the F.1A by the F.3 in 1965 the T.4 was redundant. No trip to the OCU for this trainer as it was purchased by BAC for conversion to T.54 standard arriving at Warton on 6 April 1966. A similar fate befell XM992 which had previously served with 111 Sqdn before flying to Lancashire in July. Both squadrons in Germany ultimately received single examples of the T.4. No.19 Sqdn gained XM994 whilst still at Leconfield in November 1962. Their companions, No.92 Sqdn received XM995 that same month. As the number of T.4 operators reduced, more were delivered to Germany until ultimately both units had at least three on their inventories. In common with the single-seaters the trainer also adopted camouflage during the 1970s, a finish they were still wearing when withdrawn in 1977. With their flying career ended the T.4s, in company with the F.2As found themselves listed as 'special display' aircraft more commonly known as decoys.

Apart from XL629 ensconced at the A&AEE main gate no other preserved examples of the T.4 exist. Most were to end their days on various fire dumps throughout the country. Such a fate befell XM969 which after 1,887 flying hours became 8592M at Binbrook. Fire and crash-rescue training continued until

Once the OCU had received its operating complement of T.4s the Lightning fighter squadrons also gained examples. That allocated to 74 Sqdn at Leuchars was XM974 'T', redolent in yellow 'T' bars with black fin and spine. (*CP RUSSELL-SMITH*)

Other squadrons that operated the T.4 included 111 Sqdn whose XM992 is pictured at Le Bourget in 1965. (*CP RUSSELL-SMITH*)

Anything a single-seater can do I can do better, thus XM995 of 92 Sqdn is finished with a blue fin and spine plus the obligatory yellow 'T' bands at Farnborough in 1964. (*CP RUSSELL-SMITH*)

December 1987 when its remains were sold to a scrapyard at Sutton on the Forest, Yorkshire. Coningsby gained XM987 for a secondary use, that of battle damage repair airframe, a task that began in June 1974. The violent machinations of the BDR instructors using a sharp instrument and a hammer to simulate shell damage eventually rendered the Lightning fit only for the fire dump and later scrap. Waddington, once home of the mighty Vulcan, also received a Lightning T.4, XM972, late of 226 OCU for fire and crash rescue practice.

Once ensconced on the firedump it blended in well with the other inmates, a matt-green Varsity and an all-white Vulcan B.2 that had latterly been painted gloss dark green. It too was to expire quickly being blown up on at least one occasion. A T.4 with a restricted operational career was XM997 which in its eleven years of service managed only one diversion from the OCU when it spent a few months with 92 Sqdn as 'T'. Withdrawn from use it ended up at 60 MU in store although this was more of a paperwork exercise as spares recovery was taking place. By now no more than a basic airframe XM997 was allocated for crash-rescue training at Leconfield. The fire crews at this station must have been fairly gentle as the remains were later transported to the Fire Training School at Catterick in 1976. Here they remained until later removed for scrap.

An interesting and intriguing title surrounded those redundant Lightnings left in Germany after the disbandment of the Gütersloh fighter Wing. To most of the human race they are decoys, to RAFG they rejoiced in the title of special display aircraft. Such a fate awaited XM970 and XM973 when, as 8529M and 8528M, they went on to grace the spare dispersals at Bruggen. Both wore fashionable green upper surfaces although in earlier days they had served with the OCU and wore brighter colours. XM973 had also served with 111 Sqdn as 'T' and later 23 Sqdn at

Once the LCU had evolved into 226 OCU their aircraft became some of the most colourful ever flown by a conversion unit. In September 1963 XM972 heads the line-up at Middleton St. George. (*CP RUSSELL-SMITH*)

A few years later in 1965 the OCU was based at Coltishall and, although still wearing the colours of 145 Sqdn, T.4 XM994 is decidedly less colourful. (*CP RUSSELL-SMITH*)

Leuchars as 'Z'. Before their unglamorous end both aircraft had been on the strength of 19 Sqdn. Once a stalwart of 92 Sqdn with whom it served for its entire fourteen-year working life, XM995 ended its days as a Wildenrath decoy with the maintenance number 8542M.

In common with the other Lightning variants the T.4 was also operated by other, smaller units for short periods of time. One such was the AFDS, part of the CFE at Binbrook, which by February 1966 had disappeared only to re-emerge as the Fighter Command Training Unit. Later as tactical requirements changed it too followed the Lightning into history and disappeared.

Developed in parallel with, and intended to complement the forthcoming F.3 fighter the Lightning T.5 encompassed all those changes that marked the second generation aircraft. Gone were the lower powered Avon Series 210 engines, in their place appeared the Avon 301 ECUs with a dry thrust rating of 13,220 lbs, an increase of nearly 2,000 lbs. The cockpit also became more high-tech with the full implementation of the OR946 navigation and attack suite complete with Mk.2 MRG and strip display indicators. The radar system had also undergone a revamp resulting in the appearance of the more capable AI.23B from Ferranti. In addition to the already well-established Firestreak guidance mode, the new system also incorporated the necessary extras for the all-aspect Red Top missiles. As with the T.4 that preceded it, the T.5 also had its cannon armament provision deleted, this was considered no great loss, in this the age of the missile, although once the lessons of Vietnam had come home to roost the lack of such a weapon was missed in the training of pilots in air-to-air firing.

The first T.5 had its origins as the second T.4, XM967, which made its first flight from Filton on 29 March 1962. Complete with its new square fin XM967 began the usual round of handling and performance trials, as before these were a combined effort between the manufacturers and the A&AEE. By 1964 the Lightning had completed the full range of handling trials and was therefore passed to Boscombe Down for the requisite pre-service C(A) release programme. These occupied the greater part of 1964 and successfully cleared the T.5 for RAF service, XM967 continued to act as a support and trials aircraft, this time engaged as a chase-plane for the TSR2 replacing the earlier T.4, XM968.

Evaluation flights by the Venezuelan Air Force followed in 1966 at Warton. This approach finally proved abortive as the costs projected in upgrading Venezuela's airfields would have far outweighed any gain from operating the Lightning.

Since the demise of T.4s XL628 and XM966 due to fin failure English Electric and later BAC had kept a watchful eye on this particular item. To confirm that all was well with the larger area of the T.5 fin XM967 found itself allocated to airborne fin-load stress evaluation throughout 1967. For this purpose a series of interconnected strain gauges were fitted inside the fin's structure. Airborne readings gleaned from each flight would then be compared with a similar specimen undergoing testing on the ground, thus could the health of the structure and its mountings be assessed. Apparently all was well as XM967 was demodified and loaned to RAE Farnborough for further trials programmes. Arriving in May 1968 the T.5 eventually ran the gamut of apprentices' instructional play thing before ending its days as 8433M on the Kemble firedump.

The other T.4 allocated to the T.5

development programme, XM966, was not so fortunate. Flown and operated in the T.4 trials for three years it was not until 1962 that the aircraft was flown to Filton for conversion to T.5 standard. Completed quickly XM966 first flew in its new guise in March 1963. There then followed the usual selection of trials and assessments at A&AEE during 1964–65. During the first quarter of 1965 XM966 was fitted with a pair of Firestreak missiles for airborne evaluation throughout the flight envelope. On 22 July 1965 with 263 flights and 152 flying hours to its credit XM966 suffered a catastrophic fin failure. As with the earlier XL628 the aircraft became uncontrollable leaving the crew, J. Dell and G. Elkington, with no option but to eject. Unlike John Squier in XL628 however their sojourn in the Irish Sea was short, both being rescued quickly.

The loss of XM966 notwithstanding, a contract was placed in August 1962 with the Preston division of BAC for twenty aircraft. Others were ordered but subsequently cancelled. Components produced for this latter batch were incorporated in the Lightnings destined for the Middle East. Filton was eventually chosen as the construction base for the nose sections, mainly because Samlesbury was loaded to full capacity and the Bristol factory already had experience in T.5 conversion. A unique series of nose construction numbers appeared outside of the normal range – each now being prefixed B1/95xxx. Upon completion each nose was shipped to Lancashire where it was attached to its waiting F.3 fuselage.

As the T.5 was conceived as the equivalent of the F.3 fighter it comes as no surprise to find this latest edition entering service quickly with 226 OCU for which an extra separate flight was formed.

The first production T.5 to fly was XS417, the second production example, which left the Samlesbury runway on 17 July 1964 piloted by J. Dell. Following on from this a series of company flights were performed before XS417 was passed to the A&AEE who were to add a further forty-seven before clearing the type for service use. From Boscombe Down the Lightning was returned to Warton where, after a quick overhaul, it was declared ready for collection on 25 May 1966. Not the first arrival at Coltishall by any means, XS417 was quickly slotted into the OCU's operational rota. Its tenure at Coltishall was to be short however as in December XS417 flew north to the Leuchars-based 23 Sqdn where it was coded 'Z'. Six months after arrival however, the Lightning was badly damaged in a heavy landing whose repair was to keep a combined workforce from BAC and 60 MU fully occupied for the next four years.

A return to flying with 23 Sqdn heralded five years of productive service before XS417 was transferred south again. This time the recipient was 56 Sqdn at Wattisham where the Lightning arrived, having diverted via Binbrook along the way for servicing. Initially coded 'Z', later 'W', XS417 remained at Wattisham before changing owners again in August 1976. This time the LTF, the replacement for the now defunct 226 OCU, operated the Lightning and continued to do so until late 1979 when XS417 transferred to 11 Sqdn. Wearing the fin code 'T' the T.5 remained on the 11 Sqdn flightline until February 1983 when it returned to the LTF this time as 'DZ'.

Unfortunately some thirteen months later the Lightning successfully blotted its copy-book by bursting all tyres upon landing. The mumbling, moaning and swearing that went on as the Binbrook ground crew struggled to replace the wheels and brakes can only be imagined, although their efforts were successful

By the time the T.5 reached 56 Sqdn their colourful days were long over. XS417 'Z' was the unit's trainer when pictured at Wattisham in 1976. (*CP RUSSELL-SMITH*)

Binbrook being declared open again a few hours later. Further repairs kept the aircraft grounded until it rejoined the LTF in July 1986. The aircraft's final operator was 11 Sqdn with whom XS417 remained until withdrawn from use on 18 May 1987. Total flying time was 2,603 hours. Fortunately for future generations XS417 still exists as it currently resides at the Winthorpe home of the Newark Air Museum. Its delivery however was far less dignified than the museum's other famous resident, Vulcan B.2 XM597. XS417 minus amputated wings and fin arrived by road although all has now been carefully reassembled to produce an outstanding exhibit.

Joining XS417 at the OCU in 1965 were T.5s XS416, XS418–XS423, XS449, XS452, XS453, XS455 and XS457–XS459, the last of which arrived in September. The rest of the production run was diverted to the operational squadrons – XS450 joining 111 Sqdn and 56 Sqdn received XS456, both at Wattisham, whilst No.5 Sqdn gained XS451 at Binbrook. One T.5 completely avoided RAF service, this being XS460 which had first flown in February 1966. After company flying had been completed the aircraft was then purchased by BAC to fulfil a slot in the RSAF export programme. Renumbered 55–710 the Lightning was later written-off after crashing at Warton at the end of a test-flight.

Those aircraft with the OCU continued to wear the markings of 145 Sqdn until June 1971 when the earlier variants in the inventory of the OCU, the F.1A and T.4, broke away to become No.65 (shadow) Sqdn. The T.5s and their complimentary F.3s then became 2T Sqdn. During 1972 those T.5s which had not already experienced Binbrook and its interesting weather did so when the OCU decamped en masse whilst the runway at Coltishall received attention from the maintenance contractors. Two years later in June 1974, 226 OCU disbanded, its F.1A's going into retirement whilst the better condition T.4s were dispatched to Germany for 19 and 92 Sqdns. The days of the interceptor F.3 were also numbered, therefore an organisation the size of an OCU was no longer deemed necessary.

Those T.5s not already with operational squadrons were moved to Binbrook where they initially formed 'C' flight of 11 Sqdn. The burden of extra administration, especially of a dedicated training unit, was soon recognised as being outside the squadron's prerogative and thus the Lightning Training Flight came into existence. As a Binbrook unit their aircraft were soon adorned with the station's blue lion on the fin with the letters LTF underneath. Operating alongside the F.3 and F.6 fighters, the T.5 contingent stayed active as the backbone of this unique unit until it too finally disbanded on 1 August 1987.

Of the trainers dispatched to the OCU XS416 eventually ended its days on the LTF as 'DU' having passed through the hands of 11 Sqdn as 'T' previously. XS419 also ended its RAF career with the LTF having flown with 5, 11 and 23 Sqdns as 'T'. Its continued existence past December 1965 reflects the fact that each and every T.5 was desperately needed to train new pilots, however Cat4 damage was incurred during landing and had it happened a few years later it would have resulted in the aircraft being scrapped. Fortunately both it and the approach lights at Coltishall were soon returned to working order. In its final guise the Lightning last flew as 'DU' of the LTF, completing some 2,600 flying hours. Originally purchased by G. Beck (Tanks and Vessels) Ltd for preservation it has sadly since been scrapped.

The fifth production Lightning T.5, XS420, has also led a charmed life. Prior to leaving the OCU the aircraft was seriously damaged by an in-flight fire in January 1973. Once repaired XS420 left the OCU to enter storage at Binbrook. The T.5 eventually emerged from ASSF as 'V' of the LTF in September 1976 and was to spend the rest of its RAF service with them before finally retiring in May 1983 with nearly 2,300 flying hours to its credit. Another survivor, XS420 is now safely in the hands of Wellesley Aviation at Narborough, Norfolk.

Crashes feature heavily in the histories of all aircraft and the Lightning T.5 was to prove no exception. Fortunately only two of the RAF allocated aircraft succumbed in this manner. The first was XS435 which as part of the OCU was being piloted by Fg Off Fish on his first T.5 solo. No dramatic fire and explosion, components suffering structural failure – just a jammed undercarriage that it was considered unsafe to land with. After a successful egress he watched his hapless aircraft crash into the sea off the Norfolk coast. The last RAF Lightning T.5 accident occurred on 6 September 1972 when XS453 of 5 Sqdn had to be abandoned near Spurn Head after total hydraulic failure. To complicate matters for the ejection seats and their performance envelopes, the crew had been practising aerobatics, fortunately they escaped safely. One other T.5 also managed a close call when on 8 March 1967, XS454 had just begun its take-off roll when the undercarriage collapsed. In this instance the Lightning was deemed repairable and the accident report stated that the crew 'made a safe and controlled exit'. Six months later XS454 was returned to flight status and was operated firstly by Min Tech followed by a return to the RAF and 11 Sqdn. It last flew in June 1975 with 1,449 hours on the clock. For a short period afterwards it became 8535M as a Binbrook decoy before going for scrap in June 1987.

Undercarriage problems also plagued XS418. After a short tour with Boscombe Down it joined the OCU in May 1965. During a trip from Coltishall to Stradishall on 13 August 1968 the Lightning had just touched down at the latter station when its undercarriage retracted leaving the aircraft scraping down the runway on nose ring and ventral tank. Repairs lasted the following two months from which XS418 returned to the OCU before moving to 5 Sqdn and Binbrook in 1974. Initially slated for disposal in September 1976 as 8531M the Lightning later travelled to

Star of the BBC series *Test Pilot*, Lightning T.5 XS422 still survives in preservation. In 1982 it is pictured here wearing ETPS marking and landing at Boscombe Down. (*CP RUSSELL-SMITH*)

Catterick for fire training practice. Damage must have been minimal as by September 1983 it had returned to Binbrook for use as a decoy. For a further few years it stood out on the airfield before finally being sold for scrap in August 1987.

Unlike the earliest Lightnings the T.5s did not feature heavily in the hands of the Test and Trials organisations, possibly because there were so few built. One that did however was XS457 which after a long and successful career with 11 Sqdn, 226 OCU and the LTF was operated by the ETPS on behalf of MoD(PE). It resumed its career at Binbrook in 1983 before finally being grounded in 1987. Placed on the disposal list the main part of the aircraft was sold for scrap, the nose section finding a home at the Humberside based Museum of Weapons Technology. The other T.5 in the service of the evaluators was XS422 which achieved lasting fame in the BBC series *Test Pilot* made prior to its final flight in September 1987, having flown 2,210 hours. Before joining the ETPS in 1975 XS422 had been operated by 226 OCU, 111 Sqdn as 'T', 29 Sqdn as 'Z' and 23 Sqdn also as 'Z'. After its flying career had ended XS422 was placed in Boscombe Down's famous Weighbridge hangar for use in apprentice training. Purchased by Wensley Haydon-Ballie the T.5 has joined the collector's other aircraft at Southampton Docks, although there are strong rumours that the whole collection has moved *en masse* to the United States.

Other escapees from 226 OCU include XS450 which managed to fly in 5 Sqdn's colours before being scrapped in 1987, although two earlier aircraft, XS423 and XS449, had managed to reach Binbrook only to end their days as decoys. However XS449 did manage one trip away from Lincolnshire when it appeared on static display at Gatwick in 1977. Both were eventually sold for scrap in 1987.

More fortunate was XS452 now part of the Arnold Glass cache at Cranfield. From the OCU XS452 became 'T' of 111 Sqdn in 1971 followed by a tour with 29 Sqdn. A return to 111 Sqdn occurred in 1973 although this was shortened when the Lightning was despatched to Cyprus and 56 Sqdn in early 1974. Not long after arrival however the aircraft had left 56 Sqdn to become part of the Akrotiri station flight who emphasised their ownership by painting the fin pink with a large white flamingo overlaid.

This silliness ended in 1975 when the aircraft returned to Britain to become 'T' of 11 Sqdn at Binbrook. As with all aircraft within the Binbrook regime XS452 was moved around between 5 and 11 Sqdns, storage and the LTF so that fatigue life consumption could be controlled and equalised within the fleet. During 1976 the Lightning served with both 5 Sqdn and the LTF, acquiring a coat of dark green upper surface camouflage along the way. This was soon brightened up by the addition of a large Maltese cross on the fin, applied during a squadron detachment. Having finally left 5 Sqdn XS452 became part of the LTF inventory remaining with them until 1983. Recoded 'BT' it appeared on the 11 Sqdn flightline although it alternated between them and the LTF before finally settling at the LTF as 'DZ' in 1986. It made its final service flight on 29 June 1987 bringing its flying hours total up to a respectable 3,000 hours. On 29 June 1988 XS452 made its final flight to its new owner at Cranfield who was to register it as *G-BPFE*. Plans were made to fly the aircraft on the display circuit, but apparently over the years they have come to naught.

Possibly one of the strangest places for a military aircraft to end its days is with a farming organisation, such is the fate that befell XS456 when it ceased flying in April 1987 having some 2,300 hours to its credit. Prior to that however the Lightning had enjoyed tours with 56 Sqdn as 'A' and the

In its element, Lightning T.5 XS458 of 145 Sqdn/226 OCU overshoots at Coltishall in 1968. (*CP RUSSELL-SMITH*)

Wattisham TFF. Returning to 56 Sqdn and recoded 'X' it too joined the exodus to the sun in 1967. A return to the more dismal climes of Britain saw the Lightning in service with 11 Sqdn as 'T' followed by the LTF, still as 'T', then finally as 'DX' of the same organisation. It now resides in total contrast at the premises of T.A. Smith Ltd of Wainfleet.

Another of the Arnold Glass fleet in store at Cranfield is XS458 which had also started its career as an OCU stalwart. Moving on it served with both 5 Sqdn and the LTF with whom it sported an experimental blue-grey camouflage finish on its upper surfaces. By 1979 a more normal scheme had been applied and XS458 alternated between 5 and 11 Sqdns as required, a situation that continued until 1986 when the LTF resumed full ownership. Flying as 'DX' the Lightning remained in use until 24 June 1988 when after 3,168 hours of RAF flying, it was sold to Arnold Glass and dispatched to Cranfield by air where it has remained ever since.

Another surviving T.5 is XS459 which was the 19th aircraft built. It too served with the OCU before moving to 29 Sqdn as 'T' in 1972. This was followed by an MoD (PE) loan for which the under and port side of the aircraft were painted in white fuel-sensitive paint. Fuel flow and leakage trials completed XS459 resumed its interrupted career with 29 Sqdn in May 1972. In 1975 XS459 was grounded for servicing from which it emerged to join 56 Sqdn. With the demise of this unit as a Lightning operator in 1976 the aircraft was transferred to the LTF as 'X' with whom it remained in the training role until 1984. A transfer to 5 Sqdn as 'AW' then followed, XS459 remaining with the squadron until withdrawn from use on 18 March 1987. Sold on 21 June 1988, the Lightning is now part of the Wellesley Aviation collection.

During 1965 a further order was placed with BAC for a further two aircraft that were eventually serialled XV328 and XV329, both making their maiden flights in December 1966. From Warton XV328 flew to 60 MU for storage before finally entering service with 29 Sqdn at Wattisham as 'Z' in April 1967. In contrast XV329 was flown to the Short Bros airfield near Belfast where it was prepared for shipment to Singapore. It has always struck the author as strange that the T.5 was not flown out to the FEAF as the trainer was compatible with the standard Lightning refuelling probe. However, by ship XV329 was destined to travel, unfortunately precautions against the salty sea environment had proven insufficient. Upon unloading the aircraft was found to have severe corrosion on the tailplane with further damage on the rear fuselage. Once repairs had been completely XV329 finally joined 74 Sqdn as 'T'. XV328 meanwhile remained a British-based aircraft serving first with 5 Sqdn, later moving on to the LTF and finally 11 Sqdn. When finally grounded the Lightning had notched up a respectable 3,021 flying hours after its last flight on 29 June 1988. It now resides at Cranfield awaiting a decision upon its future. XV329 returned to the UK in 1971, eventually running a whole gamut of operators before finally succumbing to the scrapman's axe.

In all good stories, whether truth or fiction, the highpoint is always kept till last. Such a fate befalls XS451 which is scheduled to fly – all outside agencies permitting – in 1994. First flown on 2 June 1965, the Lightning began its RAF career as part of 5 Squadron's inventory before moving onto 226 OCU in November 1971. With the demise of the OCU in 1974 XS451 was again at Binbrook this time with 11

Binbrook became the final home for the RAF's Lightning force from 1977 onwards. In 1975 XV328 was on the strength of 5 Sqdn. Of note is the white dorsal panel that covered the AVPIN starter tank. *(CP RUSSELL-SMITH)*

Sqdn although it was soon to appear on the roll of the LTF. For reasons best known to the powers-that-be, XS451 was grounded on 25 November 1976 having only 1,596 flying hours to its credit. Unwanted, the T.5 sat in the Binbrook hangars acting as a 'Hangar Queen', donating parts to its more fortunate bretheren. A move to the CTTS at St. Athan as 8503M followed before the Lightning decamped by road to the Missile Training School at Newton, this station being more probably associated with the training of RAF Police than missile technicians. When the school moved to Cosford XS451 was left behind redundant. Placed on the disposal list, first nibbles of a sale came from Flight Systems Inc of Mojave. This sale fell through and XS451 moved to the Vintage Aircraft Team's premises at Cranfield. Fortunately forethought had seen the Lightning properly dismantled for its journey. Arriving in April 1988 XS451 stayed at Cranfield in kit-form until sold to Plymouth Executive Aviation based – where else – at Plymouth Airport.

XS451 was granted the civil registration G-LTNG by the CAA on 8 November 1989, possibly in the belief that the aircraft would never fly and the registration would subsequently be cancelled. Restoration work began almost immediately. Led by Barry Pover, the Lightning Flying Club, as the support organisation became known, soon stripped the aircraft down to its component parts leaving just the bare bones. All items removed have undergone rigorous maintenance whilst the aircraft's structure has undergone extensive and exhaustive NDT checks.

Re-assembly is now almost complete, the major stumbling block to G-LTNG flying apparently being the CAA which has suddenly realised that the current regulations do not adequately cover the operation of Mach 2-capable two-seat ex-military aircraft. If the major obstacle of paperwork is overcome G-LTNG should soon fly to join its bretheren at Exeter Airport where new modern accommodation is being provided to house the LFC's fleet of aircraft.

Chapter 6
The Square Fins

THE SQUARE-FINNED interceptor variants of the Lightning fall quite satisfactorily into three distinct categories. The first, a pure missile-armed interceptor, was a logical extension of the earlier F.1 and F.2 series fighters, being designated the F.3. The second started life as a far more capable and longer-ranged version of the preceding F.3 and was designated Lightning F.6. To complete the picture the F.2A appeared in the late 1960s as an interceptor which combined the aerodynamic advances of the F.6 with the multi-cannon armament of the original F.2.

The first Lightning F.3 to fly was XP693 which made its maiden flight on 16 June 1962 piloted by J. Dell. Ordered as part of contract KC/2D/049 CB. (7)b dated June 1960, this first of the square-finned Lightnings preceded a further sixty-nine of the same ilk, although fourteen did not see service with the RAF in their original guises, being converted to F.6 standard and its overseas equivalent before delivery. The batches as ordered were serialled XP693–XP708, XP735–XP765, XR711–XR728 and XR748–XR751.

It has often been wondered over the years why further F.3 aircraft were not converted to full F.6 standard. Some of the answers it would appear lie in the relevant defence white paper estimates, fatigue consumption and the costs generated by such work. Even though many of the Lightning F.3s had short

Doyen of the F.3 and F.6 Lightning variants is XP693 now on the civil register as G-FSIX. This scene captures the aircraft in its final form at Boscombe Down in 1971. (*CP RUSSELL-SMITH*)

service careers, their high utilisation rate and the need to reduce spares costs for other variants, allied to the premature forecast withdrawal of the type in front-line service put paid to such ambitious plans. Defence white papers outlining Britain's shrinking overseas commitments were also to play their part in the demise of the F.3.

Even so, the F.3 was a quantum leap forward in technology. The power-plants were uprated Avon 301/2 series engines complete with full variable reheat which replaced the earlier four-stage versions. Weaponry became purely missile orientated, the Lightning F.3 being capable of toting either the Firestreak or the Red Top as required. Cannon and its provisions were omitted completely, in hindsight possibly a serious oversight. A LOX breathing system was incorporated as standard as was the full OR946 navigation/attack system. The Ferranti radar in the nose bullet had changed to the far more capable AI.23B which featured the necessary software for Red Top collision-course guidance. Externally the only visible change was the fin which, being squared-off, gave the F.3 better longitudinal stability when a full load was carried, otherwise, except for modifications, the remainder of the airframe remained unchanged.

Although XP693 had flown in mid 1962 it was to be a further two years before this latest Lightning entered RAF usage. The interim period was fully occupied however by evaluation of the aircraft and its systems. XP693 therefore spent the period 1962 to 1967 fully employed by both the manufacturers and A&AEE being put through its paces. Handling and the establishment of performance parameters took place during 1962/63, whilst the following three years saw the aircraft undergoing structural trials in both hot and cold environments, with the added bonus of radio and ferry trials being thrown in for good measure. The flight of the second F.3, XP694 in May 1963, brought another aircraft to the test programme. Operational reliability trials occupied the remainder of the year whilst the period 1964–67 saw pilots from Ferranti, BAC and A&AEE carrying out airborne proving trials on the AI.23B. By the end of 1967 the two aircraft were to go their separate ways; XP694 was routed through 60 MU at Leconfield for servicing before joining 29 Sqdn. Two tours with the LTF/LAF followed by a spell with 11 Sqdn came to an end in 1984 after 2,552 flying hours. The aircraft was finally sent to die on the Otterburn ranges in 1988.

XP693 on the other hand went on to a long and illustrious career as a development and test airframe. In 1968 its role in the F.3 programme was over, so it was flown to Warton in January where conversion to F.6, complete with cambered wings and large ventral tank, was undertaken. Conversion work completed XP693 remained at Warton where it flew as a chase-plane for other BAC products such as other Lightnings, Strikemasters, Canberras and later Jaguars. From 1972 the aircraft was employed by the company on MRCA avionics trials. Two years later XP693 was at A&AEE where development work on the MRCA, later renamed Tornado, Mauser 27mm cannon installation began. Employed basically on programmes destined mainly for RAF use it came as no surprise that the Lightning was officially transferred to the MoD (PE) in 1981. Since that date XP693 has seen use as a chase-plane for Tornados, for the first EAP, now Eurofighter 2000, and as a high-speed target for the Foxhunter radar fitted to the Tornado F.3. Flying under an RAF serial number ended on 16 December 1992, one day before the end of the MoD contract. With comparatively few hours and a generous fatigue life left, XP693 was undoubtedly a prime target for preservationists. By 23 December XP693, now registered as

No.111 Sqdn was the counterpart of 56 Sqdn at Wattisham in the 1970s. Pictured here is XP749 from the squadron. (*CP RUSSELL-SMITH*)

During 1984 two F.3s were allocated to Binbrook's display pilots. BK2 is XP749 resplendent in air defence greys. Its companion was not unsurprisingly coded BK1. (*CP RUSSELL-SMITH*)

G-FSIX, arrived at Exeter airport having been purchased by Barry Pover on behalf of the Lightning Flying Club. Also arriving with G-FSIX was another post-MoD contract redundant Lightning F.6, this being G-OPIB, the former XR773. Although the roar of the military Avon is now quieted, hopefully their resurrection as civilians will leave them only muted.

One other F.3 was to see use in the type's development programme. The 9th production aircraft, XP701, had first flown in September 1963. As well as trialing Mod 4051, a modification designed to remove undercarriage hang-ups, both in the air and on the ground, XP701 also found time to trial the auto flight control system in conjunction with the A&AEE. Further trials involved the engine and airframe ice-detection system and its associated auto anti-icing equipment. After four years as a guinea pig XP701 was refurbished and delivered to 29 Sqdn at Wattisham on 8 September 1967.

The first RAF unit to receive production F.3s was not surprisingly the CFE at Binbrook. During January 1964 both XP695 and XP696 arrived for evaluation purposes being followed very quickly by XP749 and XP750. All four helped the RAF write the tactical doctrine for this advanced interceptor. The former pair eventually returned to Warton in 1967 for an overhaul before entering RAF usage whilst the latter aircraft returned to Warton for possible conversion to F.6 standard. XP695 ceased flying in 1980 and finally disappeared from Binbrook as scrap in January 1988 whilst its companion ended its days as a target on the PEE range at Foulness Island. XP749 and XP750 were not converted to F.6 standards after all, both finally entering service with 111 Sqdn at Wattisham. Both were to end their days as Binbrook decoys before meeting the axe of the scrapman.

The first front-line squadron to receive the Lightning F.3 for service use was No.74 Sqdn based at Leuchars as part of the 'Scottish Air Force'. Their first aircraft was XP700 which arrived from Lancashire on 14 April 1964. Immediately nabbed by the Squadron Commander to become 'A' it was soon followed by others to fill the spaces in the alphabet.

The next Lightning to arrive in April was XP751 being followed by XP702 in May whilst June saw the squadron accepting XP703–XP705, XP752 and XP753, July witnessed further deliveries viz XP754. The last Lightning for 111 Sqdn was XP 764 which finally appeared in November. With a T.5 on loan from the OCU, conversion to the new fighter was rapidly accomplished – by July the squadron's old F.1A Lightnings had been completely replaced.

On 9 March 1963 No.23 Sqdn arrived at Leuchars as the second unit equipped with the all-weather Javelin. The days of the Gloster product were numbered however, as by August 1964 new equipment in the shape of the Lightning F.3 began to arrive. First deliveries from BAC comprised aircraft XP707 and XP708 which landed on the 19th. They were joined by nine more aircraft these being serialled XP737, XP756–XP761 and XP763 which pitched up on 27 October. To speed the process of 23 Sqdn becoming an operational unit, air and ground crews were drawn from other Lightning squadrons and were subjected to intensive training to weld them into a cohesive whole. As for the Javelin crews, they either moved to other FAW squadrons or retrained as Lightning pilots.

Anxious to show-off their new acquisition to the public, No.74 Sqdn designated a squadron pilot to display the aircraft at the forthcoming Battle of Britain show in September 1964. This display was never to take place, as on 28 August, whilst running through his routine, the pilot Flt Lt Owen, appeared to misjudge his height causing the aircraft, XP704 'H' to crash on the airfield. To compound matters, many of the squadron and station personnel had been released from their duties to witness the practice.

Fortunately the Leuchars squadrons overcame this tragedy and both were declared operational in early 1965. Like its predecessor the Lightning F.3 suffered from a shortage of range, therefore flight refuelling practice was to play an important part in the day-to-day training of the operators. Unfortunately for the RAF the Valiant tanker fleet had been grounded in 1964 due to the discovery of fatigue cracks in the rear wing spars. To fill the ensuing gap USAF KC-135 tankers fitted with drogue adaptors on the boom were utilised. This state of affairs ended in 1965 when deliveries commenced of the converted Victor tankers. Thus began a long partnership between the Lightnings and the Victors that was to endure until the former was finally phased out of RAF service. One of the first deployment tasks to be evolved was the best way of supporting the fighters during their long transit flights to overseas bases. This finally settled down to performing an airborne version of dot and carry, with Victors placed at strategic points down route. With radio warning in advance the waiting tankers could be in position to meet and refuel the thirsty fighters. The previous Victor that had mothered them to that point would then land whilst the replacement would escort the Lightnings to either their next hand-over or landing point.

Being based in Scotland with a large area, mainly over the sea, to patrol the Lightnings of 23 and 74 Sqdns found their Victor companions most useful, as one would automatically be scrambled to provide support whenever QRA was activated. Many were the incursions before the days of *glasnost* and *peristroika* by the Russians in their Bear and Badger bombers probing the defences of UKADGE. Each incursion required a response and, so it would appear, the aircrew of the USSR laid bets on the time taken to intercept them. Nowadays the Bear has visited these shores in peace, although it is still subject to interceptions but this time by the Lightning's purest successor – the Tornado F.3.

With the Lightning F.3 safely ensconced at Leuchars with Nos.23 and 74 Sqdns of the Scottish Air Force it became the turn of their southern counterparts at Wattisham to trade in their earlier fighters for the new Lightning. No.111 Sqdn received its first F.3 in December 1964 when XP741 arrived to become 'D' in the inventory. The New Year saw further deliveries to Wattisham comprising XP740, XP742, XP762 and XR711–XR713. With their initial complement in place 111 Sqdn bade farewell to their old F.1As and began the process of achieving operational status on their new mounts. As befits aircraft of such a famous squadron it is hardly surprising that their aircraft were soon bedecked with a black fin and spine offset by a yellow insert, similar to that on their earlier aircraft. Soon rivalling 111 Sqdn in the displaying of brightly coloured aircraft was that other Wattisham resident No.56 Sqdn. The Firebirds began to receive their new Lightnings in February 1965, finally having ten aircraft on strength, many of which had been drawn from storage at 33 MU Lyneham for service issue. Displacing the previous occupants of the flightline in a matter of weeks, the squadron's new mounts were serialled XP744–XP748, XP765 and XR717–XR721. To rival 111 Sqdn the Firebirds adorned their Lightnings with red and white checked fins and a red and white arrow on the nose where it replaced the earlier checks. Only during the interwar years of the 1930s had the RAF been so brightly coloured with reminders that the aircraft was a fighter first and foremost soon came to the fore. From on-high came the edict that squadron finishes were to be more restrained unless authorised for special reasons by higher authority. Thus ended the second period of colour in the history of the RAF, although during the late 1980s short attempts at a revival were made by squadrons celebrating various anniversaries.

Beating the Firebirds at their own game, 111 Sqdn assumed the mantle of the Fighter Command Aerobatic Display team once their full complement of fighters had arrived. The main formation of each display consisted of eleven single-seaters whilst the twelfth aircraft was the squadron's T.5. Although a big beast the Lightning was capable of spectacular turns and tail slides and this, coupled with reheat in copious quantities, made each performance noisy and spectacular. Unfortunately noise and spectacular flying does have a tendency to mask faults in individual aircraft. Such a fated machine was XR712 which, piloted by the squadron display artiste, Flt Lt Doyle, suffered a violent disintegration of No.1 engine whilst thrilling the crowds at Exeter in June 1965. With all caption warnings flashing wildly in the cockpit, the proposed flyby was abandoned and an immediate diversion to St. Mawgan – the team's operating base – was made. Although many improvements in fire containment had been incorporated in the Lightning the severity of the ensuing fire led to the failure of the aircraft's flight control systems. Discretion is the better part of valour, therefore Flt Lt Doyle took this maxim to heart and safely ejected, leaving his doomed fighter to fall into the sea. Crashes and accidents are a fact of life in high-performance aircraft although in most cases the pilots escaped using that fine product from Martin-Baker – the ejection seat. 111 Squadron had its fair share of crashes as XP739 was also to crash in 1965. In-bound to Wattisham in September, the pilot was unlucky enough to experience a double engine failure. Unable to initiate a relight and too low to glide, he took the only sensible option and ejected.

The squadron managed another eight months without incident before losing any further aircraft. This was XR714 which, upon departing Akrotiri as part of a formation take-off, suffered an undercarriage retraction before rotation. Although the pilot was to escape unhurt, the damage to the Lightning was so extensive as to preclude repairs. Much of the Lightning's routine flying took it over the North Sea near the east coast. During such a training flight XP742 became engulfed in flames following an engine fire. Luckily the sea was fairly calm in May 1970, as the unfortunate pilot spent some time upon it as his doomed fighter plunged into the depths to join all those others based at the mythical 'RAF Dogger Bank'.

Two further accidents were to take place in 1971, one of which was a mid-air collision. This occurred on 20 May near Colmar, France, when XP752 collided with a Dassault Mirage III during air combat exercises. The pilot retained enough control to land the aircraft safely, although it was soon declared Cat 5 spares recovery after in-depth repair assessment. The last 111 Sqdn F.3 loss took place on 29 October when XR711 stalled on take-off from Wattisham. The unfortunate Lightning was later declared a write-off, the pilot was far luckier and escaped virtually unscathed.

Although 56 Sqdn only lost two Lightning F.3s in service, the first was to be marred by tragedy when XR721 crashed on approach to Bentwaters on 5 January 1966 after a double engine failure. The pilot remained with his doomed fighter in an attempt to avoid some buildings in the path of the aircraft. In this he was successful although such bravery cost him his life. The squadron's final loss involved a 29 Sqdn aircraft, XP744 on loan to the Akrotiri-based fighter squadron. It occurred on 10 May

1971, the Lightning being successfully abandoned after a fire-warning caption had illuminated in the cockpit.

No.23 Sqdn in both its incarnations managed to contain its losses to just one aircraft, XP760 which crashed following an engine fire in August 1966. Although a certain percentage of Lightning F.3s were struck from the inventory due to crashes, enough remained viable to equip new units as others traded up to the more capable F.6. Expanding and changing overseas commitments led to 74 Sqdn abandoning its earlier F.3s to re-equip with the F.6. The aircraft released by the move enabled 29 Sqdn, previously operating with Javelins, to re-equip in May 1967 at Wattisham where they replaced 56 Sqdn which had decamped to Akrotiri to replace 29 Sqdn.

In-flight refuelling had played a vital part in this operation although another method being put forward to extend the Lightning's range had first appeared in September 1965 at Cranwell. Here XP765 of 56 Sqdn had been spotted in the line-up with a pair of dummy overwing tanks. Prior to their permanent move to more sunnier climes the Firebirds had enjoyed a period in Malta, during October 1966, where they took part in that years ADEX exercises. The release of F.3 aircraft from the various squadrons allowed 226 OCU to fully equip its 2T squadron with fighters capable of complementing its already established inventory of T.5 trainers.

1965 had also seen the visit of General Amer Khammesh the CAS of the Royal Jordanian Air Force. Arriving at Wattisham in December, he was treated to the rare sight of 56 Squadron's Lightnings being outmanoeuvred by an attacking force of Hunters being guided by an expert ground control interception service. Bearing in mind the shifting and volatile tensions ever present in the Middle East, the General perhaps was seeing in his mind's eye his air force, equipped with Hunters, taking on the might of Saudi Arabia – soon to equip with Lightnings.

No.29 Sqdn continued as a Lightning F.3 operator until December 1974 before disbanding to reform as a Phantom unit. Many of its remaining aircraft were to be broken-up for scrap after extensive spares recovery had been effected, a sad sight these once fine aircraft made on the Wattisham fire dump. When first formed at Wattisham however it had on strength the following aircraft: XP698, XP700, XP702–703, XP735–XP736, XP745, XP747, XP751, XP753, XP755, XP757, XP763–XP765 and XR715.

One fatal accident involving aircraft of the squadron took place on the night of 16 February 1972 when XP698 and XP747 collided. The pilot of XP698 ejected safely, his aircraft crashing near Ipswich whilst the occupant of the other Lightning was less fortunate in being killed. The wreckage from this aircraft was to land in the sea. Other losses incurred by 29 Sqdn during flying operations included three in 1971. XP705 crashed during an APC detachment to Akrotiri, XP763 ended its days in the North Sea whilst XP756 also ended up in the sea – its USAF exchange pilot ejecting safely. 1972 was fairly quiet with only XP700 being lost after seriously damaging its rear fuselage after an overtight rotation during take-off. The last Lightning to leave the 29 Sqdn inventory due to an accident was XR715 in 1974.

With the disappearance of the Lightning F.3 as a front-line fighter in 1975 most would assume that the type's RAF career was over. This was not to be the case however, as at least seventeen remained in service use to form the training and support flights of 5 and 11 Sqdns and a major part of the LTF in 1972 and 1974 respectively. Of the total of sixty-nine built, twenty-two were written-off in accidents, twelve appeared as interim F.3As whilst one, XP722, became a fully-fledged

F.53 in Saudi Arabian service. Of the others, eight were scrapped, XP745 became a gate guard, leaving the final four to appear on the books of MoD for trials work.

XP697 had first flown as an F.3, minus ventral tank, on 18 July 1963 piloted by D. Knight. A transit flight to Filton followed during August where the aircraft was transformed into an F.6. The maiden flight of XP697 in its new guise was undertaken by R.P. Beamont on 17 July 1964. Destined never to see any RAF service, the Lightning spent the intervening years until 1981 engaged on 2-inch rocket installation tests.

A period of aerodynamic flight-testing for the over-wing tank installation was undertaken by this aircraft during the period February 1970 to October 1978. Concurrent with the over-wing tank programme was a trial that covered fuel flow metering of both the ventral and over-wing installations. Active flying ceased for XP697 in 1981, the aircraft returning to Warton for use in the ground static fatigue-testing role. This was to continue until 1983 when the Lightning was declared surplus to requirements and scrapped.

Lightning XP699 remained as a standard F.3 throughout its working life, the first four years of which were spent in tropical operations evaluation of all systems. Much of this essential work was undertaken at Wheelus AFB, Libya. It eventually joined the Royal Air Force in 1966. Another Lightning that was to join BAe at Warton was XP703 which completed its career with the RAF first, before departing for Lancashire in 1981. Very little trials work was undertaken by this aircraft and after a period in storage it eventually found its way onto the Warton firedump for crash-rescue training. In contrast, many of the other retired Lightning F.3s ended their days in a far more violent way, being allocated as targets to the ranges at Pendine and Otterburn.

The Lightning F.3 soldiered on at Binbrook, its final home, before finally being withdrawn from use by 1987. Prior to that, much of the missile equipment had been removed and they spent their remaining days in Lincolnshire being used in the conversion and continuation role. Use of the F.3 in this manner reduced the consumption of fatigue life by the far more versatile F.6s. Air display work was also one of their duties which in their lightened form they undertook brilliantly, performing before delighted crowds at such venues as the International Air Tattoo at Greenham Common.

Many were also in service when the Lightning celebrated its 25th birthday during which the opportunity was taken to repaint some of them in the markings of squadrons long since re-equipped with other aircraft types. By the time the 'Last Lightning' show had taken place, most were in store or out on the airfield as decoys although in typical rainy Binbrook conditions, it was difficult to tell the live ones from the dead ones!

Thus ended the career of the Lightning F.3 in RAF service, a mere handful survive in RAF and private hands, the survival of the former must be deemed parlous given the purported state of the nations finances.

Even as the F.3 was making its slow entry into squadron service via the maintenance units the last seven of the contract, XR723–XR728, were making their first flights as F.3s during the early months of 1965. Held back at Warton they eventually appeared as F.6s. Complete with cambered wings, large ventral tanks and improved radar capability for the AI.23B system, they also featured a one-shot ventral hook located aft of the tank. Later, in line with the rest of the Lightning F.6 fleet, they were equipped with the twin Aden cannon package located at the front of the ventral tank.

Tengah AFB, Singapore, was the home for 74 Sqdn during the 1960s and 70s. Approaching the squadron's flight-line complete with over-wing ferry tanks is XR770. (*CP RUSSELL-SMITH*)

Release dates for this batch occurred during 1967 with XR723 joining 11 Sqdn whilst XR724–XR726 became part of the 5 Sqdn line-up. The next two Lightnings XR727 and XR728, were also converted to F.6 standard, joining 23 Sqdn in 1967. Prior to the delivery of full standard F.6 Lightnings for service use, BAC had persuaded the Royal Air Force that the 'Super F.3' might be the answer to their needs. Thus in January 1962 contract KC/2T/079 was issued to the company.

Sixteen aircraft were to be built as F.3s, thirteen were to appear as F.6s whilst the remainder, XR752–XR767, were to be built as F.3A/F.6 interim aircraft. In this form they were a stepping-stone between the two main square-finned variants being fully equipped as the F.3 but with only some of the systems intended for the F.6.

With the preceding Javelin FAW.9 reaching the end of its useful life, No.5 Sqdn at Binbrook became the first squadron slated to receive the new type. Using the by now established practice of forming each new squadron from a basis of experienced practitioners, operational readiness was to be quickly achieved. Deliveries of new equipment began in December 1965 when XR755 and XR766 landed at Binbrook. The first aircraft were quickly followed by the rest of the squadron's allocation, XR757–XR765, during the first three months on 1966. Of the other five Lightnings in this batch, four – XR752/753 and XR766/767 entered service with the CFE where they were put through their paces as the unit began the task of compiling the tactics handbook for the type's pilots. The remaining aircraft, XR754, had made its maiden flight on 8 July 1965 and was to arrive at the A&AEE for evaluation and pre-service C(A) release on 3 December. Delays in the deliveries of the Lightning T.5 had resulted in modified Hunter T.7s being allocated to each squadron as required for conversion and continuation flying purposes. Fully fitted with OR946 instrumentation they pre-dated a similar situation that was to afflict the Buccaneer.

Slow production, as evidenced by continued lack of government support, continued to plague the Lightning throughout the 1960s. During an exchange visit between a Lightning unit and one of their NATO F-104 Starfighter counterparts, the opportunity arose for squadron pilots of both air forces to fly in the trainer variant of each type. The response from the European pilots was overwhelming enthusiasm for the BAC product, whilst that of the RAF concerning Lockheed's finest, was noticably muted. Could the BAC product with good government support have won sales in Europe on technical merit alone? Possibly, although as events unfolded in the 1970s concerning the European fighter deal, BAC would have been outclassed by the lubrication supplied to the various people involved in this sale of the century.

Production-standard Lightnings began to be cleared by Warton for delivery during 1966. First despatches from the thirty-nine strong production run left BAC on 1 August when XR768 was delivered to 74 Sqdn at Leuchars by a squadron pilot. Arrivals into RAF service continued at a trickle and it was not unusual to see both new F.6s and the preceding F.3s sharing a squadron's flight-line for many months. By the end of the year however, the 'Tigers' had received their allocation of twelve aircraft – the inventory consisting of XR769–XR773, XS893, XS895–XS897 and XS920–XS921. Lightning F.6 XR770 prior to delivery had masqueraded as a RSAF aircraft, complete with Saudi markings, at the 1966 SBAC show.

Their redundant Lightning F.3s then went to re-equip the newly-formed 29 Sqdn at Wattisham where they were to partner No.111 Sqdn whose original companions, 56 Sqdn, had recently decamped to Akrotiri on 11 April 1967. The earliest months of the year had seen 74 Sqdn working up to operational status at an unprecedented rate. Trials with the new over-wing tanks plus air refuelling managed to stretch some sorties past the five hour mark. Another innovation tried on 74 Squadron's aircraft was the one-shot arrester hook, so called as it needed resetting on the ground, which was used in conjunction with the Rotary Hydraulic Arrester Gear(RHAG). This was far and away the more popular option to the widespread runway end barrier normally installed on military airfields. The latter was fine for those aircraft with smooth nose contours, unfortunately an aircraft such as the Lightning festooned with probes et al was prone to excess damage due to displacement of these objects.

The in-flight refuelled sorties occupied much of March 1967 whilst the following month was to be dedicated to live missile firing. As the Lightning F.6 had Red Top missiles as its only armament at that time, proficiency with the missile and its guidance was required. Unfortunately pre-issue trials by the manufacturers and A&AEE had revealed a number of problems with this all-aspect weapon. Further trials had apparently shown that all problems had been resolved. This however was not the case as the first two operational launches showed. The first missile was released in copy-book style and seemed to be tracking its target well, however the lock was lost and instead of re-acquiring the target the errant missile threw itself about the sky shedding components as it did so, before plunging into the sea in disgrace. The second round nearly brought down the carrier aircraft when it exploded just after launch. Although the pilots of 74 Sqdn were to bemoan their aircrafts' lack of cannon, they and those that followed would have to wait a few more years before the gunpacks were installed.

The purpose of all this intensive activity was to clear 74 Sqdn for its FEAF deployment to Tengah AFB, Singapore. Codenamed 'Operation Hydraulic' the transfer process began on 1 June when Britannias of Transport Command deposited transit servicing parties at Akrotiri, Masirah and the island of Gan in the Indian Ocean. Flying departures began on the 4th when the first six Lightnings departed Scotland. They were followed by five more on the following day whilst the final three left on 6 June. As related earlier the squadron's T.5 was shipped by sea, suffering extensive corrosion on the way. Aerial support came from the Victor Tankers of Nos.55, 57 and 214 Sqdns from Marham. Seventeen aircraft were involved in the relay operation, extensive use being made of the converted NBS radar and navigation systems which enabled the Victor 'motherhen' to guide her chicks accurately from way-point to way-point. All had been safely delivered by 11 June, the squadron being declared operational the next day.

Even as 74 Sqdn was charging around Britain preparing for its duties in the Far East, a further fighter squadron was trading in its aged Javelins for the new single-seater. Initially based at Geilenkirchen No.11 Sqdn had returned to Leuchars in April 1967 to become a Lightning F.6 operator. First aircraft to arrive was XS928 on 4 April and this was joined by others over the next two months. The remainder of the month saw XS918–XS919 and XS929 arriving whilst May marked the appearance of XS930–XS9931. June revealed XS932– XS934 also present on the flight-line. No.5 Sqdn was also trading up to new equipment, in their case replacing the interim F.6 model for the full standard production version. Their new inventory was comprised of the following aircraft – XS894, XS898, XS903 and XS922–XS926. Their original Lightnings were then returned to BAC Warton for modification and refurbishment before being passed to

Near the end of the Lightning's service life, air defence grey became the norm. Although the marking were miniaturised the re-appearance of normal colours was quite effective. Modelling the look is XS928 of 11 Sqdn at Abingdon in 1983. (*CP RUSSELL-SMITH*)

No.23 Sqdn in May 1967 to replace the earlier F.3s.

By the end of the year the Lightning force stood at No.5 Sqdn at Binbrook with the F.6, Nos.11 and 23 Squadrons at Leuchars also with the Lightning F.6, nos.19 and 92 Squadrons in Germany with the F.2/F.2A, whilst Wattisham was blessed with the presence of Nos.29 and 111 Squadrons with the Lightning F.3. Overseas the Lightning was represented by 56 Sqdn at Akrotiri with the Lightning F.3, whilst further east the Lightning F.6s of 74 Sqdn patrolled those sunny skies. This was to be the high point in the deployment of the Lightning in squadron service, as less than ten years later only two UK based and two RAFG squadrons remained so equipped. the other squadrons had either disbanded or, as was the situation in most cases, been reformed on the McDonnell Douglas F-4 Phantom. The irony of this situation is of course that the American replacement failed to outlast its predecessor by any appreciable length of time.

For the four years of their existence as part of FEAF, the pilots of 74 Sqdn made the most of their exotic posting. Although the heat and humidity required a period of acclimatisation, both air and ground crews adapted well. Even so, better air conditioning and canopy de-misting for Lightnings on QRA duty was felt to be a necessity. Trials of a new installation were undertaken upon XR770 with a supposedly better system. After days of test-flying and a certain amount of rectification, a sweat-drenched pilot finally reported that the original unit was as – if not more so – effective than the proposed modification. Therefore XR770 was restored to normal and the idea was quietly dropped.

No.74 Sqdn were also to be taught the same lesson that had previously been inflicted upon 56 Sqdn in Britain, that a well flown lower and slower aircraft can outfly a sophisticated aircraft such as the Lightning. This took place during a joint exercise between the Singapore Air Defence squadron and Sea Vixens of the FAA. Using diversionary tactics involving high and low altitude decoys to draw-off the fighters, the Sea Vixens from HMS *Eagle* designated as bombers were able to clock up a respectable seventy-five per cent success rate.

Further proof, if any were needed, that such circumstances could arise occurred at Binbrook. Utilising a Spitfire PR.19 the trials proved that the Lightning could itself be outflown – although its missiles could not. Such trials were felt necessary due to the tendency of the neighbouring Indonesians to carry out attacks on Malaysian territory. Aerial support for many of these attacks was the venerable P-51 Mustang, thus the need for comparison flying against a similar aircraft. Lessons from both these occurrences were taken to heart and were to be applied vigorously during February 1968 when a series of exercises in conjunction with local friendly air forces were held. From the RAAF came a mix of Mirages and Sabres based at RAAF Butterworth, whilst the RAF was to provide further attack forces drawn from the airfield at Changi in the shape of the resident Canberras, Hunters and Meteors. Possibly the most interesting aircraft encountered by the pilots of 74 Sqdn during these exercises was the Australian Mirage IIIEO. Although the RAAF pilots lost only one aircraft in simulated air combat prior to weapons release, the ensuing dog-fights conclusively proved that the Lightning could quite easily outfly the delta Mirage throughout the full flight envelope. The culmination of these exercises gave the Lightnings an overall sixty-five per cent success rate with thirteen simulated kills being achieved in twenty-nine sorties.

Light relief in the form of mock harrassing attacks on hapless passing American aircraft broke the monotony of training and standing air patrols. These victims were not however the standard medium-altitude traffic, but high-altitude reconnaissance machines operating out of Taiwan. Although the Lightnings tried frequently to catch any passing U-2, there is no record in the public domain of them succeeding.

However they did on at least one occasion pop up alongside a cruising RB-57F whose crew were convinced that the only peril they may be facing would be SAMs. One of the squadron's final exercise detachments in the area was to Darwin in mid 1969, where joint missions with and against the RAAF took place. Support tanking was provided by the Tengah-based Victor detachment. Seven days and a good tally of simulated kills later 74 Sqdn and its aircraft returned to their FEAF home.

During 1970 the squadron was to suffer its only losses when two aircraft were to crash, a third was also removed from the inventory in that year when XS928 was severely damaged by fire on the ground. Fortunately extensive repair work would ensure that the latter would fly again. Lightning F.6 XS930 was the first squadron aircraft to be lost when it entered an uncommanded steep climb immediately after take-off. Obviously out of control it passed through two loops before crashing into a Malay village, such was the force of the aircraft's gyrations that the pilot was unable to eject. The pilot of the second Lightning to go down, XS893, was by far luckier. On 12 August, less than three weeks after the first incident, the Lightning was on approach to Tengah when the port undercarriage leg failed to lower after a down selection. After many attempts to move the offending item the pilot, Fg. Off Rigg, was ordered to take his aircraft out to sea then eject, a belly landing having been ruled out as the ventral tank contained flammable fumes not the less volatile AVTUR. Once over the sea at 12,000 ft the pilot began the ejection sequence which started its cycle faultlessly, however once clear of the Lightning the main parachute deployed immediately. As this was far earlier in the sequence than intended, the force of the deployment caused damage to the harness and serious bruising to the pilots lower body.

As this was a pre-planned escape his time in the water was commendably short, being only thirty minutes. His recuperation time was appreciably longer however. During the enquiry that followed it was discovered that the barometric setting of the ejection seat had remained at the old UK setting of 5,000 metres, thus on ejection the chute had deployed instantly. Remedial action in the form of resetting the seats to a higher altitude filled the squadron's pilots, and their groins, with relief.

No.5 Sqdn now fully equipped with standard Lightning F.6s were also making forays to sunnier climes in 1968. Not only was the routine trip to Cyprus successfully accomplished, transit flights to Bahrain non-stop and 4,000 miles later, were also achieved. A deployment by the squadron to 74 Squadron's home base at Tehgah was also undertaken during 1970 for air defence exercises. Possibly the high point of the previous year had been the six-aircraft formation flypast provided for the Investiture of the Prince of Wales at Caernarvon Castle.

The sojourn of No.74 Sqdn in the Far East was to come to an end in 1971 when, due to defence cuts and a reduction in Britain's overseas commitments, it was withdrawn. The alternative strategy then enacted was a policy of providing detachments from home-based squadrons to be reinforced in times of need by rapid deployment using tanker support. The journey home for 74 Sqdn followed the route, in reverse, that had been used to reach Tengah. Tanker support came as before, from the Marham Wing, with one unusual change, that of a landing in Cyprus. At Akrotiri the more serviceable Lightning F.6s were left behind for 56 Sqdn whilst the Tigers brought home their earlier F.3s for disposal. Once officially returned to the UK No. 74 Sqdn itself disappeared from the battle plan of the Royal Air Force.

Whilst 74 Sqdn was wending its way home No.5 Sqdn was sweeping the trophies board. With the Dacre Trophy for weapons' proficiency under their belts for the previous two years, it came as no surprise when the squadron won the Huddleston Trophy for Best NATO Interceptor Squadron in May 1970. Operating in Europe against the best Starfighter, Mirage, Delta Dagger and other Lightning Squadrons the culmination of two months hard work was well earned.

No.23 Sqdn, still part of the 'Scottish Air Force' also traded in their Lightning F.3s for the more capable F.6 model. New production aircraft in the form of XS936–XS938 arrived in August 1967 whilst XS935, another new airframe, arrived in January of the following year. The remaining Lightnings delivered for the squadron's inventory were drawn from the earlier interim F.6s that had been refurbished at Warton. Included in this batch were: XR752, XR754, XR756, XR763 and XR765. On 28 August 1968 two of the squadrons Lightnings, XR725 and XS936, were flown with tanker support to Canada. Both aircraft were later adorned with Air Canada slogans and performed outstanding shows in front of enthralled Canadians at the Canadian National Show at Toronto. A week later on 3 September, both Lightnings returned home, yet again with Victor tanker support.

1971 saw a major change in interceptor fighter philosophy. Gone was the dogmatic total reliance on missiles and in came the idea that cannon might be a good idea. Much of this change of heart was the result of the USAF experience in Vietnam where missiles had proved singularly useless in a close-combat situation. As the Lightning F.6 had no provision for a cannon fit the decision was taken to install them in the forward part of the ventral fuel tank. Although this reduced the available fuel from 610 to 535 gallons, the trade-off was considered worth it in view of the increased flexibility offered. Another benefit of such an installation was the elimination of muzzle flash that had been known to cause havoc with the night sight of pilots in the earlier Lightning variants.

Conversion work was undertaken by teams drawn from either BAC or 60 MU who travelled to the various airfields to carry out the work. Other aircraft were modified at Leconfield as they underwent major servicing. Although Red Top reliability had improved tremendously, the fitment of cannon to the Lightning was to cheer the pilots up considerably, especially those on QRA duty.

Russian incursions into British airspace had really begun to escalate in 1969 with Tupolev Bears and Badgers plus the occasional Il-18 probing UKADGE. These unscheduled inbounds certainly kept the Leuchars squadrons in tip-top condition. Originally the southern-based Lightning QRA had dealt with those aircraft moving down the east coast. As soon as it was realised that whichever sector was being probed would need tanker support the decision was taken to alternate the duty between the northern and southern QRAs. Those not on duty still had to retain a pair of aircraft on one hour stand-by should extra support be needed. British Lightning operation did not just stop at QRA cover, exercises were also a significant part of a fighter pilot's life. Northern Wedding held in late 1974 involved aircraft and ships from all the NATO allies, except Greece and Turkey. It was during one of the interception flights that an 11 Sqdn pilot reported a Waddington Vulcan for frightening the living daylights out of him! It would appear that the fighter was approaching from directly underneath when the bomber opened its bomb-bay doors. Close up this would have been a frightening enough experience, it was made more so by a piece of ducting that fell out of the bomber – passing close by the Lightning as it did so.

Further reductions in Britain's overseas commitments were triggered by the revolt of the Cyprus National Guard against the Island's President, Archbishop Makarious. With nationalistic stances being adopted by both Turkey and Greece and fearing for the aircraft within the British Sovereign Base Area, the decision was taken to return the majority of the based aircraft home to Britain. The Vulcan bomber Wing returned to Waddington and Scampton whilst the transport and maritime assets returned to the main airfields associated with each type. This left 56 Sqdn and its Lightnings to safeguard all the British citizens within the Akrotiri SBA. A full emergency was declared during the period 20–27 July and was characterised by a serious increase in Turkish aerial activity. Over 200 standing air patrols were flown during the period of which 110 were fully armed battle sorties. Aerial activity continued past the 27th with 56 Sqdn continuing its intensive air patrols for the next four days.

Such intensive flying proved a point that is seldom realised, that such a rate of operation does not result in defects in aircraft, the opposite in fact holds true. A study of the engineering returns for that period shows very few serious defects occurring in the squadron's Lightnings.

The Cypriot National Guard revolt having triggered the removal of much of the Royal Air Force's Mediterranean airpower, then prompted the government to undertake a defence review. This paper published in 1975 confirmed everybody's worst fears, except for an SAR helicopter squadron, No.84, the RAF presence would be reduced to virtually nil. The precursor of this decision had seen 56 Sqdn returning home to Wattisham in January 1975.

Having operated as one of the busiest RAF stations in the world Akrotiri now looked like becoming a lazy backwater or closing altogether. This however was not to be as it was soon realised that this island in the sun would be an ideal place for Armament Practice Camps. These gatherings already had a place in RAF history, the earlier venue for the Lightning Force being RAF Valley where their missiles chased a Jindvik trailing a heat source. Weapons used for these camps were normally the earlier Firestreak which was on the point of being phased out of service. Weapons firing for the Cyprus APC was mainly cannon-orientated, much to the relief of the Canberra crews of 100 Sqdn who provided the target tow facilities. Tanker support was essential for the transit flight as each F.6 required five baskets en route whilst the accompanying F.3s and T.5 required ten. The inclusion of the shorter ranged F.3 and T.5 in the line-up enabled the former to provide air combat targets for camera gun recording whilst the latter was used for familarisation flight for the squadron's junior pilots. To help keep morale up amongst the ground crew, competitions were held during the five week detachment to win places in the T.5 for air experience flying.

Chasing the Seed Trophy for gunnery, each squadron tried to achieve its best score during its annual APC. First sorties are always camera gun and were flown until each pilot was considered safe to fly with ammunition. This being live was limited to twenty rounds per gun and was painted in different colours so that upon hitting the banner a trace would be left. Whatever

Camouflage somewhat depressed the Lightning's exuberance although good lighting did enhance the dull finish. Wearing the 'DA' code of the LTF is F.3 XR720 at Lossiemouth in 1983. (*CP RUSSELL-SMITH*)

Although the nose bars are miniaturised on this 1973 shot of XN731 in 1973, the full-size fin badge and bright colours more than offset the green upper surfaces. (*CP RUSSELL-SMITH*)

angles of approach were used the pilots were cajoled to attack within laid down limits. A good percentage of hits on the banner qualified the pilot for his ACE firing qualification, a definition for which was laid down by SHAPE, and was common to all NATO air forces.

Even as the Lightning was continuing to prove itself an agile and versatile fighter plans were being drafted to transfer the majority of units to the F.4 Phantom. No.23 Sqdn disbanded in October 1975 to reform the next month on the big American fighter. No. 29 Sqdn had earlier, in December 1974, reformed in January as a Phantom operator. In contrast 56 Sqdn was to retain its Lightnings until July 1976 before it too followed the McDonnell Douglas route. This left Nos.5 and 11 Squadrons at Binbrook as the only two British-based Lightning users. Second-line support units had also disappeared, 226 OCU disbanding in July 1974 to be replaced by the Lightning Training Flight. By 1976 therefore the remaining F.3, T.5 and F.6 Lightnings had congregated at Binbrook. Many were placed in store as the mammoth task of calculating fatigue lives and inspections began. The rota that eventually evolved saw aircraft moving to a squadron for a set period of time which would be followed by a period in storage. From ASSF the Lightning would then normally undergo a tour with the LTF which would be again followed by a further period of inactivity. Using this method of alternating flying and storage, each aircraft's fatigue life consumption could be evened-out thus extending the working life of each airframe. Each squadron operated the F.6 as their primary equipment although a small number of F.3s and T.5s were allocated for continuation and conversion flying. The F.3s also acted in the high-speed target role for their larger bretheren.

Tone-down had become the NATO buzzword in the 1970s, it had gone green mainly with paint, although some areas had become festooned with that other popular camouflage material – grass. Binbrook was obviously affected by this change in policy, the resident Lightnings soon losing their bright metal finish. Bedecked with grey and green the aircrafts' roundels and fin flashes also changed with the white being eliminated. The unfortunate side-effect of this policy was that although the aircraft were fairly inconspicuous on the ground their dark colouring made them stick out like the proverbial sore thumb in the sky.

Squadron markings also underwent a change, becoming smaller in size. Initially single-letter tail codes remained the norm although this soon changed to a two-letter designation. Codes prefixed 'A' were allocated to 5 Sqdn whilst 11 Sqdn flaunted 'B' codes on their fins. The LTF Lightnings, complete with the blue Binbrook Lion on their fins, prefixed their aircraft codes with 'D'. The third letter 'C' was not used, being held in reserve for a third promised squadron that did not, in the end, form. Much speculation was engendered in the aviation press as to its identity, many pundits plumping for the popular 74 Sqdn which had disbanded in 1971. To enhance Binbrook's front line capabilities, without the added cost of creating another squadron, the LAF was formed.

Supposedly to be manned by desk-bound pilots on ground tours and members of the LTF, the concept was short-lived and the diverted aircraft were soon returned to their respective units. Lightnings known to have been allocated in this way include XR773 and XP750 from 1980 until 1982.

By the late 1970s concern was being expressed about the fatigue cracks appearing at the Lightnings' wing roots, this was especially apparent on the heavier F.6. A wing root strengthening programme was therefore initiated in 1979 which then terminated in 1983. With so many aircraft to choose from, repair work was confined initially to those already in store although when this phase was complete Lightnings entering the portals of ASSF for servicing were slotted into the programme. Some of the trainers also underwent this process, but the lighter F.3s were left untouched as the results from NDT monitoring and their remaining short service lives militated against it.

All this of course was in the future, although they were destined to be the last Lightning operators in the Royal Air Force the two squadrons continued their policy of overseas detachments as before. An 11 Sqdn detachment to Malta took place during 1976, the purpose being to act as the attack force for aircraft deployed to the NATO training base at Decidemanou. No.5 Sqdn found itself on a NATO exchange visit the following year whilst both units deployed to Cyprus in alternate years for APC training. Possibly the highlight of the Lightning's career took place when its 25th Anniversary was celebrated at Binbrook on the weekend beginning 3 August 1979. Former pilots, many of them by now senior officers, arrived by a variety of transportation methods although the star of the show, besides the grand old lady herself, was to be R.P. Beamont.

For this special weekend those squadrons that had since disbanded were represented once more, their colourful markings standing proud against the drab grey and green. A much promised flypast of twenty-five aircraft failed to materialise as the infamous British weather intervened – producing the obligatory downpour. Even so, reports of the event state that a good time was had by all.

The dull grey and green finish soon began to give way to a selection of medium and light greys during the 1980s. This was

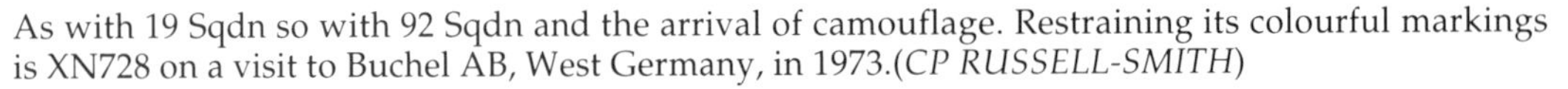

As with 19 Sqdn so with 92 Sqdn and the arrival of camouflage. Restraining its colourful markings is XN728 on a visit to Buchel AB, West Germany, in 1973.(*CP RUSSELL-SMITH*)

Also at Buchel in 1973 was another 92 Sqdn Lightning, this time the aircraft is XN732. (*CP RUSSELL-SMITH*)

When the Lightning celebrated its 25th Anniversary in August 1972, F.3 XR757 was withdrawn from ASSF stocks for repainting in 111 Sqdn markings. (*CP RUSSELL-SMITH*)

No.5 Sqdn had by 1983 painted its C.O's aircraft with a red fin. The wearer this time was XR770. No.11 Sqdn was to reply with a black fin, whilst the LTF stuck with Binbrook blue. (*CP RUSSELL-SMITH*)

accompanied by toned-down and reduced roundels, flashes and squadron markings. Also over-wing tanks began to make their appearance as a permanent fixture at this time. Such a change in policy was explained by delays with the forthcoming Tornado F.3, therefore the Lightning's service life was to be extended to cover the shortfall. The fitment of the over-wing tanks reduced the amount of low flying, the number of landings required and extended sortie times, all being angled towards reducing fatigue-life consumption. Although the new grey finishes were not as drab as the earlier scheme they still lacked sparkle. In an effort to combat this the resident units began to brighten up their aircraft. For 5 Sqdn this took the form of a bright red tail for their squadron commander's aircraft, always coded 'AA', whilst 11 Sqdn replied with a black fin for their leader's aircraft which was coded 'BA'. The LTF produced 'DA' with a blue fin upon which was placed a white disc containing a blue lion. APCs in Cyprus also saw the squadron commander's aircraft of 5 Sqdn sporting shark's teeth under the nose mainly on XR7700 'AA' and later on XR754 'AE' of the same unit.

Airshows were also still being spectacularly performed by the Lightning although the preference for the display aircraft slot was the lighter F.3. The 11 Sqdn contribution for 1986 consisted of two aircraft XR718 'BK1' and XP749 'BK2'. The last major air show to see the Lightning really pulling the stops out was the 1983 International Air Tattoo at Greenham Common where the attending crowd were thrilled by the awesome power and manoeuvres executed by this ageing fighter. All good things must come to an end however and for the Lightning 1987 marks the start of its rundown. Prior to disappearing from the RAF order of battle, the Station Commander at Binbrook, Group Captain John Spencer, threw the Station open to the public for the 'Last Lightning Show'. Once OC 11 Sqdn, the 'Boss' still retained his own aircraft, XR728 'JS', which although bearing the pilot's initials on the fin was in fact part of the LTF inventory. Binbrook has always been a magnet for Lincolnshire's bad weather and 22 August 1987 was to prove no exception. It rained, it poured, it turned Binbrook into a quagmire. Even so, the roads for miles around were jammed solid with Lightning enthusiasts coming to say farewell to a bastion of Britain's air defence. As well as the base's resident complement of fighters, active stored and decoys, two special guests in the shape of P.1A WG763 and BAe Warton development aircraft XP693 put in an appearance. Although the weather demolished the flying programme an attempt was made to run a portion of it. One of the few promised highlights that made it into the air was the diamond-nine of Lightnings that managed to perform a truncated version of their display.

The rest of the Lightning's career was to be somewhat anti-climatic, the LTF having disbanding officially on 1 August some three weeks before the show. No.5 Sqdn followed on 31 December reforming on the Tornado F.3 in May 1988. The last Lightning operator was therefore 11 Sqdn which put on a series of farewell photo sorties for the press, aviation and local, before that fateful final day. After sixteen years as a Lightning Squadron No.11 Sqdn RAF finally bade farewell to Britain's only single-seat supersonic fighter on 30 April 1988, a few months later the squadron was to be resurrected as a Tornado F.3 unit.

This is not the end of the Lightning story in RAF markings, as a handful of aircraft moved to BAe Warton where they were to be used as high-speed targets for that incoming young upstart, the Tornado F.3 Equipped with the Foxhunter radar system the fighter Tornado had been experiencing problems with its acquisition, tracking and targeting modes. Although the Lightning presented a slab-sided appearance to the human eye, to a radar scanner its signature was quite small. Therefore it was the ideal target, small, agile and fast – precisely the target needed to calibrate the troublesome radar.

The resident Warton Lightning, XP693, was soon joined by XR724, XR773, XS904 and XS928 for the MOD (PE) inspired contract. All were to retain over-wing tanks as standard fitment thus increasing the airborne time. The first of the four to be withdrawn was XR724 which had arrived at Warton on 12 April 1988. Flying continued until 27 June 1990 when the Lightning was flown to 27 MU for storage and eventual disposal. Placed on sale by July 1991 it was quickly purchased by the Binbrook-based Lightning Association who immediately registered it G-BTSY.

Fourteen months of frantic activity by the Association, British Aerospace and the Lightning Flying Club resulted in the aircraft flying from Shawbury to Binbrook on 23 July 1993 piloted by BAe pilot Peter Gordon-Johnson. Safely ensconsed in Lincolnshire the aircraft is maintained in a flyable condition, although the closest it gets to leaping skywards is a high-speed taxi. Also preserved at the base is Lightning F.6 XR725, also in the care of the Association.

The MoD contract was to finally expire on 17 December 1992. On 16 December two of the Lightnings, XP693 and XR773 were flown to the new Exeter Airport base of the Lightning Flying Club, whilst XS904 was flown to Bruntingthorpe for the Lightning Preservation Group, an earlier abortive sale to the Deutches Museum in Munich having fallen-through. Joining the already resident XR728 it is intended that both will remain in

The blue fin and spine of 92 Sqdn was perpetuated on the F.2As after conversion. Beautifully clean is XN772 pictured at Wattisham in 1968. (*CP RUSSELL-SMITH*)

taxiable condition. The last of the quartet that had joined BAe Warton was XS928. It too had a short career as a Tornado quarry being grounded in 1991 and placed in store. Destined to grace the gate at Samlesbury, the aircraft was purchased for spares by the LFC. With all usable spares removed XS928 was handed back to BAe so that it would fulfil its destiny.

Having purchased two F.6 Lightnings the LFC registered them on the civil register with XP693 becoming G-FSIX and XR773 assuming the mantle of G-OPIB. It is intended that one of the single-seaters will resume flying as soon as possible once G-LTNG has flown. As the LFC has already shown that they can exceed the stipulations laid down by the CAA by a handsome margin, that day should not be long in coming.

Faced with the most politically sensitive task ever to face a pair of fighter units, Nos. 19 and 92 Sqdns coped admirably with their role of patrolling the German border. Both squadrons were based at Gütersloh by 1968, having not served together since their days at Leconfield. Their aircraft, the Lightning F.2, had always been regarded as the stepping-stone between the F.1A and the more advanced F.3. When the first development F.3 had flown in June 1962 the quantum leap forward in handling and performance had been patently obvious. Thus a programme was formulated to convert the F.2 to F.3 standard. The decision to use the F.2 airframe was based primarily on the four-cannon installation that gave the RAFG fighter squadrons a useful ground-attack capability.

The first aerodynamic vehicle was XN799 which had been fitted with the squared fin and enlarged tank of the F.6, the wing for the moment remaining unchanged. Once test results had been absorbed by BAC it soon became apparent that a series of modifications based on the F.6 not the F.3 would serve the RAF better. XN795 was therefore retained mainly for the F.3 development programme whilst the definitive airframe settled on an F.6 lookalike albeit still retaining the original Avon 210 engines and with no provision for over-wing fuel tanks. The conversion process began in earnest during 1967 when the first of thirty aircraft, XN789, made its maiden flight on 12 October. After company flying the Lightning was despatched to A&AEE, Boscombe Down for pre-service C(A) release assessment. The second conversion was XN781 being the first to return to Germany for 19 Sqdn use in February 1968. The first convert for 92 Sqdn was XN773 which arrived in June. By September 1969 all the designated aircraft had been converted and returned to Germany. A handful of aircraft were left unconverted and they served on both squadrons as continuation, conversion trainers and fulfilled the role of TFF aircraft.

The bright aluminium finish and in 92 Squadrons case their blue fins, were to disappear from 1971 when camouflage was specified for all front line aircraft. The first Lightning to go 'green' was XN786 'M' of 19 Sqdn in May 1972. Upper surfaces were then finished in dark green although the undersides were left in aluminium. National markings also changed, those on the green paint losing their white centre ring. Fin markings remained virtually unchanged however providing a splash of colour to the otherwise drab finish. Maintenance in Germany became the responsibility of the Brüggen-based 431 MU and they found themselves dealing with the results of many an accident. One such was XN776 which, flying as 'C' of 19 Sqdn, successfully damaged its lower fuselage during cannon firing practise. Actual losses amongst the F.2A community were rare however. XN772, 'N' of 92 Sqdn crashed on 28 January 1971, whilst XN788, 'P' of 92 Sqdn blotted its copy-book on 29 May 1974 when the port undercarriage collapsed after a brake-chute failure.

A different crash and the only recorded shoot-down by a Lightning F.2A took place in 1972 during their sojourn in Germany when the Gütersloh Battle Flight was called into action to down a wayward Harrier. Abandoned by its pilot after an engine shut-down, the force of the ejection had re-started the power-plant and the crewless aircraft headed for the German border. To avoid diplomatic repercussions the decision was taken to shoot the Harrier down – which the Lightnings duly did. Another duty for the Gütersloh battle flight was that of shepherding wayward Warsaw Pact aircraft back over the border, most were inexperienced students whilst others were spotted as deliberate probing flights.

The Lightnings of RAF Germany did manage some overseas trips mainly for APC purposes. These flights were regarded as good value for money, encompassing a range of skills that were not in common usage. The primary benefit was in the honing of in-flight refuelling, for, although the RAFG Lightnings carried out some practices over the North Sea their use of the technique was not as extensive as that of their British counterparts. Described by its pilots as the ultimate single-seat fighter – in short a pilot's aeroplane – the days of the Lightning F.2A were numbered. Having played such a vital part in maintaining the peace and the *status quo* whilst patrolling the German border, the time came for a change of aircraft type. Both squadrons were to lose their Lightnings to re-equip with the Phantom. No.19 Sqdn was the first to go, disbanding on 31 December 1976 being followed by their counterparts, 92 Sqdn, on 31 March 1977. Both squadrons then reformed on the F-4 whose crews had been flying as 'designated' squadrons from Wildenrath. The redundant Lightnings mainly found new roles as 'special display' decoy aircraft on bases throughout Germany and Britain.

Although most conventional Lightning developments managed to leave the drawing-board and achieve flight status there were some more fanciful variants that proceeded no further than the design stage.

The Lightning fighter project itself had settled down to produce a point defence aircraft capable of supersonic performance. Tactical thinking within the Royal Air Force then decided to move the goal posts, postulating that the era of the high-altitude, easy to find intruder had passed. In its place was revealed the low-level intruder cruising in at 400 kts with a supersonic dash speed over the target aided and cloaked by extensive electronic countermeasures. Those familiar with aircraft design will immediately recognise the philosophy behind the Convair B-58 Hustler.

To counter such a threat the Air Ministry issued requests for a design study under Specification F155 D/T (OR329) which called for a day/night all-weather fighter, capable of intercepting a target travelling at 6,000 ft with a theoretical dash speed of M=1.3. To allow for airframe and engine growth the English Electric response, designated P8, was based on the P.1B, but featured an area-ruled fuselage, the crew seated in tandem and the missile armament mounted on wingtip launch rails. The wings themselves were extended in span and featured the cambered leading edge first tested on WG760. Another major design change from the basic Lightning was the removal of the undercarriage from the wings to area-ruled bulges in the rear fuselage, thus turning the whole wing into an integral fuel tank. The proposed power-plants were a pair of Rolls-Royce RB 126 engines equipped with concave convergent-divergent nozzles or alternatively an exhaust ejector system. Dry thrust was imagined to be in the region of 13,400 lbs st which would give a climb-rate of 500 kts IAS to 40,000 ft after which, still in dry thrust, the aircraft would accelerate to Mach 2 plus. Having overcome all the design problems that wind-tunnel testing had thrown up English Electric felt confident enough to approach the government for development funds. As with many outstanding design concepts of the 1950s, the project came to a grinding halt in the débâcle that was the 1957 Defence White Paper.

Obviously down-hearted by this blunting of British fighter design technology, a case in point being the purchase of the Phantom instead of developing the Lightning, the English Electric, later BAC, designers continued to develop their product. Design number P15 appeared in February 1956 and covered the specification for a dedicated photo-reconnaissance version of the Lightning. This appeared in a watered-down form for foreign export only, using a Vinten camera pack in the forward lower fuselage. Projects P18, 19 and 23 revealed studies for a low-altitude bomber variant of the aircraft in late 1956, an upgrade beyond F.6 standard fighter and an unspecified design respectively.

Design study No.P33 was part of a vain attempt to sell the Lightning to the Australian government. The project portrayed a two-seat strike fighter based upon the T.5 whose specifications were later to be met by the General Dynamics F-111C. P.34 postulated about the same time, took the F.2/F.2A design a stage further to provide a dedicated ground-attack aircraft

After conversion the Lightning F.2A strongly resembled the later F.6. Only the inability to carry over-wing tanks and a four-cannon fit differentiated the aircraft externally. Pictured on a visit to Croxyde, Belgium in 1968 is XN776 of 19 Sqdn. *(CP RUSSELL-SMITH)*

Awaiting ground runs is 19 Sqdn Lightning XN783 pictured at its home base of Gütersloh in 1970. *(CP RUSSELL-SMITH)*

Awaiting its pilot at Gütersloh in 1970 is 19 Sqdn F.2A XN735. Of interest is the fitment of the upper nose cannon. Many of the aircraft were normally fitted with cannon in the two lower positions. (*CP RUSSELL-SMITH*)

for the RAF. As history now shows, none of these ideas was proceeded with.

Possibly one of the most interesting and ambitious designs to appear was that created in response to a Naval requirement, AW406, which appeared in the late 1960s. AW406 called for a supersonic fleet-defence fighter capable also of strike and reconnaissance. The BAC response was based in the T.5 and featured an extended ventral fuel tank which coupled with an increased wing capacity would have given a total internal fuel load of 1,300 gallons. Naval features such as a tail skid and arrester-hook would have of course been added. The undercarriage mounting points would have been moved to the outboard wing panels, the whole structure being then strengthened to allow for a sink rate of 20 ft/sec. All this extra weight, including four 1,000 lbs bombs on external pylons, would have raised the all- up weight to 47,000 lbs.

Encouraged by the response of the Royal Navy the next set of design proposals were ready almost immediately. It was proposed to develop the wing into a swing wing with the pivot-points located just outboard of the repositioned undercarriage. The wing sweep would have given a span of 48 ft 2 inches fully forward for take-off and landing, whilst in supersonic cruise the span would have reduced to 36 ft 7 inches. To give clearance within the carrier hangar decks the fin tip was designed to fold, thus reducing the overall height to 10 ft 6 inches. The radar system was to be based on the AI.23B and would have had its dish increased in diameter to thirty inches. As design-weight was growing, a change to Rolls-Royce RB168/1R engines, instead of the previous Avons, was projected. As these power-plants were larger in diameter an area-ruled larger rear fuselage was added to the design and to cope with the increased air flow demands a pair of cheek mounted intakes with variable controlled ramps and boundary-layer bleed-off would have been necessary. At this last stage the total fuel capacity had grown to 2,000 gallons whilst the take-off weight with Red Top missiles fitted brought the launch weight to a projected 44,950 lbs. In the strike role with four 1,000 lbs bombs, the launch weight would have reached 47,450 lbs. The proposed range for the aircraft in the attack role was 825 nm, a wind-over-deck component of 24 kts IAS being required to launch.

A development programme was put forward by BAC which included two T.5s flying with the wing in the swept-forward position and a further airframe modified with a fully variable wing. The Fleet Air Arm was by now very interested in the BAC proposal, here at last was a chance to steal a march on the Americans and provide the fleet with a multi-capability fighter instead of the earlier subsonic types previously in service.

Unfortunately British defence policies throughout the period were completely inconsistent, with threats of the carriers firstly being withdrawn and then reinstated. Eventually the whole idea was dropped to be replaced by the Buccaneer in the attack/strike role and the F-4 Phantom in the fleet-defence role. With the demise of all these projects died Britain's chances of remaining a world leader in supersonic fighter design. This was only partially regained in later years by the appearance of the Tornado F.3, another Warton product.

Two years later and XN732 sits on the Gütersloh flight-line after a hard day's flying. (*CP RUSSELL-SMITH*)

Chapter 7
Lightnings in the Sand

POSSIBLY ONE of the strangest sights to greet British eyes, more used to military drabness, occurred in January 1986 when, in two waves, a total of twenty-two shiny Lightnings swept over the fence at Warton. Arriving in the standard British 'howling gale' reserved for such occasions, complete with lashing rain, it struck a complete contrast to their earlier residence amid the sands of Saudi Arabia.

The English Electric Company had been preparing studies of various derivative Lightnings tailored to fit the needs of interested countries. Austria, Japan, Germany, Singapore, Nicaragua and Brazil had all requested details on behalf of their respective air forces. Unfortunately for the E.E. Co. they were fighting a lone battle – against them were ranged the prime aviation companies of France and the United States, all of whom received government assistance in the pursuance of overseas sales. All of the British company's efforts were to come to naught as lack of positive response from British officials drove potential buyers into the arms of better supported suppliers.

One potential contract that did come close to fruition was that for Nicaragua which was proceeding quite nicely until two insurmountable difficulties came to light. First, air delivery was ruled-out as none of the country's airfields were then capable of accepting an aircraft such as the Lightning, whilst the second option, delivery by sea was also discounted when it was realised that serious demolition of property would have been required for the aircraft to have been towed clear of the docks. Also political unrest, always an ingredient of Latin American politics, would have been inflamed by such a move.

Before criticisms arise, there had been a plan to modernise an airfield to accept the aircraft which would have been placed in storage before use. It is also interesting to note that a second attempt was made to sell Lightnings to Austria when they were in the market for an air defence fighter to replace the ageing SAAB 105s. The ex-Saudi Lightnings were offered at an advantageous price which would have included full spares and support packages. This second venture also failed, the Austrians finally settling for another SAAB product, the Draken. Some other interested parties had at least flown the Lightning. A few with a view to buying, the rest so that they could report on the competition to their own governments. In the former category fall India, later to buy MiG series fighters, Australia whose airforce became equipped with Dassault fighters and Venezuela which also travelled the Dessault path. In the latter category falls the United States, determined to sell its country's products throughout the world. To be fair however, many USAF pilots did take part in the RAF/USAF exchange programmes and had nothing but praise for the Lightning.

With plans afoot to extend the range and capabilities of the Lightning, BAC management felt it was time to take up the cudgels again and begin another export drive. This time the target was the Middle East and in particular Saudi Arabia. Playing a key role on behalf of BAC and other interested parties was a British businessman, Mr Geoffrey Edwards.

Trouble with insurgents along the Yemen border as well as careful negotiation finally brought the desired result. The Royal Saudi Air Force, Al-Quwwat Al Jawwiyaal-Malakiya as-Sa'udiya, had only existed for a dozen years or so and was currently equipped with outdated and aged F-86 Sabres and Douglas B-26 Invaders. Ranged against them were MiG-17s and Il-28 Beagles, ostensibly of Yemini Air Force origin, but in reality equipment belonging to the Egyptian Air Force, courtesy of President Nassar. The troubles had first flared up in 1962 upon the death of the Yemini ruler Iman Ahmed. Egypt, at the time Communist and anti-Zionist, was supporting with Russian aid any insurrection that came to light in the region. The Saudi nation was, and still is, extremely royalist and was therefore giving its full backing to the rightful claimant to rule Yemen.

Upon the death of King Ibn Saud his son, Crown Prince Faisal, acceded to the throne and concerned for his country's safety he was determined to use some of the wealth gained from oil exports to update the equipment of the Saudi military. Geoffrey Edwards had moved to the capital, Jeddah, by this time and after a change of government in Britain to a Labour cabinet in 1964, his task of convincing the Saudis to buy British became easier. Even the dubious argument of not 'exporting arms to the Middle East in case it accelerated the local arms-race' soon disappeared.

To push the sale of its aircraft even harder BAC borrowed a Lightning F.2, XN730, from a detachment in Cyprus and flew it to Bahrain from whence it would depart to Saudi Arabia to be displayed before the King, his cabinet and the myriad of Generals that such events attract. On 3 July 1964 XN730 piloted by BAC pilot Jimmy Dell departed Bahrain for Jeddah. Unlike the situation today, Saudi airspace lacked sophisticated navigation and guidance systems, therefore navigation was very much by the seat of the pants. Fortunately the sky was free of sandstorms and the pilot quickly located the main Riyadh to Jeddah road. After a safe touchdown the Lightning was prepared for its display flight the next day.

Before the august Saudi assemblage Dell put the aircraft through its paces. Suitably impressed, the Saudi hierarchy gave favourable indications of a large forthcoming contract. To cement the deal a Saudi airforce pilot, Lt Hamdan, was sent to Warton for some hands-on experience flying. Conversion sorties were carried-out in a borrowed T.4, whilst the Lieutenant was to fly an F.2, XN723, for the trials sortie. The chase-plane was an F.3 on loan from the RAF. During his only sortie in the F.2 the Saudi pilot not only pulled away from the F.3 chase aircraft, but is rumoured to have exceeded M=2.1, well in excess of the design limits set for RAF service. With the safe completion of the flight, coupled with the pilot's enthusiastic support, the Saudi Arabian government had no hesitation in awarding the contract for the first batch of aircraft. The completion of the contract on 21 December 1965 followed by full authorisation in the following May marked the beginning of Operations Magic Palm and Magic Carpet.

Operation Magic Palm, the first phase of the programme, covered the delivery of six Lightnings, six Hunters and a battery of Thunderbird surface-to-air missiles. The Lightnings, two T.4 trainers and four F.2

Lightning F.6 XR770 masqueraded as an F.53 of the RSAF at the SBAC show at Farnborough in September 1966. (*CP RUSSELL-SMITH*)

fighters, were drawn from surplus RAF stocks. Serialled XN796, XN770, XN767, XN797 for the F.2s and XM992 and XM989 for the T.4s they were later joined by XN734 and XN729. Conversion work was carried out at Warton and the refurbished aircraft were consequently redesignated; the single-seaters became F.52s being re-serialled thus: 52-657 (ex XN769), 52-656 (ex XN770), 52-655 (ex XN767) and 52-658 (ex XN797). At a later date the three survivors were to be renumbered again becoming 56-610, 609 and 611 respectively.

The trainers were redesigned T.54 after conversion and became 54-651 (ex XM992) later 608 and 54-650 (ex XM989) later 607. Another airframe also underwent the Saudi conversion process this being XN734 which was later flown in 'B' class markings as G-27-239 being retained at Warton for training purposes.

Lightning 52-657 was the first Saudi delivery departing these shores on 8 July 1966 piloted by Tim Ferguson. Don Knight flew 52-656 to Saudi two days later and both pilots were to fly the last two aircraft to their new owners on 22 July. Both T.54s had been flown to Saudi Arabia by the same pilots on 6 June.

Showing-off the new airpower of the Saudi airforce to both friend and foe alike became the first item on the agenda. Unfortunately this was not without its hazards as the loss of 52-657 was to show. Rotating far too early during a full reheat take-off, the Lightning entered into a stall from which it was far too low to recover. Wisely the pilot ejected safely and thus the RSAF lost its first Lightning on 20 September 1966. It was soon replaced by another however as XN729 was converted to F.52 standard as 52-659, later 612, being delivered on 9 May 1967.

Having thundered about the sky impressing the natives and frightening the camels it was now time for the Lightning force to impress the Yemini incursionists. Accordingly the airbase at Khamis

The genuine article, F.53-666 wearing the B class registration G-27-2 is seen here on a flight-test from Warton. Of note are the rocket pods under the wings. (*BAe WARTON*)

Mushyat was chosen as the nearest to the troubled area. As built, however, the runway was at right-angles to the prevailing wind and this was to cause havoc on the wheels and brakes of the slab-sided fighters. Most of the air, ground and support personnel were recruited by Geoffrey Edwards – many being ex-RAF and this was to be a precursor for the later BAC support contract days.

In the meantime Airworks held the prime responsibility and it was under their auspices that the first Lightning arrived at Khamis on 7 August 1967. An F.52 and the pair of T.54s arrived first, two of the pilots later returning to Riyadh to collect the remaining two fighters. The notorious Khamis cross-wind defeated the first attempts of the second wave aircraft to land on 14 August, the aircraft having to wait a few days more before succeeding. Although only fifty-four miles from the border, Khamis is some 7,000 ft above sea-level and this rise in altitude had not been considered by either BAC or Airworks. The resulting fiasco saw AVPIN-fired starters producing the familiar whine which was followed by a burp then a deadly silence. Much fiddling, tweaking and adjustment was then required before the Avons regained their more familiar mighty roar. To celebrate, a pair of aircraft beat-up the airfield breaking windows, derendering walls and generally waking up all and sundry.

Introducing a new type of aircraft into service is always a tricky business for any air force, especially in the area of spares support. This came to a head on 20 September when supplies of LOX had run out for No.6 Sqdn and its Lightnings. However the situation had been resolved by 14 October and a more permanent solution in the shape of a LOX plant was then provided. On 13 November 1966 the Lightning flight of No.6 Sqdn RSAF was declared fully operational.

Their first alert began in January 1967 when the Hunters and Lightnings of Khamis came to full readiness status. Increased tension along the border had resulted in flare-ups of fighting between ground forces and the possibility of air incursions was regarded as very real. Further trouble in February was driven home by the arrival of a signal which placed all aircrew on permanent stand-by, not primarily to defend the airfield but to evacuate the aircraft should the need arise. Awareness of the potential of the Lightning force finally penetrated the Yemeni High Command and border tensions were considerably reduced. A fortunate turn of events as the base by that time had virtually run dry of aircraft fuel. The arrival of the replacement F.52, 52-659, on 9 May 1967 brought the Lightning flight up to its full operating strength, although it was soon to be depleted by the loss of 52-658. On 29 November 1968 whilst inbound to Khamis attempting a single engine approach, the pilot, Major Ghimlas, let his aircraft drop both altitude and speed. It flew into the ground killing the pilot.

The Magic Carpet contract finally expired on 31 March 1968. Personnel from the Pakistani Air Force then arrived to take over the duties previously assigned to those employed by BAC/Airworks. Unfortunately the Hunters and the Lightnings were beyond the skills of the PAF technicians, therefore Airworks resumed its contract work to maintain them. Pilots by this time were receiving £12,000 per annum, a significant growth from the £4,000 available previously. They and the support crews were to move into a better standard of accommodation thus setting the pattern for years to come. As for the Lightnings, they remained at Khamis Mushyat to form the Lightning OCU. Only one other aircraft was lost in service, this being 52-659 which crashed on approach on 2 May 1970 near Khamis. Of the two trainers only one was to suffer any form of major damage, this being 54-608 which had a starter fire on 26 October 1970, this required Cat 3 repairs to rectify. Not long after these early aircraft were withdrawn from service although some were to assume new roles as gate guards. At Riyadh is F.52 52-656 whilst Dharan is graced by T.54 54-650 in company with F.52 52-655. One other Lightning worthy of mention is pre-production aircraft XG313 which had been shipped out to Saudi to act as a training aid in 1968. Located at Riyadh at Riyadh Technical Training School it was eventually scrapped after many years of service.

When the announcement was made in the House of Commons in 1965 that BAC had clinched the deal with Saudi Arabia it marked the start of one of the biggest export contracts ever procured in financial terms, by 1984 it was worth £1.5 billion. Figuratively speaking Operation Magic Palm covered the delivery and support of thirty-four single-seat fighters and six two-seat trainers.

Although destined to bear the F.53 designation the resulting aircraft owed more to the later F.6 than to the earlier F.3 being in essence an F.6 with multi-mission capability. Pylons were available for weaponry both above and below the wings whilst the lower fuselage Red Top missile package could be replaced by either Microcell rockets or a reconnaissance pod. The twin Aden cannon package as fitted to the F.6 was incorporated as standard. The trainer, designated T.55, also owed much to the F.6 being more akin to an F.6 with a T.5 nose more than, as its designation suggests, a development of the basic T.5 as flown by the RAF. Fortunately design and wind-tunnel testing had already been undertaken for such a version of the Lightning, therefore it was more a case of producing prototypes in a hurry than rushing a series of design modifications through onto the production line as the order was being built. The F.53 prototype was an ex-RAF machine, XR722, that had been in store at Warton for possible F.6 conversion. This had failed to materialise, but the availability of the requisite components meant that the conversion could be undertaken relatively quickly.

Thus the rebuilt Lightning, the first of its kind, undertook its maiden flight on 1 November 1966. Development work on weapons-release parameters kept the aircraft at Warton until 28 June 1969 when it finally left Britain to join No.2 Sqdn RSAF at Khamis on 5 December.

Prior to departing however it had undertaken the full range of weaponry trials. Ground cannon firing in May 1967 was followed by air firing in December. Full flying and handling trials with various weapons began in earnest during September. Underwing pylons first made their appearance in January 1967 whilst SNEB MATRA pods were first flown in the February. Air-to-ground firing of the rocket pods was undertaken during April 1968.

This Lightning was to be eventually lost in a non-fatal crash on 6 February 1972 whilst on loan to 6 Sqdn. The first trainer followed a similar path as its fighter counterpart as it too was an ex-RAF aircraft in this case XS460. Conversion work continued apace alongside 53-666 thus the first T.55, serialled 55-710, made its first flight two days after the fighter. It too remained at Warton for development flying although its career was to be spectacularly short. Inbound to Warton on 7 March 1967 55-710 encountered a strong and unpredicted cross-wind gust. Such was the strain on the airframe upon touch-down that the right-hand undercarriage leg collapsed with the result that the Lightning veered across the runway. Further excessive side loads caused the fuselage to break at the rear cockpit pressure bulkhead joint. This in turn

Surrounded and festooned with rockets, bombs, fuel tanks and all manner of unfriendly things is 5 Sqdn F.6 XS903. The occasion was the 1967 Paris airshow and the aircraft had been mocked-up to represent an overseas export variant. (*CP RUSSELL-SMITH*)

released the canopy and caused the left-hand ejection seat to be thrown clear of the aircraft. Fortunately for the pilot the disturbance failed to start the seat firing sequence. The pilots, J. Dell instructing from the right-hand seat on behalf of BAC, and P. Williams of Airworks both suffered major leg injuries and required nearly a year of treatment and recuperation before resuming their flying careers. The Lightning not surprisingly was a complete write-off.

Prior to the flights of the Saudi Air Force prototypes BAC had displayed mock-ups at Farnborough. Warton's own F.6, XP693, carried dummy pylons embellished with rocket pods and was the centre piece in a static display surrounded by a profusion of weapon loads. The flying side was covered by another F.6, XR770, which performed its displays adorned in Saudi markings.

Disasters notwithstanding, production of the Saudi order continued. Meanwhile training of RSAF pilots had begun under the auspices of 226 OCU at Coltishall. The Saudi Air Force's own trainers were soon to appear in East Anglia where they formed a separate training flight to operate alongside those of the OCU. The first aircraft in the production batch, 55-711, made its first flight on 28 September 1967, finally joining the training programme on 2 February 1968.

The second T.55, 55-712, arrived at Coltishall on 15 February having been used before delivery to fly Colonel Yanada of the Japanese Air Force in the previous November. Two other aircraft of the six ordered also joined the RSAF flight at 226 OCU these being 55-713 and 714. Coded 'C' and 'D' respectively, the previous pair becoming 'A' and 'B', all remained in East Anglia before being delivered to Saudi Arabia in the latter half of 1969. The final pair, 55-715 and 716, also departed for their purchaser's homeland in 1969. 55-716 had appeared as a replacement for the ill-fated 55-710. Unlike their British counterparts the Saudi aircraft remained as part of the Lightning Conversion Unit at Khamis throughout their entire working lives. Only one is confirmed as having crashed in service, this being 55-712 which was lost whilst performing an inverted low pass over Half Moon Bay on 21 May 1974. The crew Colonel Ainousa and Lt Otaibi were unfortunately killed. Of the remaining five, four returned to Warton in January 1986 whilst the last aircraft, 55-716, is reported to have acted as a conversion trainer for the fighters that remained on inventory. Operated by BAe these last Lightnings, reported to be four fighters and the aforementioned T.55, were employed as high-speed targets for the Tornado F.3s of the RSAF. Their activities, similar to those duties undertaken by their British counterparts, finally ceased when Iraq invaded Kuwait in August 1990.

Single-seat aircraft production was running roughly parallel to that of the trainers. This allowed the first fourteen of the thirty-three-strong contract to be delivered to Jeddah in 1968. Serialled 53-667 to 682 and 55-684 they were flight refuelled on the way by RAF Victors with diversion staging if required being centred upon the RAF base at Akrotiri, Cyprus.

All flew with British civil 'B' registrations in the series G-27-37 to 52 and G-27-54. Lightning F.53 No.681 is of interest as this was the flight-test carried out by R.P. 'Bee' Beamont on 28 March 1968 before he retired from the programme. During the thirteen years that he had been involved with the project he had made 1,300 flights in twelve different variants.

The remainder of the fighters were delivered during 1969 following the same procedures as the preceding deliveries. Prior to their leaving British shores two of

The international airport in Kuwait City was the first and last home for the KAF Lightnings. Seen in 1984 is a full line-up of redundant aircraft soon to find other homes throughout the country. (*AL CHURCHYARD*)

the F.53s had found time to appear at Farnborough, 53-686 registered as G-AWON had provided the static display centrepiece complete with the obligatory display of weaponry and the Queen's Award to Industry badge on the nose whilst 53-687, registered as G-AWOO, but only in the cockpit, had provided the thrills of air display flying.

For those Lightnings deemed serviceable enough to fly direct, the journey time was between six and seven hours which was not the odious task it had been in some earlier generation fighters. With its advanced auto-pilot and navigation systems backed-up by those of the accompanying Victor, the pilot's cockpit workload was reduced considerably. The last eighteen aircraft delivered to the RSAF were serialled 53-683 and 53-685 to 689 with 53-691 to 699. They too were emblazoned with 'B' class registrations thus avoiding any offence or claims of provocation from other countries in the region. For the record their registrations were 683 as G-27-53 with 685 to 689 being given G-27-55 to 59. Lightnings 691 to 699 were adorned with G-27-61 to 69. One aircraft is missing from the sequence this being 53-690 which suffered a severe fire in the rear fuselage which eventually made the aircraft uncontrollable. The pilot, J. Cockburn, sensibly egressed courtesy of Martin-Baker, leaving the burning Lightning to crash near the village of Pilling, Fylde, on 4 September 1968. To replace this loss and bringing the final Saudi total up to thirty-four new-build fighters, a final F.53 53-700, was constructed in 1971. It made its maiden flight on 29 June 1972 and was the last Lightning built. Delivery to Saudi, in this case straight to Khamis, was undertaken on 4 September.

Upon arrival the Saudi Lightnings were used to form Nos.2 and 6 Sqdns RSAF. In the No.6 Sqdn inventory they displaced the earlier F.52 and T.54 aircraft which, combining with the newly delivered T.55 trainers, formed the LCU at Khamis. During their long and varied careers the Saudi Lightnings saw service at Tabuk in the north and at Riyadh and Khamis again. Support and training were always an important part of this on-going package. As well as the BAC Lightnings and Strikemasters that were delivered, the converted F.2, XN734, last seen as an F.52 had metamorphosised into a hybrid F.2A/F.53 for ground school use at Warton. Finally made redundant, the aircraft currently resides at Cranfield with the Vintage Aircraft Team.

During their service in Saudi Arabia the

Lightning F.53 fleet suffered a number of losses; 53-667 was to be written-off on 15 April 1973; 55-647 crashed in September 1972; 53-694 was lost in LCU service in April 1973 whilst 53-697 crashed in May 1970. To confuse matters and historians the Lightnings of the RSAF changed their identities at least once. The new serial range was reported to identify an individual aircraft within a squadron – thus 53-667 became 202 within No.2 Sqdn. Found to be an awkward system to manage, open as it was to confusion regarding servicing and maintenance documents, the numbering soon reverted to the earlier sequence. Throughout the 1970s the Lightnings were to give sterling service to the RSAF, but change was looming on the horizon.

With even more oil revenues to spend the air force went shopping. From the United States came the F-15, whilst BAe (the successor to BAC) provided the Tornado GR.1 and F.3, Hawks, Jetstreams and Tucanos. Withdrawn from front-line use the redundant Lightnings were placed in storage at Dharan to await their fate.

Part of the deal struck with BAe was that they would remove the greater portion of stored aircraft from Dharan, thus Operation Dhonanyi was born. After much discussion between BAe representatives and Strike Command, the plan put forward covered the aircraft returning in two waves of twelve and ten respectively. Pilots for the Lightnings would be drawn from the Binbrook Lightning units whilst tanker support would be the province of 101 Sqdn with their VC-10 K2/3 aircraft operating from Dharan to overhead Palermo, Sicily. From Palermo Victor K.2 aircraft would escort the Lightnings home.

Positioning of the tankers took place during 11 January 1986, the return journey being completed three days later. As Saudi Arabia, quite understandably, refused to allow the Lightnings to transit in RSAF markings, RAF roundels, flashes and serial numbers in the ZF range were substituted. Those returned in the first wave included F.53s ZF577-581, 583, 585, 588, 591, 594 and T.55s ZF597 and 598. The final batch of ten aircraft followed a similar path arriving at Warton on 22 January. This wave consisted of F.53s ZF582, 584, 586-590, 592, 593 and T.55s ZF595 and 596 in company. Prior to departing from Dharan the pilots were treated to a farewell banquet whilst the detachment commander was presented with a silver Lightning medal that was to proudly adorn the Officers Mess at Binbrook until the base closed.

With no obvious use in view for the returned Lightnings they were placed in storage to await eventual disposal. Feelers were put out to the RAF for possible usage of these low-time good condition aircraft, unfortunately their different modification state, to that which pertained to the RAF aircraft, would have rendered them an expensive proposition, therefore the offer was rejected. The attempt that followed to sell the entire batch to Austria also fell-through and thus the Lightnings remained in open storage. Even though no buyer was in prospect they all underwent periodic engine runs, maintenance and movement, the latter being required to stop tyres distorting and undercarriage legs seizing.

During 1988 it had become obvious within British Aerospace that no buyer was forthcoming for the aircraft therefore during late 1988, early 1989 they were disposed of to interested parties for a nominal sum, ZF578 departed for Cardiff, ZF580 appeared at Samlesbury, ZF583 went to the Solway Aviation Society, ZF584 travelled north to Ferranti at Edinburgh whilst ZF588 now graces the East Midlands Aeropark. The NEAM at Sunderland acquired ZF594 whilst the Haydon-Ballie Aircraft and Naval Museum acquired the

Displaying the final fate that awaited many of the Kuwait Lightnings is F.53 418 'L' at Ali Salem AB in 1983. Once G-27-86 and G-AXEE it had been displayed at Paris prior to its Kuwait delivery. (*AL CHURCHYARD*)

remainder. Of the four two-seaters only ZF598 moved to the Midland Air Museum at Coventry, the other three became the property of the Haydon-Baillie Museum collection based originally at Southampton docks. It has since been reported that the whole collection of Lightnings has been shipped to America.

The Saudi ban on returning aircraft wearing RSAF markings also extended to their display in museums. Therefore it is highly likely that those remaining in Britain will eventually wear spurious RAF squadron markings. Of those Lightnings that remained in Saudi 53-699 became the Tabuk gate guardian whilst the remainder are reportedly back in store awaiting disposal after their time as high-speed targets. As such flying ceased due to events in the Gulf it is only a matter of time before they appear as gate guardians or as scrap.

KUWAIT

Situated to the northeast of Saudi Arabia is the small oil-rich state of Kuwait. Having already undergone some mistreatment by a troublesome neighbour, in this case Iraq in 1962, some form of air defence was deemed necessary by the ruling Sabah family. Already entwined with Britain by a defence treaty, which placed a military mission from all services within the country, it came as no surprise to find Kuwait ordering Lightnings at the same time as her larger, mightier neighbour. Although in numerical terms a small order, only two T.55 trainers and a dozen fighters, the total package in financial terms was considerably greater. The depth of support and length of contract in no way matched that from Saudi Arabia, even so it provided BAC with another useful source of steady income.

The first Kuwaiti Lightning airborne was one of the T.55K trainers, No.410, which made its maiden flight on 24 May 1968. It was followed by the first F.55K, No.412, on 21 June. Astute readers will note the 'K' suffix applied to these aircraft, it was only necessary for recording

Against a contrasting sky is Kuwait T.55 G-27-78 also marked as 55-410'A' on a test-flight from Warton prior to delivery. (*BAe WARTON*)

purposes as from all practical angles the differences between the export Lightnings was minimal. The second Kuwaiti T.55 made its maiden flight on 3 April 1969, both trainers being delivered to the KAF in December of that year. As deliveries to the RSAF inventory were still ongoing it was not unusual to find aircraft of both countries being delivered together. Deliveries of F.53 fighters began with 53-412 in December 1968 with the other eleven airframes, 53-413 to 423 arriving at various times throughout the 1969. Before leaving Europe however two of the Lightnings, 53-418 and 419, appeared at the 1969 Paris Air Show with the civil registrations G-AXEE and G-AXFW respectively.

Upon their arrival in Kuwait the Lightnings were initially based at the International Airport. However as this was subject to intense civil flying operations it soon became apparent that operating the Lightnings in such an environment was impractical. Therefore bases were reconstructed at Ahmed al Jaber and Jakra to take the new supersonic fighter. Unfortunately neither airfield was fully or properly equipped with the necessary infrastructure that was required to operate such a complex and advanced aircraft. Flying therefore became at best intermittent due to this grevious lack of support facilities. The final crunch came when the KAF offered the survivors for sale in 1973. Interest was originally expressed by the Egyptian Air Force, but was to fail when it was revealed that a large amount of money would be required to bring the Lightnings to a common flyable standard. For a further four years the KAF struggled on with the Lightning before finally grounding them in 1977 in favour of the far simpler Mirage F.1K.

Although their career in the KAF was short, the airforce still managed to lose three of their aircraft; 53-414 crashed on 10 April 1971 whilst on approach to the International Airport. The resulting spread of wreckage killed three civilians in a shanty town whilst the pilot was to die on his way to hospital. A second fighter was lost that year when 53-419 was destroyed in a take-off accident on 2 August. In this case the pilot ejected safely from his stalled Lightning. The final crash involved 53-420 which went down in 1975. A further Lightning, 53-413, was permanently grounded in that year due to damage caused by ground handling operations.

Now redundant, the eleven survivors went into open storage at Kuwait International although some were soon on the move to other locations throughout the country. By 1985 F.53s 412 'C', 413 'E', 415 'H', 422 'P' and 423 'B' still remained at the airport whilst others of their ilk viz 53-416, 417 and 420 appeared on display at Ahmed al Jaber AFB. 53-418 was also located here, outside the KAF station headquarters. The last mentioned airframe had moved on by 1987 appearing on display outside the station headquarters at Ali Salem AFB. The final single-seater came to rest up a pole in front of the KAF headquarters building at the International Airport. Of the trainers 55-410 appeared on display at the University whilst its compatriot, 55-411, became a feature at the Officers Club at Messila beach where it was bedecked with fairy lights.

The Iraqi invasion of Kuwait in August 1990 and the moves taken to ensure their subsequent expulsion has understandably obscured the fates of many of the Lightnings. It is known that many if not all were used as targets by invading Iraqi troops. During the author's visit to Kuwait not long after hostilities had ceased, Lightning F.53s 418 and 421 were observed in a tatty, but relatively undamaged state at Al Salem AFB. Hopefully as the fog and debris of war are cleared more news concerning their fates will become available. Although the Kuwait experience with English Electric's mighty beast was not destined to be a happy one it is pleasant to note that all the other Lightning operators were more than pleased with their product which had achieved the task laid down for it so admirably.

Part II: After the Thunder

ALTHOUGH THE distinctive shape of the Lightning no longer graces the skies of Britain or the Middle East, nor assaults our eardrums (for the time being) a large percentage of the prototype and production runs still exists. It is the intention of this section to cover the histories of each of the surviving ex-RAF aircraft in a thumbnail sketch and to point readers towards their current locations for closer personal inspection. The situation regarding the ex-Saudi and Kuwaiti aircraft is rather different as much of their historical background is unrecorded. For those individual histories recorded here I am most grateful to those organisations that went out of their way to assist.

Many of the complete surviving airframes exist in a static and mostly non-flyable condition in museums throughout the country. In total contrast are the endeavours of the Lightning Flying Club whose avowed aim is to return a Lightning to flying condition for use on the display circuit. To that end their first project, G-LTNG, is approaching completion at Portsmouth and once flown should proceed to Exeter Airport where it will be stabled alongside the two F.6s already in residence. By June 1994 the LFC was awaiting the final clearance by the CAA for a permit to fly, in the meantime they are operating a Hunter T.7 G-BVGH (ex XL573) in the continuation training role, a mission it had carried out during its RAF service with 5 Sqdn at Binbrook. Other Lightnings are maintained in a close-to-airworthiness condition – three notable aircraft being those resident at Binbrook, Bruntingthorpe and Elvington.

The static exhibits, on the other hand, were mainly moved by road to their new owners and those with an appreciation of the Lightning's construction will be well aware that it was not designed for easy dismantling, therefore in most cases the outer wing panels and fin were cut off for transportation. Fortunately the restorers of these aircraft have managed quite admirably to refit these items and hide the joins.

Space and money are also a constraint that many preservation organisations face when purchasing artifacts. Therefore in many cases only the nose sections have been purchased for display. Other sections are owned by such organisations as the RAFEF at St. Athan and the Museum of Weapons Technology.

Hopefully before too long, the slab-sided aggressive shape of the Lightning will again grace our skies in the shape of those aircraft from Exeter and once again the roar of the mighty Avons, combined with outstanding agility, will thrill the waiting crowds.

English Electric P.1A
WG760/7755M
Cosford Aerospace Museum
f/f 4.8.54. Pilot R.P. Beamont. 11.8.54 Mach 1 achieved. Used for general handling, supersonic research and performance trials. 1956 reheated AW Sapphires installed. 10.57 cambered wings and inset ailerons fitted. 17.2.58 in company with XA847 to CFE team at Warton for supersonic familiarisation. 3.3.58 ret'd E.E. Co. 9.58 to RAE Bedford for crash-barrier trials followed by infra-red radiation detector trials. Uprated AW Sapphires fitted in this period. 7.6.62 grounded, hours flown 268 hrs 17 mins. To Weeton for GI use as 7755M. 1966 from Weston to 4S of TT St. Athan for GI use, then to 71 MU Bicester for restoration. 11.66 to Henlow parade ground in AFDS colours. 29.7.82 to Binbrook for preservation. 6.5.85 allocated Cosford Museum, arrived 1.86.

English Electric P.1A
WG763/7816M
Manchester Museum of Science
f/f 18.7.55. Pilot R.P. Beamont. 9.55 to SBAC Farnborough for display. 1955/56 engaged in supersonic gun firing and gas ingestion trials plus stability handling with ventral tank fitted (installed 7.10.55). 21.6.57 moved to National Aircraft Establishment (later RAE) at Bedford. Until 4.8.63 used by RAE, A&AEE and E.E. Co. for extensive testing of all aspects of type operation. 5.8.63 grounded, to Henlow as 7816M for GI/display used in company with WG760. 1982 to Hendon RAFM care but allocated to Manchester Museum of Science and Technology, arr 17.8.82.

English Electric P.1B
XA847/8371M
Air and Naval Museum, Southampton
f/f 4.4.57. Pilot R.P. Beamont. To E.E. Co. for handling performance trials including roll coupling behaviour. 1958 first firing of Firestreak missiles at RAE Aberporth in company with XG308. 25.11.59 Achieved Mach 2 piloted by R.P. Beamont. 1959 ventral tank fitted for trials as was refuelling probe. 17.1.58 to 3.3.58 operated by CFE, then to AIRPASS proving trials. 21.4.66 to RAE Farnborough for braking trials, wfu 1966, hours flown 205 hrs 30 mins, 468 flights. 1972 to RAFM Hendon, replaced by Lightning F.6 4.88. To Aviation and Naval Museum store, Southampton.

English Electric P.1B/F.1
XG329/8050M
Norfolk & Suffolk Museum, Flixton
f/f 30.4.59. Pilot R.P. Beamont. Aw Coll. 4.12.59. To C(A) for service release trials 12.59. 6.4.66 to DH Props for Firestreak programme. 21.12.66 returned E.E. Co. for stress loading trials of F.3 fin. wfu 8.7.66, to Cranwell as 8050M for GI use. 7.85 abortive sale to Waterbeach Museum, later cancelled. 23.9.86 flown as underslung load to Swinderby for display. 7.89 placed on disposal list. Sold to Ian Hancock, Essex, for display at Norfolk and Suffolk Aviation Museum, Suffolk, arr 10.93.

English Electric P.1B/F.1
XG337/8056M
Cosford Aerospace Museum
f/f 3.9.59. Pilot J.K. Isherwood. Aw Coll. 10.4.60. To C(A) 31.7.60 for free loan/trial use at A&AEE. 12.60 to RSRE/RAE for Auto ILS trials. 12.61 transferred to MOA for general handling trials. 15.1.63 to E.E. Co. then DH Props for JSTU trials of Red Top. 12.66 wfu to E.E. Co. as GI after 698 flights. 1962 to 2S of TT, Cosford, for GI as 8056M coded 'M'. 13.12.83 to Cosford Aerospace Museum.

English Electric T.4(P)
XL629
A&AEE Boscombe Down gate.
f/f 29.9.59. Pilot R.P. Beamont. To E.E. Co./A&AEE for handling trials. 1961 radar and auto ILS trials. 6.61 to A&AEE for stall and spin evaluation. 1964 Interaction trials in all flights axes. 13.5.66 to ETPS coded '23'. ETPS from

Farnborough to Boscombe Down 20.12.67. wfu 3.11.75 used as GI. To gate 1982, Firestreak missiles fitted later.

Lightning F.1
XM135
Imperial War Museum, Duxford.
f/f 14.12.59. Pilot T.M.S. Ferguson. Aw Coll. 25.5.60, to AFDS. Coltishall as 'D'. 9.61 to 74 Sqdn, Coltishall as 'B'. To E.E. Co. 1.8.62 for Mods. Ret'd 74 Sqdn 28.2.63. 24.2.64 74 Sqdn to Leuchars. 7.64 to 226 OCU/145(S) Sqdn, Coltishall. 13.1.65 to 33 MU, Lyneham for Major Serv. 21.9.66 to Leuchars TFF as '135'. 10.1.69 Cat 3 ROS by CWP. Ret'd TFF 26.3.69. 24.3.70 Cat 3 ROS by 60 MU, Leconfield, ret'd TFF 5.5.70. 21.1.72 to 60 MU, Leconfield for storage and spares recovery, instead used as MU 'hack' with inscription '60 MU Flagship' wfu 31.7.74 flying hours 1,343 hrs. To IWM as gift 20.11.74. Now repainted in 74 Sqdn colours.

Lightning F.1
XM172/8474M
RAF Coltishall gate.
f/f 10.10.60. Pilot J.K. Isherwood. Aw Coll.12.12.60. 14.12.60 to 56 Sqdn, Wattisham as 'S', later to 'B' in 1962. 1963 used as part of 'Firebirds' display team. 4.5.63 to 226 OCU/145(S) Sqdn, Coltishall. 12.10.71 Cat 3 ROS by 71 MU, Bicester, ret'd 226 OCU 8.2.72. Cat 3 repairs by 71 MU 7.7.72, ret'd 226 OCU 25.8.72. wfu 10.7.74 Cat 5GI as 8427M, placed on gate at Coltishall. Placed on disposal list 1990, sold to Haydn-Ballie Collection although remains on display at Coltishall.

Still flying at Coltishall's gate is F.1A XM172 which currently wears the markings of 145(S) Sqdn/226 OCU. (*CP RUSSELL-SMITH*)

Although up for tender and awaiting disposal Lightning XM192 'K' still looks magnificent at Wattisham's main gate. (*CP RUSSELL-SMITH*)

Lightning F.1
XM173/8414M
RAF Bentley Priory
f/f 1.11.60. Pilot J.K. Isherwood. Aw Coll. 30.12.60. To 56 Sqdn Wattisham 5.1.61 coded 'V'. Recoded 'C' 8.63 and painted in Firebirds colours. To 226 OCU/145(S) Sqdn 10.2.65. Cat 3 ROS by 71 MU 20.4.71, ret'd OCU 14.7.71. To Leuchars TFF 31.12.71. To Binbrook TFF 29.3.71.wfu 28.5.73 to Binbrook for GI as 8414M later as decoy. 1973 to Bentley Priory for display, now wears 56 Sqdn colours.

Lightning F.1
XM178/8418M
Savigny-les-Beaunes, France
f/f 30.12.60. Pilot J.K. Isherwood. Aw Coll. 31.1.61. To 56 Sqdn Wattisham coded 'U'. 9.10.61 Cat 3 landing damage ROS 71 MU, ret'd 56 Sqdn 21.12.61 as 'F'. To 33 MU, Lyneham for Major Serv. 1962. To 226 OCU/145(S) Sqdn 1963. Declared Cat 3 on following dates 4.67, 9.68 and 1.69 ROS by 60MU and 71MU. 29.2.72 to Leuchars TFF coded 'Y'. wfu 12.73, to GI as 8414M 1.2.74, to decoy 8.5.74. To Collection Association des Amis du Mussée du Château at Savigny-les-Beaunes in 1991 courtesy of Msr Pont.

Lightning F.1
XM192/8413M
RAF Wattisham gate
f/f 25.5.61. Pilot J.K. Isherwood. Aw Coll. 28.6.61. To 111 Sqdn Wattisham coded 'K' (Subject of Airfix kit in this guise). To 226 OCU/145(S) Sqdn Coltishall 14.1.65. To Wattisham TFF 2.10.69. Cat 3 landing accident ROS 71MU 9.12.71. Ret'd 226 OCU 10.5.72. wfu 4.1.74, flying time 2,186 Hours. To GI as 8413M, placed on Wattisham gate 28.5.74. Sold to Charles Ross 1994.

Lightning F.2A
XN728/8546M
A1 Commercials, Balderton, Notts

f/f 26.10.68. Pilot T.M.S. Ferguson. Aw Coll. 29.4.63. To 92 Sqdn, Leconfield coded 'B' 1.5.63. 92 Sqdn to Gielenkirchen 30.12.65. Mods by 60 MU 14.2.66. Ret'd 92 Sqdn 3.3.66. Cat 4 landing accident 9.1.68. To Warton 3.4.68 for repair and conversion to F.2A. To MinTech 24.6.69 until 24.7.69, then to 92 Sqdn coded 'F'. Ret'd Warton for mods 16.10.70. Ret'd 92 Sqdn 24.11.70. Cat 3 ROS 431MU, Brüggen, 23.2.71, ret'd 92 Sqdn 18.3. Cat 3 heavy landing 5.72 ROS 431 MU, ret'd 92 Sqdn 13.7.72 coded 'H'. wfu 1.4.77 at Widenrath as decoy as 8546M, to Coningsby as decoy 9.83. Sold to G.A. Wilks 3.10.83 then to A1 Car Sales

Lightning F.2A
XN730/8496M
Luftwaffen Museum, Germany

f/f 23.11.61. Pilot D. deVilliers, then to 33 MU, Lyneham, store. To 19 Sqdn, Leconfield coded 'B' 12.3.63. 19 Sqdn to Gütersloh 25.9.65. To BAC Warton for conversion to F.2A 11.67. To 92 Sqdn, Gütersloh, coded 'J' 30.8.68. wfu 1.4.77 to decoy at Gütersloh as 8496M. To Luftwaffen Museum, Uetersen 1983.

Lightning F.2A
XN776/8535M
M.O.F East Fortune, Scotland

f/f 18.10.62. Pilot D. deVilliers. Aw Coll. 13.2.63, to 19 Sqdn, Leconfield, coded 'E'. To BAC Warton for mods 5.8.64. Ret'd 19 Sqdn, Gütersloh 25.9.65. To BAC for F.2A

Very tatty and with many parts missing F.2A XN724 still conveys the full majesty of the Lightning's power. (*CP RUSSELL-SMITH*)

conversion 14.1.69. Ret'd 19 Sqdn coded 'C' 13.8.69. To BAC for mods 8.70. Ret'd 19 Sqdn 30.12.70. To 60 MU, Leconfield, for Major serv 21.8.72. Ret'd 19 Sqdn 26.1.73. Cat 3 19.2.74 cannon shell link ingestion damage ROS 431 MU, Brüggen. Ret'd 19 Sqdn 18.3.74. To 92 Sqdn coded 'C' 1.1.77. wfu 5.4.77 total flying time 3,285 hours, to Leuchars as 8535M for decoy. To Leuchars store 10.80. Sold to Museum of Flight, East Fortune 8.5.82.

Lightning F.2A
XN782/8539M
Luftarhtausstelling, Kiel.
f/f 20.11.62. Pilot R.P. Beamont. Aw Coll. 18.2.63. To 19 Sqdn, Leconfield coded 'K' 19.2. 19 Sqdn to Gütersloh 23/24.9.65. To BAC Warton for F.2A conversion, ret'd 92 Sqdn coded 'K' 26.11.68. Ret'd Warton 15.6.71 for mods then to 60 MU, Leconfield, for Major serv. Ret'd 92 Sqdn 10.11.71. wfu 1.4.77 as 8539M for decoy use. To Wildenrath as decoy 9.83. Sold to Luftarhtausstelling Museum, Kiel, Germany 27.6.86, arr 9.86.

Lightning F.2A
XN784/8540M
Air Classic München, Germany.
f/f 26.1.63. Pilot J.K. Isherwood. Aw Coll.19.3.63, to 19 Sqdn, Leconfield coded 'J', 19 Sqdn to Gütersloh 9.65. To BAC Warton for conversion to F.2A 31.1.96, ret'd 19 Sqdn 29.9.69 coded 'J'. To BAC for mods 5.70, ret'd 19 Sqdn coded 'L' 19.6.70. To BAC for mods 21.1.71, ret'd 19 Sqdn 4.3.71. Cat 3 18.3.74 ROS 431 MU, ret'd 19 Sqdn coded 'R'. wfu 1.4.77, to Brüggen by 9.83 as 854OM for decoy use. Gifted to Stadt Münchengladbach 11.7.85. arr 22.7.85.

Lightning F.6
XP693/G-FSIX
L.F.C. Exeter Airport.
f/f 16.6.62 as F.3. Pilot J. Dell. Aw Coll. 24.5.63, to A Sqdn, A&AEE, Boscombe Down. Transferred to MOA charge 4.10.63. Ret'd A&AEE 1.11.67. To BAC Warton for conversion to F.6 interim 19.1.68, then to BAC for chase-plane duties with Jaguars, Canberras, Lightnings and Strikemasters. To MRCA avionics programme 3.72. To A&AEE for Tornado cannon development 1974. To MoD(PE) based at Warton for use as Tornado F.3/EAP high-speed target. Contract expired 16.12.92. Sold to Lightning Flying Club as G-FSIX 22.12.92, flown to Exeter Airport. Expected to return to flying status.

Lightning F.3
XP706/8925M
L.L.P.S., Strubby, Lincs.
f/f 28.10.63. Pilot T.M.S. Ferguson. Aw Coll. 13.7.64, to 74 Sqdn, Leuchars coded 'L'. To 111 Sqdn, Wattisham, coded 'D' 24.12.66. Cat 3 landing accident 4.1.68, ret'd 111 Sqdn 15.1. To 60 MU for Major serv, 8.5.69. Ret'd 111 Sqdn 30.1.70. Cat 3 ROS 71 MU 9.71. Also Cat 3 ROS CWP/71 MU 7.72 and ROS 71 MU 2.73. Ret'd 111 Sqdn 19.3.73. To 23 Sqdn, Leuchars, coded 'R' 16.5.74. To Binbrook store 17.11.75. From store 4.76, to ASSF 23.8.77 then to 5 Sqdn coded 'AR'. To MEAS 1981/82. To 11 Sqdn coded 'BM' 14.9.82. To LFT coded 'DD' 24.6.83. wfu 7.85 to store, at Binbrook as 8925M for decoy use 9.2.86. Sold to Lincs Lightning Preservation Society at Strubby, arr 20.12.87.

Lightning F.3
XP745/8453M
RAF Boulmer gate
f/f 18.3.64. Pilot D. deVilliers. Aw Coll. 20.5.65, to 56 Sqdn, Wattisham, coded 'J'. Cat 3 accident ROS 24.6.66, ret'd 56 Sqdn 31.10.66. To Wattisham TFF loan 6.2.67, ret'd 56 Sqdn 31.3. 56 Sqdn to Akrotiri, Cyprus. To 60 MU Leconfield for Major serv 16.6.69. To 29 Sqdn, Wattisham coded 'H' 15.4.70 Cat 3 ROS 71 MU 27.5.70, ret'd 29 Sqdn 12.8.70. Cat 3 fire damage during engine start ROS CWP 4.6.71, ret'd 29 Sqdn 7.3.72. Cat 3 ROS 71 MU 2.73, ret'd 29 Sqdn 17.10.73. wfu 1.1.75 to Wattisham store, to 60 MU 4.2.75 as NES, to RAF Boulmer as gate guard as 8453M 31.3.76. On display 13.12.76.

Lightning F.3
XR713/8953M
111 Sqdn, Leuchars
f/f 21.10.64. Pilot D. deVilliers. Aw Coll 8.1.65, to 111 Sqdn, Wattisham, coded 'C'. Cat 3 ROS 60 MU 7.66. Ret'd 111 Sqdn 1.12.66. Loan to Wattisham TFF 1.67 to 26.5.67 when ret'd 111 Sqdn. To BAC for mods, arrester hook, 7.67 ret'd 111 Sqdn 25.10.67. Cat 3 landing accident ROS CWP 6.12.68, ret'd 111 Sqdn 13.11.69. To 60 MU for Major serv 16.2.71, ret'd 111 Sqdn coded 'A' 25.11.71. To 5 Sqdn Binbrook coded 'S' 7.10.74. Loan to LTF uncoded 6.3.76. To ASSF store Binbrook, 7.76. To 11 Sqdn coded 'O' 5.9.78. To ASSF 1980. To LTF coded 'O' 26.1.81. To 5 Sqdn coded 'AR' 29.4.81. Loan to 11 Sqdn, ret'd 5 Sqdn coded 'AP' then to LTF coded 'BC' 20.8.85. wfu 4.3.87. To Leuchars for BDR 9.3.87. To 111 Sqdn for display.

Lightning F.3
XR718/8932M
Blyth Valley Aviation Collection.
f/f 14.12.64. Pilot D. deVilliers. Aw Coll. 1.4.65, to 56 Sqdn, Wattisham, coded 'D'. Cat 3 ROS 71 MU/CWP 15.7.66. Ret'd 56 Sqdn 8.2.67. To 29 Sqdn, Wattisham, coded 'C' 1.5.67. To 60 MU for Major serv. 3.8.69. To 226 OCU, Coltishall 3.6.70. Cat 3 landing damage ROS 71 MU 6.3.71. Ret'd 226 OCU 30.6.72, Cat 3 damage ROS 71 MU 6.6.73, ret'd 226 OCU 26.6.73. To BAC Warton store for possible sale 4.9.74. To Wattisham ASSF 14.10.74. To 5 Sqdn, Binbrook, uncoded 3.6.76. To LTF coded 'C' 24.11.76. To 5 Sqdn coded 'AS'. To 11 Sqdn uncoded 9.5.84 then to LTF as 'DB' 29.4.86, later recoded 'DE' 29.10.86. wfu 9.2.87 then to Wattisham as 8932M for BDR. Sold to Blyth Valley Aviation Collection, Walpole, Staffs 1992.

Lightning F.6
XR724
Lightning Association, Binbrook.
f/f 10.2.65, as F.3. Pilot D. deVilliers. Aw Coll. 30.4.65. Conversion to F.6 Aw Coll. 15.6.67, to 11 Sqdn coded 'M' 19.6.67. To 60 MU for Major serv 4.5.68. To 11 Sqdn coded 'K' 24.6.68. Cat 3 for gun-pack fit and repairs ROS 71 MU 21.11.75. To ASSF Binbrook 4.5.76. Ret'd 11 Sqdn 10.8.76. Ret'd ASSF 19.4.78, to LTF coded 'K' then to 11 Sqdn coded 'B' 2.7.79. To ASSF for wing root mods 5.4.80. Ret'd 5 Sqdn coded 'AG' 4.1.81. 11 Sqdn loan 9.6.82, ret'd 5 Sqdn coded 'AV' 7.7.82. To 11 Sqdn coded 'BC' 4.10.83. To 5 Sqdn coded 'AE' 14.4.86. To MoD(PE)/BAC Warton for Tornado F.3 trials flight 12.4.88. wfu 27.6.90 to store 27 MU Shawbury. Declared for sale 7.91, to Lightning Association as G-BTSY. Flown to Binbrook 23.7.92, kept in taxying condition.

Lightning F.6
XR725
Lightning Association, Binbrook.
f/f 19.2.65. Pilot T.M.S. Ferguson. Aw Coll. 10.5.65, to store. Converted to F.6 to 23 Sqdn, Leuchars, coded 'A' 17.8.67. Cat 3 ROS 60 MU 26.10.67, ret'd 23 Sqdn 4.1.68. To 5 Sqdn loan coded 'A' 8.12.69. To 74 Sqdn FEAF coded 'A' 5.1.70. 60 MU, Leconfield, Major serv 22.9.71. To 56 Sqdn Akrotiri, NEAF, 8.5.72 coded 'P'. Cat 3 accident ROS 103 MU 5.6.73, ret'd. 56 Sqdn. 56 Sqdn to Wattisham 11 Group 21.1.75. To ASSF Binbrook 12.5.76. To Leconfield pool coded 'J' 2.6.76 then to 5 Sqdn still coded 'J'. To ASSF store 4.10.77. To LTF coded 'F' 15.4.80 became 'DF' in 1982. To 11 Sqdn coded 'BA' 14.10.85. Last flight after 3,870 hours 17.12.87. wfu 8.4.88 used as decoy. Sold to G. Beck (Tanks and Vessels) Ltd 24.6.88, moved by road 7.88. Sold to Lightning Association and returned to Binbrook by 16.11.91.

Lightning F.6
XR728
Lightning Preservation Group.
f/f 17.4.65. Pilot D. deVilliers. Aw Coll. 10.5.65, held at Warton for F.6 conversion. Aw Coll. 30.10.67. to 23 Sqdn Leuchars coded 'D'. 11 Sqdn loan 1.5.70, ret'd 23 Sqdn 8.6.70. To 60MU, Leconfield Major serv 13.5.71, ex-Major 24.11.71. To 56 Sqdn,

Akrotiri, coded 'D' 15.12.71. Cat 3 ROS 103MU 21.8.73, ret'd 56 Sqdn 19.9.73. 56 Sqdn to Wattisham 31.1.75. To ASSF Brinbrook 1.7.76. To 5 Sqdn coded 'J' 27.6.78, then to LTF coded 'D' named 'Tiverton Target Trainer', later recoded 'DD'. To 11 Sqdn coded 'BA' 1.2.82, recoded 'BF' 11.6.85. 5 Sqdn loan from LTF coded 'JS'. To 5 Sqdn coded 'JS' 3.11.87. Last flight 29.4.88 3,708 hours 40 mins. Placed on disposal list 23.5.88. Sold to Lightning Preservation Group, Bruntingthorpe. Maintained in taxying condition.

Lightning F.3
XR749/8926M/8934M
Teeside Airport
f/f 30.4.65. Pilot T.M.S. Ferguson. To Store Warton for poss F.6 conv 18.5.65. To TFF Wattisham 5.10.67. 56 Sqdn Akrotiri coded 'Q' 31.10.67. Cat3 ROS 103 MU 13.11.70 ret'd 56 Sqdn 7.8.71. To 60 MU Leconfield Major Serv 15.9.71. 5 Sqdn Binbrook 30.10.72. Store ASSF 30.4.76. Ret'd 5 Sqdn 18.4.78. To LTF 25.9.81. 11 Sqdn coded 'BM' 10.12.82. To LTF coded 'DA' 6.2.85. Ret'd 11 Sqdn 17.11.87. wfu 9.2.87. as 8926M later 8934M for Leuchars BDR. Sold to Buck Inn at Chop Gate, Yorks, now at Teeside Airport for restoration.

Lightning F.3
XR751
Lower Tremar, Cornwall
f/f 31.5.65. Pilot J.K. Isherwood. Aw Coll. 3.6.65 stored awaiting possible conversion Warton. To 60 MU, Leconfield for storage 11.1.68. Aw Coll. 2.12.70, to 226 OCU, Coltishall 3.12. To 29 Sqdn coded 'Q' 2.4.71, then to 5 Sqdn coded 'R' 13.11.72. Cat 3 ROS 71 MU 13.2.74, ret'd 5 Sqdn 26.4.74. Loan 11 Sqdn 15.10.75 to 5.2.76, ret'd 5 Sqdn. ASSF, Binbrook, 16.3.78. 11 Sqdn loan 15.1.79, then to LTF 8.2.79 later wore 111 Sqdn colours as 'D' later 'C' for 25th Anniversary. Ret'd ASSF 6.12.79. To LTF coded 'A' 2.4.80, then ret'd ASSF 22.10.80. To LTF coded 'DA' 23.9.82. wfu 21.9.97, 2,060 flying hours. Sold to buyer in Cornwall, moved by road 21.6.88.

Lightning F.6
XR753/8969M
11 Sqdn, RAF Leeming.
f/f 23.6.65. Pilot R.P. Beamont. Aw Coll. (as F.3A) 16.11.65, to FCTU, Binbrook, coded 'U'. Mods by 60 MU ROS, ret'd recoded 'T' 23.2.67. To 23 Sqdn, Leuchars, coded 'V' 28.7.67, then to BAC for full mods to F.6 22.3.68. To 60 MU for RAF prep 17.7.69, then 23 Sqdn coded 'A' 17.8.71. To ASSF, Binbrook, 3.11.75. 5 Sqdn coded 'F' 12.2.76, recoded 'A' 4.10.76. Cat 3 ROS CWP 25.7.77 ret'd 5 Sqdn 23.11.77. To 11 Sqdn coded 'BA' 30.7.80, ret'd 5 Sqdn. Coded 'AG' 1.9.82., later recoded 'AC' 25.3.85. To 11 Sqdn coded 'BP' 22.10.86. wfu 8.4.88 allocated Coltishall for BDR, later cancelled and flown to Leeming. Total time 4,285 flying hours. To 11(Tornado) Sqdn for display.

Lightning F.6
XR755
Callington, Cornwall
f/f 15.7.65. Pilot R.P. Beamont. Aw Coll. 10.12.65, to 5 Sqdn coded 'A' 13.12. Ret'd BAC for full F.6 conversion 7.4.67, then to 5 Sqdn coded 'O' 8.9.69. Cat 3 ROS CWP 4.7.69, ret'd 5 Sqdn 8.9.69. To 60 MU Major serv 5.4.72, ret'd 5 Sqdn 29.6.72. ASSF, Binbrook, 16.2.76, ret'd 5 Sqdn recoded 'F' 15.6.76. ASSF 14.12.79, then 11 Sqdn loan 13.2.80, ret'd 5 sqdn coded 'J' 9.7.80. To 11 Sqdn coded 'BJ' 8.8.80, recoded 'BF' 5.12.83, then 'BN' 24.3.86. Last flight 17.12.87, 4,094 hours. wfu 4.1.88, sold to buyer in Cornwall 21.6.88, moved by road 24.6.88.

Lightning F.6
XR770
Museum of Weapons Technology, Humberside.
f/f 16.12.65. Pilot R.P. Beamont. Aw Coll. 26.9.66, to 74 Sqdn, Leuchars, coded 'C' 27.9.74 Sqdn to Tengah, FEAF, 6–12.6.67. To 60 MU Major serv 14.9.70, then to 23 Sqdn, Leuchars, coded 'L' 26.5.72. To 56

Sqdn, Wattisham, coded 'D' 30.6.75. ASSF, Binbrook, 1.7.76, then to 5 Sqdn coded 'B' 28.11.79. To 11 Sqdn/LAF coded 'X' ret'd 5 Sqdn coded 'AA' 21.4.83, recoded 'AJ' 1984 then to 'AA' 13.11.85. wfu 4.5.88, 4,022 flying hours. Sold to Museum of Weapons Technology, Humberside, 10.6.88 wearing code 'JS', moved by road 18.6.88.

Lightning F.6
XR771
Midland Air Museum, Coventry.
f/f 20.1.66. Pilot T.M.S. Ferguson. Aw Coll. 24.10.66, to 74 Sqdn, Leuchars, coded 'D'. 74 Sqdn to Tengah 6–12.6.67. To BAC for mods 2.6.68 then ret'd 74 Sqdn 1.11.68. To 56 Sqdn, Akrotiri coded 'C' 9.71. Cat 3 and mods ROS 103MU 16.8.72, ret'd 56 Sqdn 4.10.72. 56 Sqdn to Wattisham 31.1.75. ASSF, Binbrook, 1.7.76, then to 5 Sqdn coded 'C' 21.11.78. ASSF 18.2.80, ret'd 5 Sqdn 30.10.80. ASSF 22.4.81, then to 11 Sqdn/LAF coded 'Y' 2.3.83. Recoded 'BA' 1.8.83. To 5 Sqdn coded 'AN' 18.3.86, ret'd 11 Sqdn coded 'BM' 4.1.88. Last flight 15.3.88, 3,554 flying hours, wfu 21.3.88, sold to Magnatel Ltd for M.A.M. 21.6.88, moved by road 15.7.88.

Lightning F.6
XR773
L.F.C., Exeter Airport.
f/f 28.2.66. Pilot R.P. Beamont. Aw Coll. 4.11.66, to 74 Sqdn coded 'F' 8.11.66. 74 Sqdn to Tengah 6.67. To 56 Sqdn, Akrotiri, coded 'N' 7.9.71. ASSF Binbrook 15.3.75, then to 5 Sqdn coded 'A' 20.9.75. To 11 Sqdn coded 'D' 27.7.76. To 5 Sqdn/LAF coded 'AH' 8.6.81. ASSF 2.10.81, then 11 Sqdn uncoded 1.11.84. To LTF coded 'DF' 24.4.86, then to 5 Sqdn coded 'AB' 21.1.86. To 11 Sqdn coded 'BR' 25.9.86. To MoD(PE)/BAe Warton 27.6.88. wfu 17.12.92, sold to Lightning

In safe keeping at the Newark Air Museum is T.5 XS417 seen here during its flying days in 1981 at Mildenhall. *(CP RUSSELL-SMITH)*

Flying Club, Exeter Airport as G-OPIB, arr 23.12.92.

Lightning T.5
XS417
Newark Air Museum, Notts.
f/f 17.7.64. Pilot J. Dell. To A&AEE 18.7.64. Aw Coll. 25.5.65 to 226 OCU, Coltishall, 26.5.65. To 23 Sqdn, Leuchars, coded 'Z' 21.12.65. Cat 3 ROS CWP/60 MU 6.6.66, ret'd 23 Sqdn 24.1.67. ASSF, Binbrook, 11.3.75, then 11 Sqdn loan 20.3.75, ret'd 23 Sqdn 11.4.75. To 56 Sqdn Wattisham, coded 'Z', later 'W' 20.10.75. ASSF, Binbrook, 1.7.76. To LTF Coningsby, coded 'W' 9.8.76. To 11 Sqdn coded 'T' 14.12.79, recoded 'BT' 30.7.80, then to 5 Sqdn as 'BT' 4.2.83. To LTF coded 'DZ' 4.2.83, then to 11 Sqdn 6.11.86. Last flight 18.5.87, 2,603 flying hours. wfu and sold to Newark Air Museum, moved by road 29.7.88.

Lightning T.5
XS420
Wellesley Avn., Narborough, Norfolk.
f/f 23.1.65. Pilot D.M. Knight. Aw Coll. 20.4.65 to 226 OCU 29.4.65. Cat 3 ROS 60 MU 14.12.65, ret'd 226 OCU 27.5.66. Cat 3 ROS CWP 31.1.73, ret'd 226 OCU 14.9.73. ASSF, Binbrook, 10.9.75, then to LTF coded 'V' 20.9.76. Cat 3 13.4.75, ret'd LTF recoded 'Y' 3.5.79. ASSF 27.2.80, 5 Sqdn loan 27.11.80, ret'd LTF coded 'DU' 17.12.80. Last flight 5.83, 2,296 flying hours. wfu 1.6.83 to Cat 5 spares and Binbrook decoy 21.9.87. Sold to M. Boulding Group 16.6.88. Moved by road to Wellesley Aviation, Narborough, Norfolk, 25.7.88.

Lightning T.5
XS422
Air and Naval Museum, Southampton.
f/f 24.3.65. Pilot T.M.S. Ferguson. Aw Coll. 28.5.65, to 226 OCU 1.6.65. Cat 3 accident ROS and mods 60 MU 14.12.65, ret'd 226 OCU 24.6.66. To 111 Sqdn, Wattisham coded 'T' 15.8.69. 29 Sqdn loan 23.6.69, ret'd 111 Sqdn 17.12.69. To 60 MU Major serv 20.5.71 then to 29 Sqdn coded 'Z' 16.3.72. To 56 Sqdn, Akrotiri, coded 'Z' 17.10.72. 56 Sqdn to Wattisham, 22.1.75. Loan to MoD(PE) ETPS, Boscombe Down, 3.7.75. Transferred to MoD charge 28.3.77. Last flight 9.87. 2,210 flying hours, to store Boscombe Down. By 1989 in store at Southampton with Air and Naval Museum.

Lightning T.5
XS451/8503M
L.F.C., Exeter Airport
f/f 3.6.65. Pilot D. deVilliers. Aw Coll. 19.11.65, to 5 Sqdn, Binbrook, coded 'T'. To 226 OCU 30.11.71. ASSF, Binbrook, 23.8.75 then to 11 Sqdn coded 'X' 17.9.75. To LTF uncoded 31.10.75. ASSF store 19.7.76, ret'd LTF. Last flight 25.11.76, 1,596 flying hours. To CTTS St. Athan as 8503M for GI 14.9.80. To Missile Training School Newton 1.4.80. Originally sold to Flight Systems Inc. 29.7.87. Sale cancelled, to store at V.A.T., Cranfield, by 4.88. Sold to Lightning Flying Club, Plymouth, by 9.89. Registered G-LTNG 8.11.89. Expected to fly 1994.

Lightning T.5
XS452
Arnold Glass store, Cranfield
f/f 30.6.65. Pilot D. deVilliers. Aw Coll. 17.9.65 to 226 OCU 20.9. Cat 3 mods 60 MU Leconfield, ret'd 226 OCU 8.7.66. 60 MU Major serv 21.1.71 then to 111 Sqdn, Wattisham coded 'T' 12.11.71. 29 Sqdn loan 12.10.72, ret'd 111 Sqdn 5.3.73. To 56 Sqdn, Akrotiri 27.2.74, then to Station flight. To 11 Sqdn, Binbrook coded 'T' 29.1.75. To LTF uncoded 1.10.75 then to 5 Sqdn coded 'Y' 2.4.76. ASSF, Binbrook, 9.8.76. To 11 Sqdn coded 'T' 10.5.77, then to ASSF store 6.12.79. To LTF coded 'Z' 30.6.80, then 11 Sqdn coded 'BT' 18.3.85. To LTF coded 'DZ' 30.6.80, ret'd 11 Sqdn coded 'BT' 18.3.85. Ret'd LTF coded 'DZ' 12.3.86, then to 11 Sqdn coded 'BT' 4.9.86. Last flight 29.6.86, 3,011 flying hours. wfu 14.8.87. Sold to Arnold Glass 24.6.88, flown to Cranfield 29.6.88, registered as G-BPFE. Sold to Tony Hulls 1994.

XS456
T.A. Smith & Co., Wainfleet, Lincs.
f/f 26.10.65. Pilot T.M.S. Ferguson. Aw Coll. 20.12.65 to 56 Sqdn, Wattisham, coded 'A' 21.12.65. Recoded 'X' 27.1.67. Loan to Wattisham TFF 23.2.67, ret'd 56 Sqdn 3.4.67. 56 Sqdn to Akrotiri 9–11.5.67. Cat 3 accident ROS 103 MU 20.1.70, ret'd 56 Sqdn 20.5.70. To 11 Sqdn, Binbrook, coded 'T' 12.2.75. ASSF, Binbrook, 9.12.75, to LTF coded 'T' 21.2.77. Loan to 11 Sqdn uncoded 15.6.81, ret'd LTF coded 'DT' 26.8.81. Recoded 'DX' 31.7.86. wfu 2,314 flying hours 21.4.87. Sold to T.A. Smith Ltd, 3.7.88, moved by road 20.7.88.

Lightning T.5
XS458
Arnold Glass store, Cranfield
f/f 3.12.65. Pilot D.M. Knight. Aw Coll. 31.1.66 to 226 OCU 3.2.66. ASSF, Binbrook 11.9.74, then to 5 Sqdn uncoded 30.9.75. To LTF uncoded 1.10.75, then to ASSF 23.2.77. Ret'd LTF coded 'B' 4.5.77, ret'd ASSF 6.6.78. To 5 Sqdn coded 'T' 15.1.79 – became part of 5 Sqdn/LAF 10.80. To ASSF 24.7.81. To 11 Sqdn coded 'BT' 29.4.82, then LTF coded 'DX' 7.8.86, recoded 'DY' 4.9.86. wfu 21.4.87, 3,186 flying hours. Sold to Arnold Glass 24.6.88, flown to Cranfield 29.6.88. Sold to Buyer in Cyprus 1994.

Lightning T.5
XS459
Wellesley Avn, Narborough, Norfolk.
f/f 8.12.65. Pilot J. Dell. Aw Coll. 13.4.66, to 226 OCU 14.4.66. To 29 Sqdn coded 'T' 29.2.72. MoD(PE) loan 7.4.72, ret'd 29 Sqdn 16.5.72. Wattisham Storage Flight 1.1.75, then to 56 Sqdn coded 'X' 6.2.75. To LTF, Binbrook coded 'X' 27.5.76. ASSF 19.7.76, ret'd LTF 4.4.78. Recoded 'DX' 3.6.80, then recoded 'DW' 17.5.84. To 5 Sqdn coded 'AW' 17.12.86. Last flight 18.3.87, 2,307 flying hours. wfu 19.3. Sold to Wellesley Aviation 21.6.88, moved by road 25.7.88.

Lightning F.6
XS897
S.Y.A.M., Firbeck, Yorks
f/f 10.5.66. Pilot R.P. Beamont. Aw Coll. 21.12.66, to 74 Sqdn, Leuchars coded 'K'. 74 Sqdn to Tengah 6.67. To 56 Sqdn, Akrotiri, coded 'S' 7.9.71. Cat 3 ROS 103 MU 13.11.74, ret'd 56 Sqdn, Wattisham, 31.1.75. ASSF, Binbrook, 1.7.76. To 11 Sqdn coded 'H' 23.9.77, then to ASSF 1.3.79. Ret'd 11 Sqdn 1.4.81, recoded 'BD' 4.1.83. To 5 Sqdn coded 'AC' 7.4.86. Last flight 14.12.87 3,392 flying hours. wfu 4.1.88. Sold to G. Beck (Tanks and Vessels) Ltd Doncaster 24.6.88, moved by road 7.88. Sold to South Yorks Air Museum, Firbeck in 1993.

Lightning F.6
XS903
Y.A.M., Elvington, Yorks.
f/f 17.8.66. Pilot D. deVilliers. Aw Coll. 15.3.67. to 5 Sqdn coded 'A' 17.3.67. 60 MU Major serv 29.6.69, ret'd 5 Sqdn 31.3.70, recoded 'C' 15.7.70, returned to 'A' 1975. ASSF, Binbrook, 1.11.76. To 11 Sqdn coded 'BC' 14.10.80, recoded 'BE' 26.3.81. Ret'd 5 Sqdn coded 'AM' 20.8.84. To 11 Sqdn coded 'BA' 15.7.87, recoded 'BQ' 1988. wfu 4.5.88, 4,055 flying hours. To Yorkshire Air Museum 18.5.88.

Lightning F.6
XS904
Lightning Preservation Group, Lincs.
f/f 22.9.66. Pilot R.P. Beamont. Aw Coll. 17.4.67, to 11 Sqdn coded 'A' 19.4.67. 60 MU Major serv 2.8.70, ret'd 11 Sqdn 28.3.72. MoD(PE)loan6.10.72,ret'd11Sqdn16.10.72. ASSF 7.4.78, ret'd 11 Sqdn coded 'D' 1.2.80, recoded 'BQ' 20.2.86. To MoD(PE)/BAe Warton Tornado F.3 trials. Last flight 16.12.92, flown to Lightning Preservation Group, Bruntingthorpe 21.1.93.

Lightning F.6
XS919
Lower Tremar, Cornwall.
f/f 28.9.66. Pilot J.K. Isherwood. Aw Coll. 11.5.67, to 11 Sqdn coded 'C' 18.5 60MU

XS923 is up for sale by its owner Arnold Glass. This photo depicts the F.6 as 'A' of 5 Sqdn at Binbrook in 1970. (*CP RUSSELL-SMITH*)

Major Serv 7.2.72, to 56 Sqdn, Akrotiri, coded 'R' 29.6.72. 56 Sqdn to Wattisham 23.1.75. To 5 Sqdn coded 'F' 30.6.76. ASSF 24.5.78, ret'd 5 Sqdn coded 'AD' 11.2.81. To 11 Sqdn coded 'BN' 29.6.84. Last flight 15.3.86, 3,987 flying hours. wfu 16.9.87. Sold to T. Hobbs 21.6.88, moved to Lower Tremar by road 6.88.

Lightning
XS925/8961M
RAFM, Hendon.

f/f 26.1.67. Pilot R.P. Beamont. Aw Coll. 28.2.67, to 5 Sqdn coded 'L' 2.3.67. Cat 4 accident, ret'd Warton for repair 14.9.68. Ret'd 5 Sqdn 25.2.70. To 11 Sqdn coded 'J' 15.8.75, ret'd 5 Sqdn coded 'L' 15.10.75. ASSF,

When XA847 left the RAFM at Hendon, its place was taken by recently retired F.6 XS925 captured here at Finningley in 1975. (*CP RUSSELL-SMITH*)

Binbrook 24.3.77, ret'd 5 Sqdn coded 'D' 19.7.79. ASSF 11.2.80. 11 Sqdn loan coded 'AD' 26.10.82, ret'd 5 Sqdn 3.11.82. To 11 Sqdn 'BD' 14.6.85. wfu 24.7.87, 4,016 flying hours. To RAF Museum, Hendon by road 26.4.88.

Lightning F.6
XS928
BAe, Warton Gate
f/f 28.2.67. Pilot R.P. Beamont. Aw Coll 4.4.67. to 11 Sqdn, Leuchars, coded 'D' 5.4. To 74 Sqdn, Tengah, coded 'L' 5.1.70. Cat 3 fire damage, flown to Warton for repair 6.4.70. To 56 Sqdn, Akrotiri, coded 'E' 18.8.72. 56 Sqdn to Wattisham 22.1.75. ASSF, Binbrook, 1.7.76 then to 5 Sqdn coded 'K' 23.9.76. Recoded 'F' 30.1.80, ret'd ASSF 24.11.80. To 5 Sqdn coded 'AJ' 7.7.82, then to 11 Sqdn coded 'BJ' 21.6.83. Ret'd 5 Sqdn coded 'AH' 19.8.85, recoded 'AD' 6.3.87. To 11 Sqdn as 'AD' 3.2.88. wfu 21.3.88. To MOD(PE)BAe Warton 14.6.88. Began Major serv 1991, not completed, wfu 3.92. Spares removed for LFC, to gate 1993.

Lightning F.6
XS929/8970M
RAF Akrotiri gate
f/f 1.3.67. Pilot T.M.S. Ferguson. Aw Coll 27.4.67, to 11 Sqdn, Leuchars, coded 'E' 28.4. Cat 3 ROS 71 MU/CWP 6.8.70, ret'd 11 Sqdn 23.12.70. To 56 Sqdn, Akrotiri, coded 'L' 12.8.73. 56 Sqdn to Wattisham 23.1.75. ASSF, Binbrook, 1.7.76, then to 11 Sqdn coded 'E' 14.12.77. ASSF 8.8.79, ret'd 11 Sqdn 11.2.81. To LTF coded 'DG' 21.8.85, then to 11 Sqdn coded 'BG' 2.4.86. wfu 4.5.88, 3,601 flying hours, flown to Akrotiri 25.5.88. On display Akrotiri 20.5.89.

Lightning F.6
XS936
Castle Air, Liskeard, Cornwall.
f/f 31.5.67. Pilot J. Cockburn. Aw Coll 25.7.67, to 60 MU store 28.7. To 23 Sqdn Leuchars coded 'B' 23.8.67. Loan to MOA 23.12.70, ret'd 23 5.2.71. ASSF, Binbrook, 3.11.75 then to 11 Sqdn coded 'G' 2.6.76. ASSF 5.9.77, ret'd 11 Sqdn 1.3.79. To 5 Sqdn still coded 'G' 26.6.81. 5 Sqdn/Binbrook pool 14.7.81, ret'd 5 Sqdn coded 'L' 2.4.82. To LTF coded 'DF' 21.7.82, to 5 Sqdn coded 'AL' 7.4.83, ret'd LTF coded 'DF' 28.11.83. Ret'd 5 Sqdn coded 'AS' 30.5.85. Last flight 24.11.87, 3,962 flying hours. Sold to T. Hobbs 21.6.88, moved by road 23.6.88 Now on plinth at Castle Motors/Castle Air by 1989.

Currently flying on a pole is XS936, once 'B' of 23 Sqdn photographed at Dijon in 1975. The aircraft's current location is Liskeard, Cornwall, in the care of Castle Air/Castle Motors. (*CP RUSSELL-SMITH*)

Selected RSAF Lightning histories

Lightning F.53
53–681/ZF583
Solway Aviation Society, Carlisle Airport.

This particular RSAF Lightning F.53 is significant as it is the last aircraft flight-tested by Roly Beamont before retirement. 53–681, construction number 95286, was first flown with the 'B' class registration G-27-51 on 28 March 1968 from Samlesbury. After test flying from Warton the aircraft, piloted by Tim Ferguson, was delivered in company with 53-682, to Jeddah on 1 July – transiting via Cyprus using Victor tankers provided by the RAF.

After arrival '681, the first true export Lightning, was placed in store at Riyadh where it was to stay until issued to 6 Sqdn, RSAF, at Khamis Mushayt on 9 December 1971. A tour with the LCS (similar to the LTF) at Dharan began on 27 February 1975. This lasted until 5 January 1976 when '681 rejoined a front-line unit, in this case No.2 Sqdn at Dharan.

No.2 Sqdn was to transfer to the RSAF base at Tabuk on 25 November, taking 53-681 with them. By April 1980 the aircraft had been coded '210', the first digit reflecting the squadron number whilst the latter two depicted the aircraft's place in the squadron. This system was to change later to a single-letter code, that of '681 being 'H', this being retained on the fin right up to the aircraft's final flight on 7 January 1986.

Seven days later 53-681 was flown home to Warton as ZF583, its silver finish recalling the heyday of the Lightning in RAF service. In its 1,872 flights the Lightning had flown 1,884 hours. On 8 January 1989 the aircraft was sold to the Solway Aviation Society based at Carlisle Airport where it arrived a few weeks later.

Lightning F.53
53–693/ZF588
East Midlands Airport Aeropark

Lightning F.53 '693 is the 28th production aircraft built for the RSAF. Given the constructor's number 95300 it first flew from Samlesbury piloted by Tim Ferguson on 9 October 1968. Fifteen days later the Lightning made its ferry flight to Warton as G-27-63 where it was prepared for the transit flight to Saudi Arabia. On 23 May 1969 the aircraft left Warton to begin the flight to Jeddah staging via Akrotiri, Cyprus on the way. Pilot for the delivery flight was Andy Love.

Preparation for RSAF service was carried out by the resident BAC team, 53-693 finally joining the LCS at Dharan as 'L' during April. When the LCS moved to Khamis Mushayt '693 was to follow on 3 December 1969. A short loan to 2 Sqdn took place during July 1970 though the Lightning returned to the LCS one month later. Also based at Khamis Mushayt was another Lightning operator, No.6 Sqdn RSAF, who were to gain '693 in May 1975. The aircraft's tenure with the squadron was short however as it returned to the LCS, now at Riyadh, in 1976.

Another tour with a front-line unit began in January 1977 when '693 joined No.2 Sqdn at Tabuk in Northern Saudi Arabia. This was to be the aircraft's last operator as this Lightning became one of the twenty-two that were sold to BAe, returning home to Warton on 14 January 1986 for storage and possible resale.

After three years in storage 53-693, still

marked as ZF588, was finally disposed of to the East Midlands Aeropark near Leicester on 8 January 1989 where it has resided ever since.

Lightning F.53
53–696/ZF594
North East Aircraft Museum, Sunderland.
On 14 November 1968 test pilot John Cockburn lifted Lightning F.53, 53-696, from the runway at Samlesbury on its maiden flight, cunningly disguised as G-27-66. Upon landing at Warton, the aircraft began a series of shake-down flights that were to culminate in its ferry trip to Saudi Arabia. The pilot on this occasion was R. Ingham and as before, the aircraft staged via Akrotiri supported by RAF Victor tankers. Arriving at Jeddah on 3 June 1969 the Lightning joined the LCS with whom it was serving when they moved to RSAF Riyadh on 26 November 1972. Unfortunately not long after arrival, on 9 July, the aircraft suffered Category 3 fire damage which grounded it for the next few months. A tour at Dharan with 2 Sqdn followed the repair work, the aircraft remaining with them until transferring to 6 Sqdn at Khamis Mushayt in May 1975.

No.6 Sqdn was to move to King Abdul Aziz AB in June 1976, taking '696 with them, although this state of affairs only lasted until 23 January 1977 when '696 joined 2 Sqdn again, this time at King Faisal/Tabuk AB in the north of the country. A short tour on the strength of 13 Sqdn as 1308 began on 18 April 1978 and continued until 1982 when the aircraft returned again to 2 Sqdn. Initially coded 226 the aircraft later assumed the code 'Y'. It was still wearing this code when it made its last RSAF flight on 13 January 1986.

The next day, painted as ZF594, the aircraft headed for Warton where it was to enter long-term storage whilst awaiting possible resale. During its working life 53-696 had flown a total of 2,057.06 hours. With no market forthcoming, 53-696 was put up for disposal, being purchased by the NEAM for a token sum during 1988. In November of the following year 53-696 was moved to the Museum's premises near Sunderland to join the rest of this burgeoning collection.

Royal Saudi Air Force Lightnings

TYPE	S No.	RAF/'B'reg.	REMARKS
F.52	52-655	XN767	del 22.7.66, to 52-609
F.52	52-656	XN770	del 11.7.66, to 52-610
F.52	52-657	XN796	del 8.7.66, w/o 20.9.66
F.52	52-658	XN796	del 22.7.66, to 52-611
F.52	52-659	XN729	del 9.5.67, to 52-612
F.52		XN734	to Saudi support unit Warton as G-27-239 (F2A) now G-BNCA Cranfield
F.53	53-666	G-27-2	del 5.12.69 w/o 6.2.72
F.53	53-667	G-27-37	del 20.9.68 2Sqdn RSAF
F.53	53-668	ZF577, G-27-38	del 8.11.68 2Sqdn RSAF rtd 14.1.86
F.53	53-669	G-27-39	del 1.10.68 2 Sqdn RSAF
F.53	53-670	ZF576, G-27-40	del 8.11.68 2Sqdn RSAF rtd 14.1.86
F.53	53-671	ZF579, G-27-41	del 11.10.68 2Sqdn RSAF rtd 14.1.86
F.53	53-672	ZF580, G-27-42	del 18.11.68 LCU,2Sqdn rtd 14.1.86
F.53	53-673	G-27-43	del 23.8.68 2Sqdn RSAF
F.53	53-674	G-27-44	del 18.11.68 2Sqdn RSAF
F.53	53-675'209'	ZF581, G-27-45	del 16.9.68 2Sqdn RSAF rtd 14.1.86
F.53	53-676	ZF582, G-27-46	del 20.9.68 2Sqdn RSAF rtd 22.1.86
F.53	53-677	G-27-47	del 23.7.68 w/o 4.9.83
F.53	53-678	G-27-48	del 23.8.68 2Sqdn RSAF
F.53	53-679'206'	G-27-49	del 16.9.68 2Sqdn RSAF
F.53	53-680	G-27-50	del 23.7.68 2Sqdn RSAF
F.53	53-681	ZF583, G-27-51	del 1.7.68 2Sqdn RSAF rtd 14.1.86
F.53	53-682	ZF584, G-27-52	del 1.7.68 2Sqdn RSAF rtd 22.1.86
F.53	53-683	ZF585, G-27-53	del 11.3.69 2Sqdn RSAF rtd 14.1.86
F.53	53-684	G-27-54	del 18.11.68 2Sqdn RSAF
F.53	53-685	ZF591, G-27-55	del 31.1.69 2Sqdn RSAF rtd 14.1.86
F.53	53-686	ZF592, G-27-56	del 17.4.69 LCU,2Sqdn rtd 22.1.86
F.53	53-687	G-27-57	del 17.4.69 2Sqdn RSAF
F.53	53-688	ZF586, G-27-58	del 17.4.69 2Sqdn RSAF rtd 22.1.86
F.53	53-689'J'	G-27-59	del 18.11.68 2Sqdn RSAF
F.53	53-690	G-27-60	del 4.9.68 w/o?
F.53	53-691	ZF587, G-27-61	del 31.1.69 2Sqdn RSAF rtd 22.1.86
F.53	53-692	ZF593, G-27-62	del 17.4.69 2Sqdn RSAF rtd 22.1.68
F.53	53-693'L'	ZF588, G-27-63	del 23.5.69 2Sqdn RSAF rtd 14.1.86
F.53	53-694	G-27-64	del 3.6.69 w/o 9.76
F.53	53-695	G-27-65	del 23.5.69 2Sqdn RSAF
F.53	53-696	ZF594, G-27-66	del 3.6.69 2Sqdn RSAF rtd 14.1.86
F.53	53-697	G-27-67	del 26.8.69 w/o 3.5.70
F.53	53-698	G-27-68	del 3.6.69 2Sqdn RSAF
F.53	53-699	G-27-69	del 3.6.69 2Sqdn RSAF
F.53	53-700	ZF589, G-27-233	del 4.9.72 2Sqdn RSAF rtd 22.1.86

T.54	54-650	XM989	del 6.6.66 to 54-607] one on disp.
T.54	54-651	XM992	del 6.6.66 to 54-608] Dharan ?
T.55	55-710	XS460	w/o 7.3.67 before delivery
T.55	55-711'A'	ZF597, G-27-70	del 27.8.69 LCU,2Sqdn rtd 14.1.86
T.55	55-712'B'	G-27-71	del 11.7.69 w/o 21.5.74
T.55	55-713'C'	ZF598, G-27-72	del 27.8.69 LCU,2Sqdn rtd 14.1.86
T.55	55-714'D'	ZF595, G-27-73	del 11.7.69 LCU,2Sqdn rtd 22.1.86
T.55	55-715'E'	ZF596, G-27-74	del 11.3.69 LCU,2Sqdn rtd 22.1.86
T.55	55-716'F'	G-27-75	del 30.9.69 LCU,2Sqdn
F.1		XG313, G-27-115	Inst A/F Dharan scrapped?

Kuwait Air Force Lightnings

TYPE	S.No.	'B' reg	REMARKS
T.55	55-410	G-27-78	del 18.12.68 'A' wfu 1977 last noted Kuwait University
T.55	55-411	G-27-79	del 3.12.69 'B' wfu 1977 last noted Messila Beach Club
F.53	53-412	G-27-80	del 18.12.68 'C' wfu 1977 last noted Kuwait Int Apt.
F.53	53-413	G-27-81	del 25.3.69 'E' w/o 1975
F.53	53-414	G-27-82	del 25.2.69 'F' w/o 10.4.71
F.53	53-415	G-27-83	del 23.5.69 'H' wfu 1977 last noted Kuwait Int Apt.
F-53	53-416	G-27-84	del 11.7.69 'J' wfu 1977 last noted Kuwait Int Apt.
F.53	53-417	G-27-85	del 23.5.69 'K' wfu 1977 last noted Ahmed Al Juber AB
F.53	53-418	G-27-86	del 11.7.69 'L' wfu 1977 last noted Ali Salem AB 2.83
F.53	53-419	G-27-87	del 26.8.69 'M' w/o 2.8.71
F.53	53-420	G-27-88	del 19.7.69 'N' w/o?
F.53	53-421	G-27-89	del 19.7.69 'O' wfu 1977 last noted KAF HQ 6.85
F.53	53-422	G-27-90	del 4.12.69 'P' wfu 1977 last noted Kuwait Int Apt.
F.53	53-423	G.27.91	del 3.12.69 'R' wfu 1977 last noted Kuwait Int Apt.

Lightnings Clinging on to Life – Just!

THE MAIN part of this section deals with those complete airframes surviving in fairly good circumstances around the world. Others are not so lucky, moving on after grounding to other establishments that treat them in a far rougher manner.

Fire training is one area of activity that fully occupies these old airframes. Three Lightnings employed in this role are XG327, used for brake fire training at Manston; XP741 in use for general burning and T.4 XM997 currently based at Catterick, although due to move when the base shuts, which finds itself occupied in a similar task.

A quick and more violent end awaits many of the other redundant Lightnings at the Pendine and Otterburn ranges where they act as targets for their airborne brethren. At Otterburn are Lightnings XP694 and XP702 whilst on the Pendine ranges lurk XM139, XM147, XP708, XP735, XP748 (the ex-Binbrook gate guard) and F.6 XS895. Another establishment that puts aircraft to a violent end is the Proof and Experimental Establishment on Foulness Island where long suffering F.2As XN726, XN771 and XN795 are now accompanied by XR756, XS421 and XS921 which act as targets for a variety of machine-gun and cannon shells.

The slowest method of aircraft destruction is Battle Damage Repair Training and this occupies T.4 XM987 and F.2A XN774 at Coningsby, this also being the fate of XR718 at Wattisham, XR749 at Leuchars and XR754 at Honington.

In contrast to the lingering Lightnings of Britain, many of those in RAF Germany find further employment as 'Special Display' or decoy aircraft. Some also fulfil the more traditional BDR role. Brüggen currently employs the most retired Lightnings, using T.4s XM970 and XM973 plus F.2As XN783 and XN789 as decoys whilst F.2A XN792 is used for BDR training in company with F.6 XS901. Wildenrath, scheduled to close soon, has XM995 and XN778 in the decoy role with XR727 in use for BDR purposes. Over at Laarbruch, the former RAFG Lightning base, are F.2A XN732 as a decoy with XN788 and XR758 being employed in the BDR role.

The Lightning also survives in smaller bits mainly in the form of noses. These are popular with the smaller museums and collections as their reduced size cuts the cost of upkeep. From the pre-production F.1 batch the noses of XG325 and XG331 survive with two ATC units, No.1312 Sqdn at Southend and No.2342 Sqdn at Innsworth. The Royal Air Force also maintains an exhibition nose – this being from XM191 which is based with the RAFEF at St. Athan. Preservation groups also acquired noses, that of F.3 XP703 going to the Lightning Preservation Group at Bruntingthorpe having survived the earlier machinations of the BAe Warton Fire Service. Also with this organisation is the nose of F.6 XS932 which came from the store at Rossington. The nose of F.6 XR757, also late of Rossington, is now at the Museum of Weapons Technology, New Waltham, where it joins earlier resident,

T.5 XS457. A museum in the making at Narborough, Norfolk, is run by Wellesley Aviation and they have gained the nose of F.6 XS933 which joins their other two complete airframes.

Other Lightnings do survive around the country, but they are not included as they are on stations due to close, thereby in danger of scrapping, or they are on fire dumps and their existence is at best tenuous. Final mention must be made of Binbrook Primary School which has a late variant fin outside which wears the colours of both 5 and 11 Squadrons.

Appendix A
Lightning Production and Contracts

P.1A
Three aircraft to Spec F23/49. Contract SP/6/Aircraft/5175 CB7a
WG760, WG763, WG765 (structural test specimen).

P.1B
Three aircraft to Spec F23/49. Contract SP/6/Aircraft/5175 CB7a
XA847, XA853, XA856.

P.1B/F
1 pre-production aircraft, 20 ordered to Contract SP/6/Aircraft/10351 CB7a
XG307–XG313, XG325–XG337.

F.1 Production Aircraft
20 ordered to Contract SP/6/Aircraft/12715 CB7a
XM134–XM147, XM163–XM168.

T.4 prototypes
To Spec T178 D&D, 2 aircraft with company designation P.11, no contract number issued.
XL628, XL629.

F.1A production aircraft
30 ordered to Contract SP/6/Aircraft/15445 CB7a
XM169–XM192, XM213–XM216 (XM217 & XM218 ordered but not built).

T.4 production aircraft
20 ordered to Contracts SP/6/Aircraft/15445 & 12715 CB7a
XM966–XM974, XM987–XM997.

F.2 Production Aircraft
44 ordered to Contract KC/2D/03 CB7a
XN723–XN735, XN767–XN797.

F.3 Production Aircraft
48 ordered to Contract KC/2D/049 CB7a
XP693–XP708, XP735–XP765.

F.3/F.6 Production Aircraft
22 ordered to Contract KC/2T/079 CB7a
XR711–XR728, XR747–XR751, XR723–XR728 & XR747–XR751 delivered as F.6.

F.3A/F.6 Interim Production Aircraft
16 ordered to Contract KD/2T/079 CB7a
XR752–XR767.

F.6 Production Aircraft
6 ordered to Contract KD/2T/079 CB7a
XR768–XR773.

F.6 Production Aircraft
33 ordered to Contract KD/2T/0139 CB7a
XS893–XS938.

T.5 Production Aircraft
20 ordered to Contract KC/2D/064 CB7a
XS416–XS423, XS449–XS560.

T.5 Production Aircraft
2 ordered to Contract KC/2D/188 CB7a
XV328, XV329.

T.55 Production Aircraft
6 ordered for RSAF
55-711 – 55-716.

T.55 Production Aircraft
2 ordered for KAF 55-410, 55-411.

F.53 Production aircraft
33 ordered for RSAF
53-667 – 53-699.

F.53 Production Aircraft
1 ordered for RSAF
53-700.

F.53 Production Aircraft
12 ordered for KAF
53-412 – 53-423.

Appendix B
P.1 and Lightning Production Airframe Totals

P.1A	WG760, WG763	2	WG765 1
P.1B	XA847/853/856	3	
P.1B/F.1	XG307–XG337	20	Test airframes 3
F.1	XM134–XM147		
	XM163–XM167	19	
F.1A	XM169–XM192		
	XM213–XM216	28	Test airframe 1
T.4/P.11	XL628, XL629	2	
T.4	XM966–XM974	8	
	XM987–XM997	12	
F.2	XN723–XN735	13	
	XN767–XN797	31	
F.3	XP693–XP708	16	
	XP735–XP765	31	
F.3	XR711–XR722	12	
F.6	XR723–XR728	6	
F.3	XR747–XR751	5	
F.6 int	XR752–XR767	16	
F.6	XR768–XR773	6	
	XS893–XS904	12	
	XS918–XS938	21	
T.5	XS416–XS423	8	
	XS449–XS460	12	
	XV328, XV329	2	
T55	55-711–716	6	
	55-410–411	2	
F.53	53-667–699	33	
F.53	53-700	1	
F.53	53-412–423	12	
Totals		339	5

Appendix C
RAF Lightning Operators

5 Sqdn RAF

Nov 62–Oct 65	Javelin FAW9	Binbrook
Dec 65–Dec 87	Lightning F.6	Binbrook
Jun 70–Sep 72	Lightning F.1A	Binbrook
Oct 72–Sep 87	Lightning F.3	Binbrook
31.12.87	Disbanded	
1.5.88	Reformed Tornado F.3	Coningsby

11 Sqdn RAF

Dec 62–Jan 66	Javelin FAW9	Gielenkirchen
Apr 67–May 88	Lightning F.6	Leuchars/Binbrook
Oct 72–May 86	Lightning F.3	Binbrook
30.4.88	Disbanded	
1.11.88	Reformed Tornado F.3	Leeming

19 Sqdn RAF

Oct 56–Jun 59	Hunter F.6	Leconfield
Dec 62–Oct 69	Lightning F.2	Leconfield/Gütersloh
Jan 68–Dec 76	Lightning F.2A	Gütersloh
31.12.76	Disbanded	
1.1.77	Reformed Phantom FGR2	Wildenrath

5 Sqdn painted red bars on the noses of their aircraft whilst their fins bore a Canadian Maple leaf. The F.6 is XS898 pictured at Leuchars in 1971. (*CP RUSSELL-SMITH*)

In later days grey and green camouflage intruded and is worn here by XP764 of 11 Sqdn in 1977. (*CP RUSSELL-SMITH*)

19 Squadron's F.2As always looked good with their big nose bars and fin badge; here XN724 displays both proudly in 1969. (*CP RUSSELL-SMITH*)

23 Sqdn RAF

Apr 62–Sep 62	Javelin FAW7	Leuchars
Aug 64–Nov 67	Lightning F.3	Leuchars
May 67–Oct 75	Lightning F.6	Leuchars
May 72–Oct 75	Lightning F.3	Leuchars
31.10.75	Disbanded	
1.11.75	Reformed Phantom FGR2	Coningsby

29 Sqdn RAF

Apr 61–May 67	Javelin FAW9	Wattisham
May 67–Dec 74	Lightning F.3	Wattisham
31.12.74	Disbanded	
1.1.75	Reformed Phantom FGR2	Coningsby

56 (Punjab) Sqdn RAF

Nov 58–Jan 61	Hunter F.6	Wattisham
Dec 60–Apr 65	Lightning F.1	Wattisham
Mar 65–Dec 71	Lightning F.3	Wattisham/Akrotiri by 11.4.75
Sept 71–Jun 76	Lightning F.6	Akrotiri/Wattisham by 21.1.75
28.6.76	Disbanded	
29.6.76	Reformed Phantom FGR2	Wattisham

74 (Trinidad) Sqdn RAF

Nov 57–Nov 60	Hunter F.6	Coltishall
Jun 60–Apr 64	Lightning F.1	Coltishall/Leuchars by 2.6.64
Apr 64–Sep 67	Lightning F.3	Leuchars
Sep 66–Aug 71	Lightning F.6	Leuchars/Tengah by 12.6.67
1.9.71	Disbanded	
19.10.84	Reformed Phantom F-4J (UK)	Wattisham

Caught just before touch-down is T.5 XV328 wearing the markings of 29 Sqdn. The location is Wattisham in 1967 and the nose bars look smaller than usual for the time. (*CP RUSSELL-SMITH*)

23 Squadron carried red and blue nose bars on their aircraft with a red stooping bird of prey on the fin. Both are worn with pride by XM178 at Leuchars in 1978. (CP RUSSELL-SMITH)

The Phoenix of 56 Sqdn sits well upon the Lightning, represented here by F.6 XR728 in 1975. (*CP RUSSELL-SMITH*)

Tiger overseas and XR773 taxies into its Tengah dispersal in 1967. (*CP RUSSELL-SMITH*)

92 (East India) Sqdn RAF

May 57–Apr 63	Hunter F.6	Leconfield
Apr 63–Jul 71	Lightning F.2	Leconfield/Gielenkirchen by 29.12.65, Gütersloh by 24.1.68
Aug 68–Mar 77	Lightning F.2A	Gütersloh
31.3.77	Disbanded	
1.4.77	Reformed Phantom FGR2	Wildenrath

111 Sqdn RAF

Nov 56–Aug 61	Hunter F.6	Wattisham
Apr 61–Feb 65	Lightning F.1A	Wattisham
Dec 64–Sep 74	Lightning F.3	Wattisham
May 74–Sep 74	Lightning F.6	Wattisham
30.9.74	Disbanded	
1.10.74	Reformed Phantom FGR2	Coningsby

AFDS/CFE

8.59	Coltishall
10.62	Binbrook
1.2.66	Disbanded, became FCTU

used Lightning F.1, F.1A, F.2, F.3, T.4

FCTU

1.2.66	Binbrook

used Lightning F.2, F.3, T.4

LCS

29.6.62	Middleton St. George
1.6.63	became 226 OCU

used Lightning F.1A, F.3, T.4, T.5

LTF ex 'C' Flight 11 Sqdn

10.74	Binbrook
3.76	Coningsby
1977	Binbrook
1.8.87	Disbanded

used Lightning F.3, T.5, F.6

Minus its previous black and yellow fin is Lightning F.3 XP749 of 111 Sqdn outbound from Wattisham in 1972. (*CP RUSSELL-SMITH*)

Complete with blue fin and spine is F.2A XN728 of 92 Sqdn captured at Gütersloh in 1970. (*CP RUSSELL-SMITH*)

In the beginning it was the LCU based at Middleton St. George. T.4 XM970 is pictured with others of its ilk in 1962. (*CP RUSSELL-SMITH*)

Once 226 OCU had been fully established its aircraft wore the markings of 145(S) Sqdn represented here by T.4 XM969 at Woodbridge in 1969. (*CP RUSSELL-SMITH*)

The need for fighter pilots in the Lightning force diminished in the early 1970s with the arrival of the Phantom. Thus the LTF was born; represented here by T.5 XS451 pictured here at Binbrook in 1976. *(CP RUSSELL-SMITH)*

Following on from 145 Sqdn came 65 Sqdn whose markings adorn T.4 XM970 in 1971. *(CP RUSSELL-SMITH)*

226 OCU

6.63	Middleton St. George 145 (Shadow) Sqdn
4.64	Coltishall
1966	Leconfield (Coltishall runway repairs)
5.71	145 (Shadow) Sqdn disbanded
5.71	65 (Shadow) Sqdn formed used F1A, T4
5.71	2T Sqdn formed used F3, T5
1972	Binbrook (Coltishall runway repairs)
17.6.74	226 OCU disbanded replaced by LTF

Wattisham TFF

1966	Formed
1973	Disbanded

used Lightning F.1, F.1A

Leuchars TFF

1966	Formed
1973	Disbanded

used Lightning F.1, F.1A

Binbrook TFF

1966	Formed
1973	Disbanded

used Lightning F.1, F.1A

60 MU Leconfield
operated F.1, F.1A at various times

Akrotiri Stn Flight
operated T.5
during 1974

(MoD(PE), A&AEE, ETPS and BAe Warton have operated all marks of Lightning at various times throughout the years.)

The Target Facilities Flights fulfilled many roles in training during the Lightning's peak. F.1A XM192 was on the strength of Wattisham TFF in 1973. (*CP RUSSELL-SMITH*)

Appendix 'D'
Lightning Crashes and Their Causes

1959

DATE	TYPE	S No.	UNIT	LOCATION	CAUSE AND DISPOSAL
1 Oct	Lightning T.4	XL628	EE Co.	Irish Sea	Fin mountings failed, uncontrollable, A/C abandoned.

It is somewhat ironic that the first Lightning to be lost was the T.4 prototype, bearing in mind that twenty-five single seaters were already engaged in active flying. For many years after the accident the truth was withheld, the only indications that a problem existed being references in the pilots' notes concerning limitations and in the servicing schedules for inspections.

1960

DATE	TYPE	S No.	UNIT	LOCATION	CAUSE AND DISPOSAL
5 March	Lightning P.1B	XG334	AFDS	Wells-next-the-Sea	U/C failed to lower fully, A/C abandoned.

This was a recurring problem on the Lightning throughout its early years of service, the main cause being close tolerances between leg, mounting and undercarriage bay structure. Aerodynamic, thermodynamic and the small vagaries of jig-built construction all combined under certain circumstances to restrict movement of the undercarriage. The solution was to allow slightly greater clearances all round, thus eliminating the binding effect.

1961

DATE	TYPE	S No.	UNIT	LOCATION	CAUSE AND DISPOSAL
6 March	Lightning F.1A	XM185	56 Sqdn	Nr. Wattisham	Total hydraulic failure followed by control loss. A/C abandoned.

1962

DATE	TYPE	S No.	UNIT	LOCATION	CAUSE AND DISPOSAL
13 Sept	Lightning P.1B	XG332	DH Props	Hatfield	Fire in rear fuselage causing control system failure. A/C abandoned.
12 Dec	Lightning T.4	XM993	226 OCU	Middleton St. George	Crashed on landing, A/C burnt out, abandoned.

Two further causes to explain Lightning losses came to the fore in 1961/62. The hydraulic-system leaks were eventually traced to chafing between pipes and the surrounding structure. This was eliminated by re-routing of some offending items whilst others were clamped at closer intervals. Fuel fires plagued the Lightning throughout its service life. One of the earliest causes was failure of the fuel pipes between the ventral tank and the airframe. Modification work eventually cured this fault.

1963

DATE	TYPE	S No.	UNIT	LOCATION	CAUSE AND DISPOSAL
26 April	Lightning F.1	XM142	74 Sqdn	Nr. Cromer	Control system failure, A/C abandoned.
6 June	Lightning F.1A	XM179	56 Sqdn	Gt. Bricett	Collided with XM171 during display practice, A/C abandoned, pilot seriously injured.
18 July	Lightning F.1A	XM186	111 Sqdn	Nr. Wattisham	Pilot became disoriented in cloud, performed wingover. A/C crashed. 1 Fatal.
31 July	Lightning P.1B	XG311	EE Co.	Nr. Warton	U/C failed to lower fully, A/C abandoned.

1964

DATE	TYPE	S No.	UNIT	LOCATION	CAUSE AND DISPOSAL
25 March	Lightning F.2	XN723	R-R	Nr. Hucknall	In flight fire caused by excess fuel leakage. A/C abandoned.
27 April	Lightning F.2	XN785	19 Sqdn	Hutton Cranswick	Pilot misjudged approach whilst landing at disused airfield. 1 Fatal
9 June	Lightning F.1A	XM191	111 Sqdn	Nr. Wattisham	Fire in rear fuselage caused failure of controls during take-off. A/C abandoned.
28 Aug	Lightning F.3	XP704	74 Sqdn	Nr. Leuchars	Pilot misjudged height above ground during aerobatics. 1 Fatal.
11 Sept	Lightning F.1	XM134	226 OCU	Nr. The Wash	ECU fire warning. A/C abandoned.

Although much effort had been expended to reduce the possibility of fuel fires in the rear fuselage their occurrence was still a cause for concern. In an attempt to eliminate this a system of 'zones and zonal checks' was introduced. These were carried out by a SNCO and covered the integrity of both fire protection and isolation on the aircraft before it flew after any form of hangar servicing.

1965

DATE	TYPE	S No.	UNIT	LOCATION	CAUSE AND DISPOSAL
11 Jan	Lightning P.1B	XG335	AFDS	Larkhill Ranges	U/C failed to lower fully, A/C abandoned.
26 June	Lightning F.3	XR712	111 Sqdn	Nr. Padstow	Pilot disoriented, crashed into sea. A/C abandoned.
22 July	Lightning T.5	XM966	EE Co.	Irish Sea	Fin failed making A/C uncontrollable, abandoned.
29 Sept	Lightning F.3	XP739	111 Sqdn	Nr. Wattisham	Fire in rear fuselage causing loss of control. A/C abandoned.

Yet another case of fin failure, this time involving XM966 which as a T.5 prototype lost its vertical flight surface. As this was the second occurrence, work was put in hand to strengthen the offending area.

1966

DATE	TYPE	S No.	UNIT	LOCATION	CAUSE AND DISPOSAL
5 Jan	Lightning F.3	XR721	56 Sqdn	Helmington, Suffolk	ECU failure, landed in field. Cat 5 spares recovery. 1 Fatal.
15 March	Lightning F.1A	XM190	226 OCU	RAF Coltishall	ECU fire. A/C abandoned
6 May	Lightning F.1A	XM213	226 OCU	RAF Coltishall	Uncommanded U/C retraction on take-off.
1 July	Lightning T.5	XS453	226 OCU	Nr. Happisburgh Norfolk	U/C failed to lower fully, A/C abandoned.
27 July	Lightning F.3	XR714	111 Sqdn	RAF Akrotiri	Uncommanded U/C retraction on take-off.
24 Aug	Lightning F.3	XP760	23 Sqdn	Nr. Seahouses, Fife	ECU failure, A/C abandoned.

1967

DATE	TYPE	S No.	UNIT	LOCATION	CAUSE AND DISPOSAL
2 Jan	Lightning T.4	XM971	226 OCU	RAF Coltishall	Radar fairing came loose causing FOD damage to engines. A/C abandoned.
3 March	Lightning F.3	XP699	56 Sqdn	Wethersfield	Fuel line failed causing fire in rear fuselage. A/C abandoned.
17 April	Lightning F.1A	XM184	226 OCU	RAF Coltishall	Fire on landing. A/C Cat 5 scrap.

7 Sept	Lightning F.6	XR766	23 Sqdn	ENE Leuchars	Entered uncontrollable spin. A/C abandoned.
13 Sept	Lightning F.1	XM136	Watt. TFF	RAF Coltishall	Reheat fire followed by control failure on approach. A/C abandoned.

1968

DATE	TYPE	S No.	UNIT	LOCATION	CAUSE AND DISPOSAL
24 Jan	Lightning F.6	XS900	5 Sqdn	Nr. Lossiemouth	Controls jammed by FOD/ECU power loss. A/C abandoned.
29 April	Lightning F.6	XS924	5 Sqdn	Nr. Beelsby, Lincs	Crashed after flight refuelling possible cause wake turbulence. 1 Fatal.
12 Sept	Lightning F.6	XS896	74 Sqdn	Nr. Tengah, Singapore	Fire in rear fuselage loss of control, A/C spun into ground. 1 Fatal.
29 Nov	Lightning F.1A	XM174	Leu TFF	Nr. Leuchars	ECU failure, A/C abandoned.

Crashes caused by the interference of foreign objects have reduced significantly over the last twenty or so years. Even by 1968 the realisation that FOD could be responsible for loss of life was strongly appreciated, therefore extensive checks were introduced throughout the RAF in an effort to eliminate the human side of the problem. Even so the loss of XS900 shows that such efforts were not always successful.

1969

DATE	TYPE	S No.	UNIT	LOCATION	CAUSE AND DISPOSAL
22 Sept	Lightning F.6	XS926	5 Sqdn	North Sea	Pilot lost control, A/C abandoned.

1970

DATE	TYPE	S No.	UNIT	LOCATION	CAUSE AND DISPOSAL
5 Mar	Lightning F.6	XS918	11 Sqdn	In sea Nr. Leuchars	Rear fuselage fire. A/C abandoned. 1 Fatal.
7 May	Lightning F.3	XP742	111 Sqdn	Nr. Great Yarmouth	Uncontrolled ECU fire, A/C abandoned.
26 May	Lightning F.6	XR767	74 Sqdn	In sea Nr. Singapore	Pilot disorientated, A/C crashed. 1 Fatal.
27 July	Lightning F.6	XS930	74 Sqdn	Tengah, Singapore	Crashed on take-off, possible uncommanded control input. 1 Fatal.
12 Aug	Lightning F.6	XS893	74 Sqdn	Nr. Changi, Singapore	U/C failed to lower fully A/C abandoned.

8 Sept	Lightning F.6	XS894	5 Sqdn	Nr. Flamborough Head	Crashed in sea, cause not determined. 1 Fatal.
19 Sept	Lightning T.4	XM990	226 OCU	Little Plumstead, Norfolk	Entered uncontrollable roll during aerobatics. A/C abandoned.

1970 was a bad year for the RAF in general with forty-three aircraft being lost in crashes. Of that total seven were Lightnings. Although much statistical analysis of the results was carried out no specific trend for the losses could be determined.

1971

DATE	TYPE	S No.	UNIT	LOCATION	CAUSE AND DISPOSAL
25 Jan	Lightning F.3	XP756	29 Sqdn	Nr. Gt Yarmouth	Zonal fire warning, A/C abandoned.
28 Jan	Lightning F.2A	XN772	92 Sqdn	Nr. Diepholz, Germany	Control lost in spin, A/C abandoned.
28 April	Lightning F.6	XS938	23 Sqdn	Nr. Leuchars	Fuel fire in rear fuselage during take-off. A/C abandoned.
10 May	Lightning F.3	XP744	29 Sqdn	Nr. Akrotiri	Zonal fire warning, A/C abandoned.
20 May	Lightning F.3	XP752	111 Sqdn	Nr. Colmar	Collided with FAF Mirage IIIE. Landed safely, declared Cat 5.
26 May	Lightning F.6	XS902	5 Sqdn	Nr. Grimsby	ECU fire, A/C abandoned.
8 July	Lightning F.3	XP705	29 Sqdn	Nr. Akrotiri	ECU failure, A/C abandoned.
22 Sept	Lightning F.3	XP736	29 Sqdn	Nr. Gt Yarmouth	Cause not determined, A/C crashed into sea. 1 Fatal.
30 Sept	Lightning F.6	XR764	56 Sqdn	Nr. Akrotiri	ECU fire, A/C abandoned.
29 Oct	Lightning F.3	XR711	111 Sqdn	RAF Wattisham	Premature rotation on take-off caused stall. 1 Fatal.

Another bad year for the Lightning fleet with no less than ten Lightnings being lost. Of this total four came from the same squadron thus prompting an investigation, the results however have never been published.

1972

DATE	TYPE	S No.	UNIT	LOCATION	CAUSE AND DISPOSAL
16 Feb	Lightning F.3	XP698	29 Sqdn	Nr. Harwich	Collided with XP747, A/C abandoned.
16 Feb	Lightning F.3	XP747	29 Sqdn	Nr. Harwich	Collided with XP698, A/C crashed. 1 Fatal.

7 Aug	Lightning F.3	XP700	29 Sqdn	Nr. Wattisham	A/C damaged rear fuselage seriously on take-off. Abandoned.
6 Sept	Lightning T.5	XS455	5 Sqdn	Nr. Spurn Head	Hydraulic failure leading to loss of control. A/C abandoned.
14 Dec	Lightning T.4	XM974	226 OCU	Nr. Happisburgh	ECU/reheat fire. A/C abandoned.

1973

DATE	TYPE	S No.	UNIT	LOCATION	CAUSE AND DISPOSAL
3 April	Lightning F.6	XS934	56 Sqdn	Nr. Akrotiri	ECU fire, A/C abandoned.
5 June	Lightning T.4	XM988	226 OCU	Nr. Gt Yarmouth	Entered spin followed by loss of control. Abandoned.
10 Dec	Lightning F.3	XP738	111 Sqdn	RAF Wattisham	U/C collapsed on landing, Cat 5.

1974

DATE	TYPE	S No.	UNIT	LOCATION	CAUSE AND DISPOSAL
13 Feb	Lightning F.3	XR715	29 Sqdn	Blyford Green, Southwold	ECU fire forced ejection. A/C abandoned.
24 June	Lightning F.3	XR748	29 Sqdn	Nr. Coltishall	Total hydraulic failure leading to loss of control. A/C abandoned.
29 Oct	Lightning F.6	XR768	5 Sqdn	Nr. Saltfleet, Lincs	Double reheat fire, A/C abandoned.

1975

DATE	TYPE	S No.	UNIT	LOCATION	CAUSE AND DISPOSAL
14 April	Lightning F.6	XR762	11 Sqdn	Nr. Akrotiri	Pilot misjudged height above sea during tail chase, crashed into sea. 1 Fatal.

1976

DATE	TYPE	S No.	UNIT	LOCATION	CAUSE AND DISPOSAL
30 July	Lightning F.6	XS937	11 Sqdn	Nr. Spurn Head	Abandoned after U/C failure.

1977

DATE	TYPE	S No.	UNIT	LOCATION	CAUSE AND DISPOSAL
24 Feb	Lightning T.4	XM968	92 Sqdn	Nr. Gütersloh	Total hydraulic failure leading to loss of control. A/C abandoned.

1978
NIL

1979

DATE	TYPE	S No.	UNIT	LOCATION	CAUSE AND DISPOSAL
25 May	Lightning F.6	XS931	5 Sqdn	Nr. Flamborough Head	Control restriction caused by FOD, A/C abandoned.
17 Aug	Lightning F.3	XP737	5 Sqdn	Nr. Valley	U/C failed to lower fully. A/C abandoned.
18 Sept	Lightning F.6	XR723	5 Sqdn	Nr. Akrotiri	ECU failure, A/C abandoned.

1980
NIL

1981

DATE	TYPE	S No.	UNIT	LOCATION	CAUSE AND DISPOSAL
27 March	Lightning T.5	XS459	LTF	Nr. Binbrook	Crashed on approach.
23 July	Lightning F.6	XR765	5 Sqdn	North Sea	ECU fire, A/C abandoned.

1982
NIL

1983

DATE	TYPE	S No.	UNIT	LOCATION	CAUSE AND DISPOSAL
26 Aug	Lightning F.3	XP753	LTF	Nr. Scarborough	Crashed in sea during unauthorised aerobatics. 1 Fatal.

1984

DATE	TYPE	S No.	UNIT	LOCATION	CAUSE AND DISPOSAL
13 July	Lightning F.6	XS920	5 Sqdn	Nr. Henslingen	Collided with power cable during ACM. 1 Fatal.
8 Nov	Lightning F.6	XR761	5 Sqdn	North Sea	ECU fire, A/C abandoned.

1985

DATE	TYPE	S No.	UNIT	LOCATION	CAUSE AND DISPOSAL
6 March	Lightning F.6	XR772	5 Sqdn	Nr. Spurn Point	Control loss, A/C abandoned.

1986

DATE	TYPE	S No.	UNIT	LOCATION	CAUSE AND DISPOSAL
15 July	Lightning F.6	XR760	11 Sqdn	Nr. Whitley	ECU fire, A/C abandoned.

1987

DATE	TYPE	S No.	UNIT	LOCATION	CAUSE AND DISPOSAL
19 March	Lightning F.3	XP707	LTF	Nr. Binbrook	Crashed during aerobatics.
1 July	Lightning F.6	XR763	5 Sqdn	Nr. Akrotiri	Double ECU failure, A/C abandoned.

1988

DATE	TYPE	S No.	UNIT	LOCATION	CAUSE AND DISPOSAL
11 April	Lightning F.6	XR769	11 Sqdn	Nr. Easington, Lincs.	ECU failure, A/C crashed into sea after abandonment.

The last eighteen years of the Lightning's service saw a continued downward trend in accidents. Such results were the outcome of better servicing standards and higher morale, although to the last the Lightning continued to produce surprises. The honour of the last aircraft to crash in RAF service falls to XR769 just prior to 11 Squadron's disbandment.

Appendix E
Lightning Colour Schemes

LIGHTNING F1. F.1A

Delivered in silver/natural metal finish overall except for fibreglass areas. Fins and spines painted as required by operating Squadrons.

LIGHTNING F.2, F.2A

Initially F.2s were delivered in silver/natural metal finish, coloured fins and spines being painted by users as required. Some F.2s not converted to F.2A standard nevertheless received the dark green upper surfaces applied to the later standard aircraft in the 1970s. They were then used as TFF aircraft. F.2As were returned after conversion in natural metal finish with coloured fins and spines of the applicable operating squadron. During 1971–73 all the surviving F.2As were repainted with dark green upper surfaces complete with toned-down markings.

LIGHTNING F.3

As with other marks of Lightning the F.3s were delivered in silver/natural metal overall with coloured fins and spines being applied by the operators. During 1971–73 Lightning F.3s were repainted in a grey-green scheme over the upper surfaces. From 1981 onwards F.3s appeared wearing either of two grey air defence schemes.

(a) Medium sea-grey uppers with light grey lower surfaces.

(b) Dark sea-grey upper-surfaces with medium sea-grey/barley-grey lower surfaces.

LIGHTNING T.4

As with the other Lightning variants the T.4s were initially silver natural metal overall complete with yellow trainer bands. Coloured fins and spines were applied as required by the various operators. Later the yellow 'T' bands were to disappear. Those T.4s employed by RAFG Squadrons painted their T.4s with dark green upper surfaces during 1971–73.

LIGHTNING T.5

As with the earlier T.4 the T.5s were silver/natural metal overall, but they did not wear yellow trainer bands. As with other variants, painted fins and spines were applied by the various operators. After the application of experimental paint schemes to the type in the mid-1970s the T.5s were repainted with grey-green upper surfaces during 1971–73. During the 1980s some of the T.5s were repainted in air defence greys similar to the F.3.

LIGHTNING F.3A/F.6

Lightning F.3A/F.6s were delivered in silver/natural metal overall, coloured fins and spines being applied as required by their various operators. From 1971 onwards operational Lightning F.6s began to wear upper-surfaces painted in grey-green disruptive camouflage. In the 1980s air defence greys were applied, starting with a barley grey/light grey scheme that soon settled to the colour schemes applied to the F.3s.

SAUDI ARABIAN AND KUWAIT COLOUR SCHEMES

The Lightnings of Saudi Arabia and Kuwait were delivered in a silver/natural metal finish that was only to be relieved by their respective countries national markings. This was to remain the case throughout their working lives.

Appendix F
Lightning Comparative Strengths

Aircraft	25th Anniversary August 1979		Last Lightning Show August 1987
F.3 XP693	Warton		BAe Warton, on show
F.3 XP694	5 Sqdn R/29 Sqdn R*		store
F.3 XP695	11 Sqdn M		decoy
F.3 XP701	11 Sqdn O	store	store
F.3 XP702	5 Sqdn P		store
F.3 XP706	store		store
F.3 XP707	5 Sqdn P	store	LTF DB store
F.3 XP737	11 Sqdn N		cr 17.8.79
F.3 XP741	11 Sqdn N	store	5 Sqdn AR
F.3 XP749	LTF A		store
F.3 XP750	LTF B	store	store
F.3 XP751	5 Sqdn S		store
F.3 XP753	5 Sqdn S	store	cr 26.8.83
F.3 XP764	LTF B		LTF DC
F.3 XR713	11 Sqdn O		5 Sqdn AP store
F.3 XR716	LTF C	store	5 Sqdn AQ
F.3 XR718	LTF C		5 Sqdn AS store
F.3 XR720	11 Sqdn M	store	store
F.6 XR723	5 Sqdn A		cr 18.9.79
F.6 XR724	5/11 Sqdns		5 Sqdn AE
F.6 XR725	5 Sqdn J		11 Sqdn BA
F.6 XR726	5 Sqdn K/23 Sqdn K*		11 Sqdn BM
F.6 XR727	11 Sqdn F		5 Sqdn AB
F.6 XR728	LTF D		LTF JS
F.6 XR747	5 Sqdn E	store	store
F.3 XR749	5 Sqdn Q		11 Sqdn BK2
F.3 XR751	LTF C/111 Sqdn*		store
F.6 XR752	11 Sqdn D		decoy
F.6 XR753	5 Sqdn A	store	11 Sqdn BP
F.6 XR754	11 Sqdn A	store	11 Sqdn BC
F.6 XR755	5 Sqdn F		11 Sqdn BN
F.6 XR756	5 Sqdn/23 Sqdn G*		11 Sqdn BH store
F.6 XR757	11 Sqdn A		11 Sqdn BL
F.6 XR758	5 Sqdn E		11 Sqdn BF
F.6 XR759	11 Sqdn H	store	11 Sqdn BJ
F.6 XR760	5 Sqdn B		cr 15.7.86
F.6 XR761	/74 Sqdn F*	store	decoy
F.6 XR763	/56 Sqdn E*	store	5 Sqdn AE store
F.6 XR765	11 Sqdn C	store	cr 23.7.81
F.6 XR769	/19 Sqdn B	store	11 Sqdn BE
F.6 XR770	5 Sqdn B		5 Sqdn AA
F.6 XR771	5 Sqdn C		5 Sqdn AN
F.6 XR772	11 Sqdn C		cr 6.3.85
F.6 XR773	11 Sqdn D	store	11 Sqdn BR
T.5 XS416	LTF V		5 Sqdn AZ
T.5 XS417	LTF W		LTF DZ store
T.5 XS419	5 Sqdn T	store	LTF DV
T.5 XS420	LTF V	store	LTF DV store
T.5 XS422	ETPS		ETPS not at show
T.5 XS452	11 Sqdn T		11 Sqdn BT store
T.5 XS456	LTF T		LTF DX
T.5 XS457	LTF Y		5 Sqdn AT store
T.5 XS458	5 Sqdn T	store	LTF DY
T.5 XS459	LTF X		5 Sqdn AW
F.6 XS895	11 Sqdn B		5 Sqdn AO
F.6 XS897	11 Sqdn H	store	5 Sqdn AD
F.6 XS898	5 Sqdn J		11 Sqdn BD
F.6 XS899	/92 Sqdn C*		5 Sqdn AM
F.6 XS901	11 Sqdn G	store	5 Sqdn AH
F.6 XS903	5 Sqdn C	store	11 Sqdn uncoded
F.6 XS904	11 Sqdn B	store	11 Sqdn BQ
F.6 XS919	5 Sqdn F	store	11 Sqdn BB
F.6 XS920	11 Sqdn E	store	5 Sqdn AF store
F.6 XS921	11 Sqdn F		5 Sqdn AB store
F.6 XS922	11 Sqdn L	store	5 Sqdn AF
F.6 XS923	11 Sqdn J		11 Sqdn BE
F.6 XS925	5 Sqdn D		11 Sqdn BD
F.6 XS927	11 Sqdn H		11 Sqdn BB
F.6 XS928	5 Sqdn L		11 Sqdn BJ store
F.6 XS929	11 Sqdn E		11 Sqdn BG
F.6 XS932	5 Sqdn F		5 Sqdn AG
F.6 XS933			5 Sqdn AJ
F.6 XS935	5 Sqdn B	store	5 Sqdn AK
F.6 XS936	11 Sqdn G		5 Sqdn AS
T.5 XV328	5 Sqdn T	store	LTF DU

Lightnings marked thus* were repainted in the markings of defunct squadrons for the Anniversary show.

Bibliography

Although much of this book has been compiled using the bare bones of Official Records, some of the flesh has come from the publications listed below.

BAC Lightning	Arthur Reed	Ian Allan	1980
British Fighter Since 1912	Peter Lewis	Putnam	1979
British Military A/C Serials 1878–1987	Bruce Robertson	MCP	1987
Gate Guards	Jim Simpson & Kev Darling	Airlife	1992
EE/BAC Lightning	Bryan Philpott	PSL	1984
English Electric P1 Lightning	Roland Beamont	Ian Allan	1985
Euromil	T. Brightman et al.	Seefive	1984
Military Aircraft Markings	P.R. March	Ian Allan	various
RAF Squadrons	C.G. Jefford	Airlife	1987
Wrecks and Relics (various eds.)	Ken Ellis	MCP	various

PUBLICATIONS AND PERIODICALS

Aeroplane Monthly	IPC
Aircraft Illustrated	Ian Allan
Air International	Key Publishing
Airfix Magazine	PSL
Air Forces Monthly	Key Publishing
Air Pictorial	Air League
Aviation News	Alan W. Hall Publications
Flypast	Key Publications
Military Aircraft Review	MAP
RAF Yearbook (various)	RAFBF
RAFAS Magazine	RAF Aviation Society
Tamiya Magazine	Traplet Publications

Abbreviations

ASSF	Aircraft Servicing and Storage Flight
A&AEE	Aircraft and Armament Experimental Establishment
AFDS	Air Fighting Development Squadron
APC	Armament Practise Camp
ATC	Air Training Corps
BAC	British Aircraft Corporation
BAe	British Aerospace
BDR(T)	Battle Damage Repair (Training)
C(A)	Controller (Aircraft)
CFE	Central Fighter Establishment
CTTS	Civilian Technical Training School
CWP	Contractors Working Party (normally from the manufacturers)
DC	Direct Current
DH Ltd	de Havilland Ltd
E.E. Co.	English Electric Company
ETPS	Empire Test Pilots School
FCTU	Fighter Command Trials Unit
FEAF	Far East Air Force
LAF	Lightning Augmentation Flight
LCS/U	Lightning Conversion Squadron/Unit
LFC	Lightning Flying Club
LPG	Lightning Preservation Group
LTF	Lightning Training Flight
MEAS	Mechanical Engineering Aircraft Squadron
MoA	Ministry of Aircraft
MoD(PE)	Ministry of Defence (Procurement Executive)
MoS	Ministry of Supply
MU	Maintenance Unit
NEAF	Near East Air Force
OCU	Operational Conversion Unit
QRA	Quick Reaction Alert
RAE	Royal Aircraft (later Aerospace) Establishment
RAFG	Royal Air Force Germany
ROS	Repaired on Site
RRE	Royal Radar Establishment
RSRE	Royal Signals and Radar Establishment (now RRE)
SASO	Senior Air Staff Officer
SBAC	Society of British Aircraft Companies
S of TT	School of Technical Training
T(D)FF	Target (Dual) Facilities Flight
UKADGE	United Kingdom Air Defence, Ground Environment

Index

Page numbers in italics refer to subjects in illustrations.